THE LIFE AND WORK OF BARBARA PYM

THE LIFE AND WORK OF BARBARA PYM

Edited by

Dale Salwak

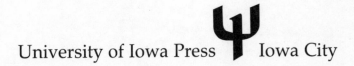

University of Iowa Press ❦ Iowa City

For Hilary Walton

Contents

Contents

Part III   In Retrospect

Preface

The rising tide of interest in Barbara Pym since 1977, when both Philip Larkin and Lord David Cecil identified her as one of the most underrated writers of the twentieth century,[1] invites a comprehensive, up-to-date survey of her life and work. This collection responds to that invitation by bringing together in one volume essays specially written for the occasion (with only a few exceptions) by nineteen distinguished men and women.

The volume is divided into three sections. The essays in Part I consider Barbara Pym's life. Those in Part II evaluate her novels from a variety of fresh perspectives. And the contributions which make up Part III discuss, in a general way, her human and artistic achievement. Together, all these provide special insight into the work, the woman behind the work, and the wide appeal of both.

Ideally the reader of this book is someone who has already encountered the pleasures of Pym's novels and wants to know more about them as well as their author. At the same time many people have heard of Barbara Pym but have not yet read her works, and I hope that this book will be useful to them as well.

Several of the contributors knew Barbara Pym. I feel deprived at never having met her. I am told that she was very much like her characters: dignified, friendly, honest, humorous and unpretentious. Photographs of her reveal the sort of gentle, intelligent face we expect to see in wise, kind teachers, reflecting an unselfishness and a patient endurance. One acquaintance wrote, 'She had that wonderful combination of quiet charm and good manners that made you feel she really wanted to talk to you.'[2] Another wrote, 'In meeting Barbara one never felt that she had missed out on any part of life.'[3]

It is appropriate that twelve of the nineteen contributors to this volume should live outside Great Britain. This offers testimony to her international readership. The reasons for her ever-growing acclaim are many and varied, of course, and on that matter I shall let the contributors speak for themselves. Certainly her appeal to the reading public lies partly in her fulfilment of the most fundamental requirements of any great writer: that she be a storyteller, a teacher, but, above all, an enchanter.[4] Barbara Pym has done what the greatest and liveliest writers usually do: she has made a world that is uniquely her own, an enchanted place both real and varied. 'In minute, breathtaking ways, she sizes up the harms, the conventions, the pleasures, and the perversities of small lives and bestows upon them the rare beauty and clarity of her own genius.'[5]

Like many admirers, I came upon her novels through the recommendation of a friend. Three years later, in 1983, after I had read everything by her and about her that I could find, the idea occurred to me to produce a volume of essays. Early in 1984 I wrote to people I knew who were familiar with her work. One colleague's response typifies the letters I received: 'You have hit me in a vulnerable place: I love Barbara Pym.'[6] That it has been possible to produce this collection within a comparatively short time is owing to the enthusiasm of the contributors. I am indebted to all of them.

I am also indebted to a number of good people who have expressed from its beginning a keen interest in this project. I should like to thank the following for their personal encouragement and professional advice: Professor John Halperin of Vanderbilt University; Professor Stephen C. Moore of the University of Southern California; Professor Edwin A. Dawes of the University of Hull; Professors David Sundstrand and Linda Humphrey of Citrus College; Paul De Angelis, Caroline Press and Jean Rawitt of E. P. Dutton; Frances A. Arnold of the Macmillan Press; Catherine Aird, Hazel Holt, Hilary Walton and the late Philip Larkin; my wife, Patricia; and my parents, Stanley and Frances H. Salwak. To all of them I am indeed grateful.

'No reputation is more than snowfall. It vanishes.'[7] True for some writers, perhaps, but Barbara Pym's reputation may be an exception. Her books are attracting an ever-widening audience as the years pass. Now the critical interest is there as well.

'Quiet, paradoxical, funny and sad,' Eudora Welty wrote in 1982, '[Barbara Pym's novels] have the iron in them of permanence too.'[8] I cannot improve upon that judgement.

Here, then, is the life and work of Barbara Pym – a writer whose time has come.

DALE SALWAK
Glendora and London

Acknowledgements and Note on References

Grateful acknowledgement is made to the following for permission to reprint previously published materials: the late Philip Larkin and Macmillan London for the Foreword to *An Unsuitable Attachment* (1982), reprinted here as 'The Rejection of Barbara Pym'; Penelope Lively and the editor for 'The World of Barbara Pym', *Literary Review*, I (1980) 8–9; Robert Smith and the editor for 'How Pleasant to Know Miss Pym', *Ariel: A Review of International English Literature*, II (1971) 63–8; John Murray (Publishers) Ltd for 'Business Girls', in *John Betjeman's Collected Poems*, 1980.

The pieces by Gail Godwin, Shirley Hazzard and Joyce Carol Oates were written to be read on the occasion of 'A Celebration of Barbara Pym', the Gramercy Park Hotel, 3 October 1984, and are here published for the first time by the kind permission of the authors and Paul De Angelis, E. P. Dutton, New York.

Page references to the novels (citing the most recent British editions, as listed in the Bibliography) are supplied in the notes at the end of the book. Letters, diaries and manuscripts lodged at the Bodleian Library, Oxford, are generally cited by manuscript number (prefixed PYM) or, in some instances, by page in *A Very Private Eye: An Autobiography in Diaries and Letters*, by the kind permission of Hazel Holt and Tim Rogers.

Every effort has been made to trace all the copyright-holders, but if any have been inadvertently overlooked the publishers will be pleased to make the necessary arrangement at the first opportunity.

Notes on
the Contributors

Frances H. Bachelder, concert pianist and teacher for over forty years, studied at the University of Massachusetts and Purdue University. She now resides in San Diego, California, and while continuing her career as pianist also writes poetry and non-fiction.

John Bayley is Warton Professor of English Literature and Fellow of St Catherine's College, Oxford. His publications include *In Another Country* (novel), *The Romantic Survival: A Study in Poetic Evolution*, *The Characters of Love*, *Tolstoy and the Novel*, *Pushkin: A Comparative Commentary*, *The Uses of Division: Unity and Disharmony in Literature*, *An Essay on Hardy* and *Shakespeare and Tragedy*.

Gail Godwin is the author of *The Perfectionists*, *Glass People*, *The Odd Woman*, *Violet Clay*, *A Mother and Two Daughters* and *The Finishing School* (novels), and two short-story collections, *Dream Children* and *Mr Bedford and the Muses*.

Robert J. Graham is Associate Provost/Dean and former Head, Division of Humanities, at the Pennsylvania State University at Harrisburg. His essays on English education and on American newspaper, magazine and book publishing have appeared in books and journals. Currently he is completing a book-length critical study of the writing of V. S. Naipaul.

John Halperin is Centennial Professor of English at Vanderbilt University. A Guggenheim Fellow in 1978–9 and again in 1985–6, he is also a Fellow of the Royal Society of Literature. Among his published volumes are *Trollope and Politics*, *Gissing: A Life in Books*, *C. P. Snow: An Oral Biography* and *The Life of Jane Austen*.

Shirley Hazzard has been a full-time writer since resigning from the United Nations headquarters staff after a decade of service.

She has published a collection of short stories, *Cliffs of Fall*, and a number of novels: *The Evening of the Holiday, People in Glass Houses, The Bay of Noon* and *The Transit of Venus*. She has also published numerous articles on literature and international affairs, and one non-fiction work, *Defeat of an Ideal: A Study of the Self-Destruction of the United Nations*. Her novel *The Transit of Venus* received the National Critics Circle Award in the United States in 1980. In 1982 she was elected to the American Academy and Institute of Arts and Letters.

Hazel Holt was born in Birmingham in 1928 and educated at King Edward VI High School. On leaving Cambridge, where she read English, she joined the staff at the International African Institute, where she worked with Barbara Pym for over twenty-five years, eventually taking over from her as Assistant Editor of *Africa*. She is Barbara Pym's Literary Executor and, as such, has prepared for press the typescripts of *An Unsuitable Attachment* (1982), *Crampton Hodnet* (1985) and *An Academic Question* (1986). She also, with Hilary Pym, edited Barbara Pym's letters and diaries, published as *A Very Private Eye* (1984). She is at present preparing for publication an anthology of some of Barbara Pym's unpublished works. She is also working on the official biography.

Philip Larkin is the author of *The North Ship, The Less Deceived, The Whitsun Weddings* and *High Windows* (poems); *Jill* and *A Girl in Winter* (novels); and two collections of criticism, *All What Jazz: A Record Diary 1961–68* and *Required Writing* – for which he received the 1984 W. H. Smith Award. He also edited *The Oxford Book of Twentieth Century English Verse*. From 1955 until his death in 1985 he served as Librarian of the Brynmor Jones Library, University of Hull. His many honours included the Queen's Gold Medal for Poetry and honorary degrees from a number of universities.

Robert Liddell was educated at Corpus Christi College, Oxford, has taught at the Universities of Alexandria, Cairo and Athens, and is a Fellow of the Royal Society of Literature. His publications include novels, short stories, travel books and the following literary criticism: *A Treatise of the Novel, Some Principles of Fiction*, a biography of Cavafy, and studies of the novels of Jane Austen, George Eliot and Ivy Compton-Burnett.

Penelope Lively is the author of eight novels, seventeen children's books, a non-fiction study of landscape history, as well as many short stories and radio and television scripts. Her fiction has twice been shortlisted for the Booker Prize. She is also a recipient of the Arts Council National Book Award, the Carnegie Medal and the Whitbread Award.

Constance Malloy is a doctoral candidate at the University of California, Davis, where she is writing as her dissertation a critical biography of Barbara Pym. She has delivered papers on the novelist at a number of literary conferences.

Joyce Carol Oates is the author of more than a dozen novels and many volumes of short stories, poems and essays, as well as plays. She has been honoured by awards from the Guggenheim Foundation, the National Institute of Arts and Letters and the Lotos Club, and by a National Book Award for her novel *them*. She is a member of the American Academy and Institute of Arts and Letters.

Gilbert Phelps, a full-time writer and lecturer, has published nine novels (including *The Winter People* – *Mortal Flesh* in the American edition – and *The Old Believer*), six volumes of criticism (including *The Russian Novel in English Fiction*, *A Survey of English Literature*, and *Fifty British Novels, 1600–1900*), several travel and general-studies books and two biographies, as well as many short stories, poems and essays. His latest work, in process of publication, is entitled *From Myth to Modernism: A Short Survey of World Fiction*. He is now working on another novel. Gilbert Phelps is a Fellow of the Royal Society of Literature.

Janice Rossen is the author of *The World of Barbara Pym*. She is currently at work on a book about Philip Larkin.

A. L. Rowse, a leading authority on Elizabethan England, is the author of many noted books on the Elizabethan age. They include biographies of Shakespeare, Christopher Marlowe, Sir Richard Grenville and Sir Walter Raleigh, plus his survey of the period in four volumes. Recent publications include *The Annotated Shakespeare* and *Prefaces to Shakespeare's Plays*, as well as *The Contemporary Shakespeare*. Dr Rowse is a Fellow of the British Academy; an

Emeritus Fellow of All Souls College, Oxford; and Benson Medallist of the Royal Society of Literature.

Muriel Schulz is Professor of English at California State University, Fullerton. She is co-author (with Ruth Wodak-Engel) of *The Language of Love and Guilt*, and is co-editor (with Cheris Kramarae and William O'Barr) of *Language and Power*. She has been a co-organiser of two international socio-linguistic conferences, one on language and gender and the other on language and power.

Robert Smith, former Professor of History at Ibadan, Nigeria, has published *Yoruba Warfare in the Nineteenth Century* (with J. J. A. Ajayi), *Kingdoms of the Yoruba, Warfare and Diplomacy in Pre-Colonial West Africa, The Lagos Consulate* and numerous articles in academic journals, mainly on West African history.

Lotus Snow received her doctorate at the University of Chicago and has taught at Hope, Albion and Keuka Colleges. She has published articles on Henry James, Virginia Woolf, Elizabeth Bowen, Muriel Spark, Ivy Compton-Burnett and Edna O'Brien.

Mary Strauss-Noll is Assistant Professor of English at the Pennsylvania State University, New Kensington. She has published articles on Faulkner, the teaching of English, and sex bias and language. She is currently writing a book about the novels of Barbara Pym.

Dale Salwak (editor) is Professor of English at Southern California's Citrus College. He was educated at Purdue University and the University of Southern California under a National Defense Education Act competitive fellowship program. His publications include literary biographies of John Wain and A. J. Cronin; reference guides to Kingsley Amis, John Braine, A. J. Cronin and John Wain; and two collections: *Literary Voices: Interviews with Britain's 'Angry Young Men'* and *Mystery Voices: Interviews with British Mystery Writers*. He is currently completing a study of Kingsley Amis, for which he was awarded a National Endowment for the Humanities fellowship in 1985.

Part I
The Life

1

Excellent Woman

Shirley Hazzard

As we cryptically say 'Proustian' or 'Jamesian', we may now say 'Barbara Pym' and be understood instantly. Only a writer with a strong original view – an implacable view, one might say – can do that for us. Having read Barbara, one cannot recast one's consciousness in the pre-Pym mould: what did one do, pre-Pym, with those observations and imaginings to which she has given voice and form?

I have the impression that poetry formed her. Poetry flows through her books – not only in outright quotations, but in suggestions, in allusions concealed not merely for the appreciative but for the loving. She is herself the poet of the lonely, the virtuous, the ironic; of the unostentatiously intelligent and witty; of the angelically self-effacing, with their diabolically clear gaze. Nothing escapes such persons; and they escape nothing.

She understood those who measure out life in coffee-spoons; and she knew, too, how they carefully count the spoons when the company has departed. She knew how dread of change can act as a brake on existence, can become an existence in itself: the lament of a transferred bureaucrat about his new office – that 'different pigeons come to the windows' (*Excellent Women*, p. 71) – is perhaps her most enviable line.

'The truth is so rare', said Emily Dickinson, 'it's delightful to tell it.' Barbara Pym's delight in telling it is what gives her work its largeness. Magnanimous, merciful, she yet could not tell a lie. Excellent woman.

2

The Quest for a Career*

Constance Malloy

'Life in 1977. Concorde, costing I don't know how many millions, flies over our heads, clearly visible from our cottage window, while the road outside is full of potholes as in the 16th-century.'[1] Barbara Pym recorded this incongruity between the old and the very new in a winter letter to her long-time friend and confidant Robert Smith, who had left England in 1959 to teach history in a Nigerian university. Perhaps she herself was feeling like a relic from the past in a modern world, for sixteen frustrating years had elapsed since publishers had last accepted her fiction. She had written six successful novels between 1950 and 1961, but since then she had amassed a large file of rejection letters from publishers, who seemed to find her books too 'old-fashioned' for current literary taste.

Barbara was sixty-four years old now, unmarried, retired from her London office job, and living with her only sister, Hilary, in a country village much like the ones that form the setting for several of her novels. Finstock, twelve miles north-west of Oxford and just on the edge of the Cotswolds, is not the quaint sort of village that attracts tourists. Barbara described it as 'an interesting mixture of carefully restored cottages and bright new bungalows with broken dry-stone walls, corrugated iron and nettles, and even the occasional deserted or ruined homestead'.[2] Several years earlier, she and Hilary had settled into their small, book-lined

* Two University of California Humanities Awards made it possible for me to do biographical research on Barbara Pym in Oxford. I am indebted to Timothy Rogers, Colin Harris, and their staff at the Bodleian Library for cheerful and patient assistance. I wish to thank Hilary Walton, Hazel Holt and Robert Smith for their time, suggestions and encouragement. And, for their ideas and editorial suggestions, I should like to thank Diane Johnson, Robert Hopkins, Max Byrd, Celeste Turner Wright, Elizabeth Hilliard and above all David Bell, who first introduced me to Barbara Pym's novels and has been an invaluable friend and adviser.

seventeenth-century cottage, with its roof of locally quarried Stonesfield slate. In this rural setting Barbara tried to content herself with growing vegetables in the cottage garden, making jam, doing patchwork, walking the countryside, attending church up the hill, taking tea with friends – in short, leading the 'uneventful' kind of life her heroines led. 'Who could ask for more?' sing the Beatles in 'When I'm Sixty-Four'. Well, Barbara Pym, for one, if she had been candid enough to say so. She fought a constant battle with despair over the failure of her writing-career, doing her best, with her sister's encouragement, to remain cheerful and useful. She could not have foreseen that after this sixteen-year lapse in publication she would suddenly become fashionable again – that she would be 'rediscovered' in this age of the Concorde.

Barbara had dabbled with writing as a child[3] and had even written a respectable though adolescent novel, *Young Men in Fancy Dress*, at the age of sixteen. She composed her first mature novel, *Some Tame Gazelle*, in her early twenties when she returned to her family home in Shropshire in 1934, after completing her degree in English language and literature at St Hilda's College, Oxford. She modelled the two main characters, the unwittingly comical spinsters Belinda and Harriet Bede, on herself and her sister Hilary, but she projected them into middle age and set them in a country village. Their lives revolved around the local Anglican church, headed by the peevish, over-literary Archdeacon Hoccleve, whose personality she patterned on that of Henry Harvey, a beau from her Oxford days.[4]

Ironically, the novel foresaw in many ways the course Barbara's own life was to take. As young women, both she and Hilary had expected to marry, and Barbara entertained occasional thoughts of marriage to Henry Harvey. Hilary did marry Alexander Walton during the Second World War, but they were divorced several years later. Henry disappointed Barbara by marrying a young Finnish woman, Elsie Godenhjelm. And, though a string of suitors throughout her life indicates that Barbara remained single by choice, the nature of that choice remains ambiguous. From her girlhood on, she tended to fall in love 'safely': she usually fixed her romantic longings on men she didn't know, on men she loved unbeknownst to them, or on 'unsuitable' men who were unstable, much younger, bisexual or homosexual.[5] At the age of twenty-five, in a letter to Henry, she was already referring to herself humorously as 'an old brown spinster'.[6] In a subsequent letter to his wife Elsie, whom she tried to cherish as a 'sister', she wrote this cryptic, Austen-like declaration: 'It is known that every woman wants the love of a husband, but it is also known that some women have to be content with other kinds of love.'[7] 'Other kinds of love' appear to be those that remain untested in reality. Like most of her heroines, Barbara had an active and romantic imagination that could bestow countless charms on certain men in her life, so long as they remained at a distance. Her ambivalence toward marriage, which surfaces in all her novels, was perhaps unconscious; she never discussed it, even with Hilary, always her closest friend.

The two sisters set up house together, first in Bristol during the war, later in London as each pursued her career, and finally in the Oxfordshire village to which they moved upon their retirement. In Finstock they came most closely to resemble the Bede sisters of *Some Tame Gazelle* – Belinda (Barbara), the elder sister, taller, more slender, reserved, sensitive and sensible, with doe-like green eyes, and Harriet (Hilary), the younger sister, shorter, a bit stouter, a sturdier sort of person with a round face and a frank and mirthful demeanour. Village life, with its coffee mornings, jumble sales, church services and local-history society, had by now become a common source of interest for the sisters. Henry Harvey, though married and divorced twice, had earlier moved to Willersey, a village not far from Finstock, and remained Barbara's friend throughout her life.

But to Barbara Pym 'a full life' (as Mildred Lathbury of *Excellent Women* would call it) included being a publishing novelist. In 1936 at the age of twenty-three she had completed the first draft of *Some Tame Gazelle* and had sent it to several publishers. All refused it, although Jonathan Cape promised to consider it again if she would make the alterations he recommended. But, when war threatened and then became a reality, Barbara's serious literary intentions were interrupted by duties to Great Britain.

At first she helped her mother care for six children evacuated from Birkenhead to the Pym house in Oswestry, near the Welsh border. As she tackled mounds of washing, ironing and mending, ideas for writing still simmered in her mind. Yet she rarely found the time or energy for anything but domestic chores and her volunteer work at the local YMCA camp for soldiers.[8]

At the age of twenty-eight Barbara was drafted into 'Work of

National Importance' – first civilian and then military postal and telegraph censorship, which took her to Bristol. By coincidence Hilary was working in Bristol with the BBC, and Barbara moved into the large house that her sister was sharing with other BBC workers. There she met and fell in love with Gordon Glover (later to become the model for Fabian Driver in *Jane and Prudence*), whose estranged wife Honor was both Barbara's housemate and close friend. Her love affair with Gordon was ill-fated and unhappy, primarily because of his personal instability. After their separation Barbara wrote in her diary, 'Even if we ever did get together again he wouldn't really want the same things as I do and surely would fail me again. . . . It's somebody else I've got to look for. Some fantastic dream lover.'[9] The diary entry is particularly telling, as most of her subsequent lovers remained literally 'dream' lovers, men to whom little or nothing of her real feelings was spoken.

To escape her misery over the failure of her affair with Gordon and to make a new start, Barbara joined the Women's Royal Naval Service (the 'Wrens') in 1943. Soon thereafter she was transferred to serve as an officer in Naples, where social life took the fore, with almost nightly cocktail parties, dinners and moonlight dancing. A series of minor romances with naval men (after whom she patterned Rocky Napier of *Excellent Women*) helped to raise her spirits.[10]

Barbara was called back to England in the summer of 1945 by the news of her mother's terminal cancer. In Oswestry, where her social life was practically nil, Barbara cooked, cleaned and cared for her mother when she wasn't in hospital. 'All days are so alike that I forget what I did on each one',[11] she wrote in her diary on 21 June 1945. To pass the time, she took up the novel she had been working on before the war. As she later recalled, 'I still had the manuscript of *Some Tame Gazelle* and had even done a little work on it – I can remember finding some solace in revising it when my mother was dying at the end of 1945 – it took my mind off what was happening in a way that nothing else could.'[12]

The war ended in August; Irena Pym died in September. Barbara had been close to her mother, a fun-loving person after whom she later patterned Jane of *Jane and Prudence*;[13] but she suppressed her grief and tried, as always, to get on with life. While Barbara was waiting to be officially demobilised, she rejoined Hilary in London and began looking for work. Through

Beatrice Wyatt,[14] aunt of Frances Kendrick, a friend from the Wrens, Barbara found a job in February 1946 as a research assistant for the International African Institute, an anthropological foundation where she helped to prepare material for publication. Meanwhile her own dream of publication spurred her to continue revision of her manuscript. In a 1946 letter to Henry Harvey she wrote, 'I have brought my typewriter back [from Oswestry] with me, so shall be able to get on with some writing. I have done a lot of alterations to *Some Tame Gazelle* and may try it again; after an interval of eight years it may be more acceptable!'[15] She worked on the manuscript during evenings and weekends. On 7 February 1949 the revised novel went off to Jonathan Cape, and this time he accepted it. 'I don't know anything equal to the thrill for a novelist at having a first novel accepted', Barbara later wrote. 'A literary career now stretched before me!'[16]

On 1 May 1950, at the age of thirty-seven, Barbara finally had the pleasure of sending Henry Harvey a copy of her first published novel, but not without some fear of his disapproval: 'Here is a copy of my book *Some Tame Gazelle* – published today – with the author's compliments. I don't know if it will amuse you, but hope that perhaps it may. Please don't notice all the places where I ought to have put commas – I am only too conscious of my shortcomings.'[17]

Whether or not Henry liked the novel,[18] Barbara Pym's readers responded enthusiastically; and two years later, when she was thirty-nine, Cape accepted *Excellent Women*, often considered her best work. She began turning out a new novel nearly every two years, and Cape published the books as quickly as she could write them. By 1961 she had had six novels published, usually stories about spinsters with a keen sense of life's absurd and comical little details, such as the curate's combinations inelegantly peeking out at the bottom of his trousers, or an eccentric old woman complaining about the 'unpleasantness' that birds have deposited on her window sill. The novels continued to be popular with the public, and Barbara received letters of admiration from writers so eminent as Ivy Compton-Burnett, Elizabeth Taylor, Philip Larkin and Lord David Cecil.[19]

Barbara Pym had enjoyed over a decade of literary success, and certainly her role as a novelist must have seemed fairly secure. But writing, as she knew, was not always a dependable source of income. Though she considered leaving the International African

Institute to become a full-time author, her practicality kept her at her editorial job.

> Dreams [she later said] are wonderful things, but I have always been prudent, even unadventurous, certainly not rash. . . . I haven't the sort of temperament to be able to write something to pay the rent – I had to have the peace of mind that a regular salary, however small, brings, and so I kept on working and writing novels in my spare time.[20]

She often awoke early to write before leaving for the IAI office in Fetter Lane; and, being adept at her research and editorial work, she also found 'spare time' at the Institute. There she discussed ideas for plots and characters with her friend and co-worker Hazel Holt, who had taken a degree in English literature at Cambridge. The two women shared a similar sense of humour and enlivened their tedious office work by inventing 'home lives' and 'field lives' for the anthropologists with whom they worked. Many a scene or dialogue was jotted on the back of old proofs, carbons of letters or even the occasional 'while you were out' slip; indeed, much of this was done when the Institute's Director, Daryll Forde, was 'out'. But, despite the rich material her working-environment provided, Barbara must have looked forward to the day when she and Hilary would retire to the country and she could write full time.

But, before this dream could be realised, something happened to bring Barbara Pym's writing-career to a halt. In 1963 when she was fifty years old, she sent her seventh novel, *An Unsuitable Attachment*, to Jonathan Cape, who had published the first six. G. Wren Howard of Cape returned the manuscript with a letter that began, 'I feel that I must first warn you that this is a difficult letter to write.'[21] In short, her publisher did not want the novel. Shocked and hurt, Barbara wrote to her friend Robert Smith,

> There is quite a lot to tell you, not all of it good. In fact 1963 has been a bad year so far. Just after the two burglaries and losing my typewriter, I had a great blow from Cape, who said they didn't want to publish my novel, which they read 'not without pleasure and interest', because they feared that with the increased cost of book production &c. &c. they would not sell enough copies to make a profit! And that after six novels and

thirteen years and even a small amount of prestige to the house of Cape!²²

A number of factors might have explained Cape's rejection of *An Unsuitable Attachment*. Jonathan Cape himself had died, and there had been a change in administrative staff; along with it came a change in policy. Barbara speculated, in the same letter to Robert Smith, that 'their whole policy is obviously to publish only best-sellers like Ian Fleming'. Then, too, perhaps her seventh novel really was not so good as the previous six. She revised it considerably over the years, and Hazel Holt did the final editing and cutting when it was published posthumously, but some critics still find it her least successful work. Barbara herself, however, seemed to fix on the explanation that her novels were outmoded. 'I don't think the book is much worse than the others, just not to present-day taste.'²³ Looking back on this rejection, the first of many, Barbara discussed the incident in a 1978 autobiographical radio talk called *Finding a Voice*:

In the early sixties, I sent my seventh novel to my publishers. And to my horror they wrote back saying they didn't feel they wanted it. I offered it to several others, but the manuscript still came thudding back through the letterbox. One publisher said: 'We think it's very well written but there's an old-fashioned air to it'; another thought that it wasn't the kind of book to which people were turning – I wasn't sure what he meant by that – while a third said curtly that their fiction list was full up for the next two years. I had never made my living as a writer so I still had my job, but my books had been published regularly and now it seemed that nobody wanted them. It was an awful and humiliating sensation to be totally rejected after all those years, and I didn't know what to do about it.²⁴

Some recent commentators err in assuming that what Barbara Pym did about it was to give up and steal away from the literary scene with a wounded ego. Although the rejection did jar her self-confidence, she never gave up. 'So I did go on writing, even in the face of discouragement', she explained in her radio talk. She revised *An Unsuitable Attachment* and sent it out to numerous publishers during these sixteen so-called 'silent years'. And she completed two new novels, *The Sweet Dove Died* and *Quartet in*

Autumn, both of which were also repeatedly rejected. She even tried using a pen name, Tom Crampton,[25] because she felt it had a 'swinging air' to it, one that might appeal to the publishers of the 'swinging sixties', which had 'swung me out of fashion', as she later wrote to a friend.[26] But, no matter what she tried, the manuscripts ricocheted back to her.

By 1977, as her correspondence reveals, Barbara Pym was struggling to balance too much optimism on the one hand with too much pessimism on the other. Certainly she enjoyed writing and even referred to it as an 'addiction', though she did ask herself, 'Is it enough to write just for ourselves if nobody else is going to read it?'[27] Fortunately, her sister and her friends encouraged her to go on, and she did have a small but faithful public following. Several fans wrote to say that they had demanded 'more Pym!' from Cape, who responded evasively. According to one, 'They replied that they had tried to persuade you to write another.'[28] Barbara's friend Robert Smith had written an appreciative article, 'How Pleasant to Know Miss Pym', published in *Ariel* in October 1971; but it failed to convince publishers that they could sell her novels. Feeling quite forgotten indeed, Barbara brought the article to the attention of Jean Mossop at Cape, adding, 'I suppose this is a kind of posthumous fame, though I'm still very much alive!'[29] She wanted desperately to see her novels in print again; but, since publication had come to seem unlikely, she did her best to accept the modest life she was now leading.

As planned, she and Hilary moved to their country cottage in Finstock; 'but then, when in theory I had all the time in the world to write I was faced with the ironical situation that no publisher wanted my books!'[30] In her retirement she kept herself busy with 'the church and the local History Society . . . cooking, mild gardening, sewing and patchwork'.[31] And she tried to remain cheerful and courageous, despite the nagging disappointment over the failure of her writing-career. She wrote to Robert Smith, perhaps more to convince herself than him, 'So easy to sink into apathy and despair, but that is not really my nature.'[32] Though apathy and despair always threatened, her nature bade her persevere – to keep writing, to keep trying her manuscripts with yet another publisher, but to steel herself for the inevitable rejection slip.

Writing had become such an important part of her life that,

rather than give it up, Barbara Pym tried to adjust her philosophy about it. 'I always determine never to write anything else, but the habit is difficult to break!'[33] she confided to Jean Mossop of Cape in 1976. In the same year she wrote to Henry Harvey, with whom she had maintained an irregular correspondence since their days at Oxford some forty-five years earlier, 'Novel writing is a kind of personal pleasure and satisfaction, even if nothing comes of it in worldly terms. But at our age we must surely have decided that fame is dust and ashes anyway?' Though perhaps Barbara wished to believe this, the question mark betrays her. The note goes on lightly to tell Henry of some seeds she planned to sow in her garden. But in a revealing aside she concluded, '(? Is gardening enough? No!)'.[34] A month later, on holiday in Greece, she went to the church on St Nicholas island: 'Inside we each burned a candle (I only for the success of my novel, perhaps an unworthy object).'[35]

Coinciding with the failure of Barbara Pym's writing-career were several tragedies in her personal life. While her sister was holidaying in Greece in 1971, Barbara discovered a lump in her left breast. Like Marcia Ivory of *Quartet in Autumn* (the novel she began the following year), Barbara had a mastectomy, performed just four days after the diagnosis of cancer. She accepted the situation stoically. 'The only snag (if that's the word) about my illness was that [Hilary] hasn't been here', she wrote to Robert Smith. 'The scar is healing well and I'm getting used to it.'[36]

Then, in March 1974, while she was still living in London and working at the International African Institute, she suffered a mild stroke that left her unable to read or write properly for nearly a month. The stroke was caused, apparently, by a thyroid condition. In her journal entry of 7 April 1974 she attempted five times, without success, to spell 'thyroid': 'thyrode thyoroyde thyroud thyoroud thyroue'.[37] Hilary wrote to Robert Smith, 'Barbara goes on getting better and is quite herself again except for the reading and writing. These may take some time. She is very objective about it and in her typical way sees the irony of the situation.'[38] Though the stroke hastened Barbara's retirement, she recovered completely and enjoyed fairly stable health until 1978.

But another disillusionment plagued her as well. In 1963, the year when *An Unsuitable Attachment* was first rejected, she became friendly with Richard Roberts, a handsome man twelve years younger than she. The relationship was ambiguous. Though not exactly a love affair, it had all the trappings of one: they dined together often, he phoned, dropped by and sent fond cards and gifts. As she told Robert Smith, who had introduced Richard to her, 'Richard brings a bit of joy into life because he is so much not of this grim everyday world.'³⁹ Like Leonora Eyre in *The Sweet Dove Died* (1978) Barbara waited anxiously for his visits and telephone calls but undoubtedly recognised the 'unsuitability' of the attachment. A fifty-year-old woman, inwardly romantic but outwardly sensible, she would never have made herself so foolish as to declare herself in love with a man of thirty-eight.⁴⁰ His calls grew less regular as he formed other attachments; and in 1964 Barbara wrote to Robert Smith,

> You ask about 'that Creole' [Roberts is an American whose family lived in the Bahamas] and hope I am seeing a lot of him. Well, perhaps not so *very* much lately . . . as it is I feel I must just leave him to go his own way and be there if needed. Of course I have become very fond of him, as you must have gathered, especially this summer, and he has been very sweet to me. I wish he could be happier but perhaps that is not in his nature. 'I love Bob, I love Richard, I love Rice Krispies . . .' says the brisk jolly voice from the pulpit, and a ripple of laughter goes through the congregation. Perhaps it is best in the end just to love Rice Krispies?⁴¹

As with the failure of her writing-career, Barbara tried to make light of the situation. But she had become attached to Richard, and his habit of disappearing and then reappearing only when he needed her finally drew this bitter comment to Robert Smith in 1967:

> [Work] has helped me overcome the depression that occasionally threatens when I think of nobody wanting to publish my novels, and my total 'failure' (if that's the word) with R. Trying to understand people and leaving them alone and being 'unselfish' and all *that* jazz has only the bleakest of rewards – precisely nothing! . . . But in the meantime I have been going on with writing because I like doing that, and you never know, perhaps one day. . . .⁴²

When she wrote to Robert Smith again six months later, the

bitterness had mellowed to sadness and resignation: 'Now, alas, I am too old to change myself but shall just be more cautious in the future – not allowing myself to get fond of anybody.'[43] Though she referred sentimentally to Richard in her private writing for a number of years thereafter, this was the 'swansong' (as Hilary later called it) of her romantic attachments.

Barbara continued to fight self-pity and did her best to avoid the pity of others, but she did welcome kind and understanding words from Robert Smith, who later reflected,

> I know that B. was much cast down over the R. R. situation and then over lack of publication. These troubles to some extent seemed to work against each other, and she continued both to complain and to laugh about them. . . . Her approach to all these troubles ('curtains for Barbara' etc.) was very robust, but she did speak of them and asked for and was grateful for sympathy.[44]

As Philip Larkin observed in 'The World of Barbara Pym', the Pym heroines are 'contented with what they have, which is more often little than much'.[45] Barbara tried to content herself with little, but she did want much, though she sometimes tried to hide the fact from her friends and even from herself. Barbara still longed for the fame that seemed to be turning to 'dust and ashes'. In her journal entry of 20 November 1975 she wrote, '"Fame did not come, but your life has made its own." (me) Only six novels published and no stories in the *New Yorker* or anywhere else.'[46] Gardening, country walks, church socials – and even writing for its own sake – all gave her pleasure, but they could not supply the same satisfaction as literary fame. Like her heroine Letty Crowe of *Quartet in Autumn* (1977), who bravely faced a bleak retirement, Barbara clung to the optimistic view that 'life still held infinite possibilities for change' (p. 218).

The change came suddenly and unexpectedly. In an autobiographical talk called 'The Ups and Downs of a Writer's Life', Barbara recalled this momentous highlight in her own career:

> One evening in January a friend rang up and asked me if I had seen the *Times Literary Supplement* where a number of distinguished critics and authors had been asked to name the

writers they considered to be the most over- and under-rated in the last seventy-five years. I hadn't seen it, so he.told me. Lord David Cecil and Philip Larkin had both named *me* as the most under-rated author – and I was the only person to be named twice in this way.[47]

What she modestly omitted in this address was the high praise that both Larkin and Cecil had offered her in the survey: Larkin had applauded her 'unique eye and ear for the small poignancies of everyday life', and Cecil had called two of her early works 'the finest examples of high comedy to have appeared in England' in the twentieth century.[48] In an excited letter to Robert Smith, she reported, 'and there was no collusion, as Philip [Larkin] afterwards told me!'[49]

But Barbara still feared expecting too much and then being disappointed, however close her dream of literary fame must have seemed when the *TLS* distinction came. She told Robert Smith, 'I am not "overly" hopeful (as Richard might say).'[50] Likewise, she tried to convince her old friend Henry Harvey, and probably herself as well, that she could be contented with 'little rather than much':

It was nice of you to write and of course I'm very pleased about the kind words in *TLS*, though I doubt if it will cut much ice with publishers. At the same time I made some rather successful marmalade, so you see where one's priorities lie. (And this morning I scrubbed the kitchen floor.) But I am also trying to get on with a novel and have been given an introduction to somebody in Macmillan. If only one could write Gothic novels![51]

As it turned out, Barbara need not have been so cautious about the possibility of further rejection, for the *TLS* survey did indeed cut ice with publishers. 'And to add a romantic note', as she later told the Romantic Novelists Association (for whom she had been judging novels), her break came on 14 February 1977, when Alan McLean of Macmillan telephoned to say that they wanted to publish *Quartet in Autumn*. 'Surely no rejected novelist ever had a more wonderful valentine!'[52]

Now Barbara could admit to the bitterness she had felt at being rejected for sixteen years by Cape and other publishers – and she could afford to gloat a bit. In the talk she delivered to the Senior Wives Fellowship in 1978 she said,

> My original publisher got in touch with me and asked what had happened to the novel I had sent them the previous summer. I was able to write back and tell them that this novel [*Quartet in Autumn*] was being considered by 'another publisher' – this of course was Macmillan, who published it.[53]

With Robert Smith she was free to reveal her feelings more candidly:

> Of course I have had quite a lot of letters from Tom Maschler [one of the directors at Cape since Jonathan Cape's death] now, even enquiring about previous novels they had rejected, but naturally I told him that I hoped Macmillan would take those, if anyone did. After all, I had to point out to him that I had in fact sent those novels to Cape but had been repeatedly told that they wouldn't sit happily on the Cape list as it now is![54]

Now, also, Barbara could admit to herself and to others just where her priorities really lay; to the Romantic Novelists Association she victoriously declared, 'This was the best thing that happened – to be in print again – a proper novelist, as it were.'[55]

After St Valentine's Day, Barbara Pym's letters take on a happy, youthful tone. Like Clarissa in Virginia Woolf's *Mrs Dalloway*, drunk on the loveliness of spring in London, alive to every sensation, she wrote Robert Smith a carefree, almost girlish, account of her meeting with her new publishers on 3 March 1977:

> It was a beautiful spring day and I found myself slipping into London as easily as if I had never left it. . . . I was to meet Alan McLean, who is one of the directors and the one who accepted the book and rang me up about it, and James Wright, who does all the sort of 'literary' work on the manuscript. As Alan McLean was at a meeting, James Wright took me to lunch ('I'm sure you're dying for a drink') and Alan McLean joined us a bit later. . . . I found them both extremely congenial and cosy – of course I would as they liked the book! We had smoked salmon and a veal thing and profiteroles and drank white wine, and

over the meal talked about titles. The book is finally to be called
QUARTET IN AUTUMN and is supposed to come out in
September.[56]

The following months brought other unexpected pleasures as
well. Shortly after accepting *Quartet in Autumn* Macmillan also
made plans for the 1978 publication of the previously rejected *The
Sweet Dove Died*, which Barbara had written in the 1960s. And, in
America, E. P. Dutton was soon to follow suit by publishing her
novels. On 11 March 1977 the *TLS* printed Philip Larkin's flattering
essay 'The World of Barbara Pym'. To Robert Smith she reported,
with her typical modesty, 'I'm glad you enjoyed his article – it has
made an impression, of course, and perhaps on people who
would otherwise have thought nothing of me. As a result of it
[Larkin] had a letter from John Bayley (Iris Murdoch's husband)
saying how glad he was to meet another BP addict, so that is
certainly unexpected!'[57] In her diary for 19 May 1977, Barbara had
simply noted, 'Tea with Lord David Cecil'; but in a letter to Robert
Smith she eagerly detailed her first meeting with the man who
had been partially responsible for her rediscovery:

We went to Dorset for a few days in mid-May and lovely
weather and had tea with Lord David Cecil at Cranborne. He
and Rachael are a most delightful pair and so easy to talk to –
the time absolutely flew. We had brown toast for tea and ginger
cake – Lapsang tea in an ordinary brown teapot and she
wheeled it all in on a trolley. On leaving he gave me a book (an
anthology he had made) charmingly inscribed.[58]

Barbara Pym's 'uneventful' life was suddenly brimming with
activity. During the previous sixteen years, while the literary
world had ignored her, publicity had become an important part of
the publishing writer's duties. Now Barbara was the centre of a
good deal of attention from the media and from groups who
wanted her to address them on the subject of her writing-career
and her philosophies as a writer. More at ease making tea than
making speeches, she was at first somewhat overwhelmed by the
new demands her career imposed. In her 1978 talk to the Senior
Wives Fellowship she said,

What I noticed most was the way the literary scene had changed since the fifties. Now there seemed to be far more publicity, though of course my rather unusual situation did attract more attention. My first radio interview 'Finding a Voice' – for Radio Oxford – made me realise how much I disliked my own voice though I have got used to it now.[59]

On the author's publicity form she received from Macmillan, Barbara wrote, 'On the whole I prefer to stay in the background',[60] but she had difficulty doing so, as it turned out. The invitations to speak were so numerous that she was forced to decline quite a few, although shyness and lack of confidence did determine many of these decisions. As she told one person who asked her to speak before a group, 'My "rediscovery" as a novelist has not done anything for my gifts as a speaker.'[61] To Paul De Angelis of Dutton she confessed, 'It is only people *en masse* that scare me.'[62] But Barbara did appear on *Desert Island Discs*, a radio programme that asks famous people what musical recordings, books and luxuries they would take to a desert island. (She chose assorted classical music, Henry James's *The Golden Bowl* and a case of white wine.) For a BBC film on 5 September 1977, *Tea with Miss Pym*, she and Lord David Cecil had tea in the garden of her Finstock cottage as they discussed her life and literary career. During the filming Barbara was not entirely at ease: 'I poured tea and tried with my left hand to fend off Nana [her cat] who had sprung onto the tray and was trying to put her paw into the milk jug. Will it be like the Mad Hatter's tea party?'[63] The producers had compiled a photograph album showing Barbara at various stages – as a child growing up in Shropshire, a teenager with a cat on her lap, a student in her cap and gown at St Hilda's in Oxford, an officer with the Wrens in Naples during the Second World War, and an editor for the International African Institute's publication *Africa*. Along with this publicity were numerous interviews and photography sessions for newspapers and magazines. To Robert Smith, who had written 'How Pleasant to Know Miss Pym' in 1971, Barbara joked, 'People will get very sick of Miss P. (How Boring to Meet Miss P.)'[64]

Some of the newspaper and magazine articles struck Barbara as particularly humorous. 'Then there were the various articles written about me that had their comic side. I sometimes think that if you put them together you would gain a rather curious impression of me.'[65] She refers, for the most part, to the article in

The Times written by Caroline Moorehead, 'How Barbara Pym was Rediscovered after 16 Years out in the Cold' (14 September 1977). For information about her, Moorehead had phoned her original publisher, Jonathan Cape. But, despite the recent survey in the *TLS*, the person she talked to at Cape 'was at first even doubtful whether she was still alive', according to the article. Cape's doubts are all the more surprising because, not so many months before, they had rejected *Quartet in Autumn* and then asked to see it again as a result of the survey. But Moorehead happily reported, 'She is very much alive, a tall, somewhat gawky woman in her early sixties, with a few sharp things to say about the fickleness of publishers.' Near the end of the article Moorehead explained that, if Barbara Pym should make a great deal of money on her new publications, 'she and her sister will go on Concorde to Latin America [because] the new Barbara Pym belongs to the seventies'.[66]

With her typical wit, even when directed at herself, 'the new Barbara Pym' created a montage of her interviewer's erroneous impressions: 'A tall, gawky woman who wants to go to South America on Concorde and who reads Ovid and Vergil.'[67] In truth, however, the volumes of Ovid and Virgil, which Moorehead may have noticed on a shelf in the cottage bathroom, belonged to Hilary, who had taken a degree in Classics at Lady Margaret Hall in Oxford. And, practical as usual, Barbara purchased books and a corner cupboard rather than airline tickets with her new income. As she later wrote to Paul De Angelis of Dutton (who had hoped she would stop by New York on her Concorde expedition),

> About my trip to South America! This was really a joke, based on a remark I made when Caroline Moorehead of the *Times* came to interview me and I happened to have seen a friend who had been on the Concorde the previous day. I think I said I would rather like to go to South America on it, but the remark seems to have been taken up, like various other things I may have said.[68]

Nevertheless, Barbara was amused by the description; she called it 'a formidable combination, but only the gawky part is true, and even that was rather a surprise to me (still, it was in the *Times* . . .)'.[69]

Now Barbara Pym was in style again, and more so than ever. Although no longer the anachronism that publishers of the 1960s and early 1970s had thought her, neither was she so very 'modern' that she wanted to soar in Concorde over the potholes of her sixteenth-century lane. Yet perhaps she had found a way to bridge the gap between the old and the new – by combining the old setting, an English village that revolves around its church, and the new times, the 1970s. In a 1977 letter to an Italian admirer of her novels, Barbara wrote, 'The novel I am writing now: I have had so many letters to write during the last few weeks that I have hardly done any work at all! But I am trying to do a novel about village life in the 1970's [*A Few Green Leaves*].'[70]

Over the following two years, 'the new Barbara Pym' continued to lead an active village life and continued to write about village life in *A Few Green Leaves*, marvelling all the while at the strange but felicitous turn her own life had taken. 'God really does move in a mysterious way', she wrote to Robert Smith, using her heroines' favourite explanation for inexplicable events. 'What is amusing (and rather saddening when you think of other good writers) is that I haven't done anything different – just plodded on. It only needed a little push and the whole thing gathered momentum – like a stone rolling down a slope – or the Gadarene swine hurtling down to sea?'[71]

But, as her career gathered momentum, the cancer recurred, this time in her abdominal region. She seems to have known that she had only a short time to finish her last novel. Always ready to see the positive side of a situation, she wrote to James Wright of Macmillan on 17 October 1979,

> I have been pretty good most of the year but now they are going to try a new drug on me and I have not been feeling too well the last few days. . . . I was given up in 1974 – but look how lucky I've been to live for my rediscovery and the joy of Macmillan. Anyway, the new novel *is* finished though I hope to improve it still more a bit.[72]

On 11 December 1979 James Wright wrote to say that 'I have now put the book into production and I don't see any reason why we shouldn't publish it in July.'[73]

Barbara Pym did not live to see the novel in print, nor did she live to read Dutton editor Paul De Angelis's praise of it, mailed on 9 January 1980, just two days before her death: '*A Few Green Leaves* is not only a work worthy of your name, but in many ways the culmination of your work.'[74] Barbara died peacefully and, according to the plan she had made with Hilary, in an Oxford hospice. Even here, she was still observing all around her rich material for new novels.

Those of us who continue to cry 'more Pym!' are grateful for the work of Hazel Holt, Barbara's co-worker, close friend and literary executor: she prepared for posthumous publication *An Unsuitable Attachment* (1982) and *Crampton Hodnet* (1985). She is currently working on an anthology drawn from assorted unpublished pieces and plans to write an official biography of Barbara Pym. She and Barbara's syster Hilary compiled the wonderful glimpse of Barbara Pym's personal life *A Very Private Eye: An Autobiography in Diaries and Letters* (1984). When I last met Hilary in Oxford, in autumn 1984, she was on her way to buy tickets to America, where she and Hazel Holt would speak with eager Pym fans. How would they travel? On Concorde, naturally.

3

The Novelist in the Field: 1946–74

Hazel Holt

It ought to be enough for anybody to be the Assistant Editor of Africa, especially when the Editor is away lecturing for 6 months at Harvard, but I find it isn't quite.[1]

Neither of the rooms we shared at the Institute for over twenty years can have been more than eighteen feet square. Taking up most of the space were two large wooden desks, set facing each other. Their cigarette-scarred surfaces were obscured by stacks of wire trays full of slipping piles of galley proofs, dog-eared folders of yellowing manuscripts and dangerously leaning towers of books endlessly awaiting review.

In a small clearing on each desk was an old-fashioned typewriter. We typed all our own letters and often some for our Director, Professor Daryll Forde, as well as the texts of any special lectures he might be giving, since no one else at the Institute could read his writing. There were also long passages of revised manuscripts to be typed, and bibliographies and indexes. We both of us typed with two fingers.

Around the walls stood a collection of olive-green metal filing-cabinets, since we also did our own filing – eccentrically but efficiently. Next to these in a wooden cabinet of considerable antiquity were kept a quantity of papers, handed down to the Institute by some long-vanished department of the (then) Colonial Office. They were a source of great interest – and, often, mystification – to anthropologists, who found the nuggets of sociological information difficult to disinter from the splendid day-to-day administrative chat, which was, of course, what *we* found most fascinating. ('The key to the jail at —— is kept under

the *mat*; I think you will have no difficulty in finding it.') Barbara
had arranged them in the most general way:

> I met John Ballard once and I think he was rather shocked
> when I showed him a rather chaotic collection of Intelligence
> Reports we have at the IAI, and when he suggested mildly it
> might be nice to have a list of them, I said roughly that there
> was certainly no hope of *that*. It might be a nice job to do on
> those long, dusty August afternoons . . . .[2]

Then there was the map cupboard. Barbara's first job at the
Institute was to produce the Ethnographic Survey of Africa. This
ambitious project, initiated by Professor Forde, was to be a
complete survey, tribe by tribe, of the whole of Africa. It was to be
complemented by a similar study of all groups of African
languages in the Linguistic Survey. Every related group of tribes
was to have its own volume, each written by a specialist in that
area and all on the same pattern: history, social organisation,
political organisation, land use, religion, and so on. Each volume
was to have its own specially drawn map.

So Barbara was in charge of the maps. They had a life of their
own and, however carefully arranged and efficiently stored,
whenever the shelves of the cupboard (which always stuck and
had to be given a special sort of tug) were pulled out, a cascade of
partially unrolled maps would tip out onto the floor. The cupboard
was only waist-high and profoundly inconvenient, so Barbara
spent a considerable time crouching (to use one of her favourite
words) on the cold linoleum searching for the relevant map of a
specific area.

She delighted in the 'mystique' of the maps and used to enjoy
little technical talks about scales and so forth with Professor
Forde, who was, originally, a geographer and sometimes expected
a deeper knowledge of such things than either of us had.

Inadequately covering the linoleum was a square of carpet ('I
am to have a new carpet – speckled black and white that won't
show the cigarette ash'[3]) from Gamages. The walls and paintwork
were a rather dingy cream colour. The cleaning at the Institute
was always rather sketchy and we both kept dusters in our desk
drawers. Once, in a fit of exasperation at the grit and grime in the
curtains (London was being rebuilt around us in the 1950s and
1960s), Barbara took them home and washed them herself.

In a bookcase behind her desk were kept the file copies of the Ethnographic and Linguistic Surveys, copies of the Institute's monographs and all the back numbers of our official journal *Africa*, of which Barbara was the Assistant Editor. There was also a miscellaneous collection of her own dictionaries, brought from home for reference – English, French, Portuguese, Italian (Naples, 1943), German (Oxford, 1934) and Polish (Katowice, 1938). Beside them a motley selection of novels and poetry of a kind that find their way onto bookshelves for no apparent reason: *David Blaize* by E. F. Benson, *No Coward Soul* by Noel Adeney, *Robert Ellesmere* by Mrs Humphry Ward, Palgrave's *Golden Treasury*, *Metaphysical Poetry from Donne to Butler* and a Gilbert Murray translation of *The Trojan Women*.

Hanging beside this bookcase was the Juju. This was constructed from various 'magical' objects: a wooden bull-roarer (brought back from Nigeria by one of our anthropologists), a Salvation Army badge, a feather, a lock of my hair (Barbara had trimmed it for me one afternoon in the office when we were feeling bored) and the signature of the Father of anthropology, Professor Malinowski, cut from a letter in the files. Occasional 'offerings' – a pressed flower or a paper-clip – were made to the Juju if we needed a new reviewer or our proofs were late – only partly in jest.

The Institute was founded by Lord Lugard in 1929 for the study of African languages and cultures, and until the 1960s remained very much the kind of learned society that Barbara depicted in *Excellent Women* and *Less than Angels*. After the war, admittedly, Professor Forde had revitalised it, but there remained, until his death in 1973, just the slightest suggestion of accomplished amateurism. He was a great fund-raiser (very like Felix Mainwaring in *Less than Angels*) and could always manage to coax just one more grant from UNESCO or the Ford Foundation for a new project. Life at the Institute in his day was always interesting.

Originally the Institute was rather grandly housed in Lower Regent Street, but financial pressures necessitated a move to Fetter Lane, just off Fleet Street, an interesting part of London. ('Hazel and I recalled Dryden living in Fetter Lane, perhaps writing *Absalom and Achitophel* in the place where our Library now stands.'[4])

The building, St Dunstan's Chambers, was old and in a bad state of repair. We occupied two floors. The library and library offices were on the lower floor, and also that little room where Deirdre and Tom were discovered sitting together on the sofa – actually occupied by our bookkeeper. The second floor housed Professor Forde's room, that of the Institute Secretary, a room for the Membership Secretary, the General Office with two typists (where tea was made, as in *Jane and Prudence*) and our room, which carried the non-committal legend 'Editorial'.

St Dunstan's Chambers became gradually more dilapidated and decayed as the surrounding buildings were demolished. Barbara, who worked from ten until six, to avoid the rush hour on the Tube, was often alone on the second floor from five until six. 'Now that the advertising firm above us have left, the place is empty except for us and you can hear the mice scuttling overhead in the evenings.'[5] It could be an eerie experience, especially in the dark winter evenings.

In March 1972 we moved from the interesting disintegration of Fetter Lane to a blank, modern block in High Holborn. As in *Quartet in Autumn*, there was a public library on one side and the Rendezvous Restaurant (which took luncheon vouchers) on the other.

Barbara had no formal title at the Institute, being simply 'in charge of Publications'. She was, of course, Assistant Editor of *Africa*, a position that gave her considerable satisfaction. It was a source of pride that, even during various printers' strikes and disputes, *Africa* always appeared (quarterly) on time.

Professor Forde, naturally, chose the articles, but it was Barbara who was responsible for editing the articles themselves, as well as for the preliminary selection of books for review ('Are you beginning to experience "some problems of a review editor"? It makes one almost *hate* people when they don't send in reviews, I find, and I have my own private black list on which it is very terrible to be'[6]). Then there was the compilation of Notes and News and the frustrated novelist complained that 'D. F. won't let me keep the bit about the coffee morning and "the beautiful lakeside campus".' She had to organise the French and English summaries for each article (*Africa* was bilingual) and annually compile the subject and tribal indexes.

She was also in charge of the advertisements for *Africa*. This was another little bit of 'mystique' which gave her great pleasure. When she was dealing with the agency that handled the more important advertisements for banks, airlines, and so on, she would assume a slightly dashing air, the faintest hint of Madison Avenue.

Each year the Institute would publish, funds permitting, two or three full-length monographs, three volumes of the Ethnographic Survey and one of the Linguistic Survey (linguists being notoriously more difficult to urge into print) and one or two volumes of seminar papers, as well as the four issues of *Africa*. Barbara saw them all through the press, at every stage, from the initial editing to the final proof-reading. I was her only assistant.

Her general air of vagueness and tentativeness hid a formidable professionalism. She never seemed to hurry; there was always time for a chat – indeed, we had the reputation of never seeming to do any work; but, somehow, the work always was done. And well, and on time.

Daryll Forde, energetic, extrovert and 'do-ish', used to say 'Barbara has no sense of urgency' and 'Barbara never initiates anything'. They lived and worked at different tempos: 'Get him on the phone right *away*, my dear', he used to say briskly. Barbara would give a compliant smile and go quietly away and write a well-turned letter instead. The results were usually the same.

It is not surprising that there should have been moments of stress between two such opposite personalities. Professor Forde mellowed with the years ('His helmet now', we used to quote, 'shall make a hive for bees'), but in the 1950s and 1960s he was forceful, and occasionally blustering. 'I work for dear Professor Forde, who is brilliant, has great charm but no manners, and is altogether the kind of person I ought to work for!'[7] His temper was short and his patience limited. Sometimes Barbara would return to our room in tears. He was essentially a kind man, but insensitive, and he obviously had no idea of the effect he had on those of a more retiring nature. One forgave him his faults because he was so brilliant. He had that rare thing, a truly clear and incisive mind that could cut straight through to the heart of any problem, financial or academic. This made him (once one had conquered one's fear of him) a most exciting person to work for. Towards the end of her time at the Institute Barbara wrote, 'It is rather nice having Daryll around more. "Stimulating" as you say, and I feel we are two old people cleaving together.'[8]

Working, as Barbara used to say, on 'the dustier fringes of the academic world', we came across many eccentrics. Anthropology being something of a grab-bag of a discipline, Barbara was able to observe the whole gamut, from scientifically oriented sociologist to traditional, Africa-based missionary. She delighted in the jargon of the anthropologist – though no one in *Africa* was allowed to say 'prior to the commencement of my second field-trip' and she had a particular hatred of 'amongst' and 'whilst'. The grammatical examples of the linguists ('I have eaten polenta to bursting') gave her great pleasure, as did certain terminological complications: 'A mother's brother acknowledged some responsibility for his sister's son, but not for the sister's son of his sister's son.'

The Institute provided fellowships for anthropological work in the field, the results to be written up in monographs, which Barbara would edit. She, therefore, had her 'own' anthropologists, whose progress she would follow with interest and whose lives she examined minutely. Some became friends, and the longueur of office afternoons would be enlivened by visits from the prototypes of Tom Mallow, Digby Fox and Everard Bone. 'These long, lonely August afternoons are ideal for receiving visitors when one is dozing over proofs.'[9]

Summer was the time for visiting American anthropologists to call. Barbara was fascinated by American academic life: the 'crushing teaching load' of four hours a week, the delicate matter of the correct address ('it can't have been as bad as when I called someone *Assistant* Professor when he was *Associate*'[10]). She also enjoyed the freshness of expression in the phraseology ('we are about five miles from the campus, portal to portal'). At one time Barbara, always a great reader of contemporary fiction, read all the novels she could find about American academic life. It seemed like another world.

As she always did in any situation, she speculated about the lives of her authors and invented sagas about them. These inventions were so vivid that it was hard to remember what was fact and what fiction. She usually got the character right, though: 'I had a card from dear John Beattie – how nice of him to write to me and so typical of the character we have invented for him.'[11]

The inhabitants of this world slipped – 'with a little polishing' – quite easily and naturally into her fictional world: Margaret Bryan became Miss Lydgate; Jean Rouch, Jean-Pierre le Rossignol; Father Van Bulck, Father Gemini; Wilfred Whiteley, Everard Bone and Professor A. N. Tucker, the little man with the suitcases apparently filled with lead.

The Institute staff also provided material: the Secretary, Beatrice Wyatt, and the Librarian, Ruth Jones, both gave her aspects of Esther Clovis; one of the library assistants was the original of Mervyn ('Mr C in the Library – he is having his lunch, eating a sandwich with a knife and fork'); and I make a brief appearance in *No Fond Return of Love* as Laurel's mother.

Even though she had six novels published during her years at the Institute, not every member of the staff seemed particularly impressed. Professor Forde read one, found it, I suspect, largely incomprehensible and read no more. Other members of staff read them and some, such as Barbara's friend Ailsa Currie (another ex-Wren officer, who was Secretary of the Institute from 1954 to 1964), appreciated and loved them.

The anthropological world, with some exceptions, however, saw Barbara's name in print only on the cover of *Africa* and in formal acknowledgements: 'I am also grateful to Miss Barbara Pym for the considerable work involved in preparing the final version of the text for the printer.'[12] She noted, 'I looked at the author's acknowledgements, the first thing I always do with books of Africa interest!'[13] Only a few Africanists, 'on the same wave length', as Ailsa Currie used to say, realised that the beady eye of a novelist was upon them and that she was engaged in her own kind of field work, which provided the basis for her fictional world.

As far back as 1949, three years after joining the Institute and just after she had attended a course of Professor Forde's lectures at University College, London (her only 'training' in anthropology), she had written a radio comedy – never, alas, accepted – about anthropologists. It was called *Parrot's Eggs*. The title refers to the custom of sending five parrot's eggs to a Nigerian chief when his suicide was required, so this probably indicates that she wrote it while engaged on one of the early, Nigerian sections of the Ethnographic Survey.

Dr Apfelbaum and Miss Jellink of *Excellent Women* ('Now, Herbert, no milk for Miss Jellink!' – p. 88) both make early appearances. She also makes her first reference to the dichotomy between the old and the new in African studies when she compares the missionary hero's *With Cassock and Surplice in Lyamboolooland* with the anthropologist heroine's *The Fission and Accretion of Certain Fragmentary Patrilineal Kin Groups in Lyambooloo Social Structure*.

Barbara had little interest in anthropology as such and certainly none in Africa – she never expressed a wish to go there. Occasional aspects, the human ones, would catch her attention – case histories or incidents in people's lives. One rather old-fashioned study of a religious leader in a small East African tribe, *The Mugwe*, was a favourite of hers. She found one of the chapter headings, 'The Vacancy in Imenti', somehow very evocative.

But some of the actual techniques of anthropology were those, in fact, that she had been employing herself for years: observation, notation and deduction. 'Not even the slightest expression of amusement or disapproval should ever be displayed at the description of ridiculous, impossible or disgusting features in custom, cult or legend', was one of Barbara's favourite quotations from *Notes and Queries in Anthropology*. That kind of dispassionate quality of examination and evaluation is present in her work, though there is amusement in abundance. Which is one of the reasons why she was a novelist and not an anthropologist.

Another rich source of material lay in the Institute itself, in the inter-relationship and 'unpleasantness' inherent in all office life. ('Great staff dramas in our office – *that* set-up suggests itself as fruitful novel material.'[14]) *Jane and Prudence* contains a lot of the Institute's daily routine: the making of the tea or coffee (the typists made the tea – tea money sixpence a week – but one made one's own coffee), the delicate balance of office hierarchy, and the oblique criticisms ('"Well, of course I have been sitting here since a quarter to ten", said Miss Clothier. "So perhaps I have got cold sitting." "Ah, yes; you may have got cold sitting", agreed Miss Trapnell. "I have only been here since *five* to ten"' – p. 36).

Sections of *An Unsuitable Attachment* are taken straight from IAI library life: '"Government in Zazzau", he declared. "The place of publication is London, *not* Oxford. It was published *by* the Oxford University Press *for* the International African Institute – do you see?"' (p. 29). And the party in the library, for the left-over readers a source of embarrassment, brings back many agreeable memories.

Quartet in Autumn gives a maturer, sadder view of office life, but Barbara's own retirement party was a considerably more cheerful affair.

My retirement party went off quite well and I didn't burst into tears or anything shaming like that. There was wine and lots of nice food. John Middleton [the Director] made a speech and everyone (almost) that I liked was able to come. . . . I was presented with a cheque but my real 'present', the new Oxford Dictionary, which I had chosen, rather typically hadn't arrived as it was rebinding.[15]

Because the Institute was registered as an official charity and funds fluctuated, depending on grants from various sources, salaries were very low. Staff, especially in the 1950s, were expected to be either married (and thus supported by their husbands) or to have private means. Barbara's salary, when she began in 1946 was £5 a week – it was still less than £1500 a year when she retired in 1974. She made a little from her novels, but it was never more than pin money. Fortunately she lived with her sister Hilary (who, as a BBC producer, had a more substantial salary) and shared expenses with her, Hilary providing the little luxuries of life for them both.

The shortage of funds at the Institute made us all very conscious of the need for economies. Though, since we had just come through the war and were still, in tne 1950s, living in a period of austerity and rationing, we were naturally frugal – as, indeed, Barbara was by nature. Every single paper clip was precious; carbon paper and typewriter ribbons were used to the point of illegibility; and all drafts and internal communications were made on the back of old manuscripts or proofs. Indeed, in those careful days Barbara was grateful for a limitless supply of scrap paper on which to write the first drafts of her novels. Just occasionally, when she had an idea or when things were a little slack, she would write a bit of a novel in the office. Often she would get out one of the small spiral-backed notebooks in which she recorded her observations and make a note of something that had caught her attention.

This note-taking would often occur when we returned from lunch. To make up for the meagreness of our salaries we had relatively long holidays (four, later five, weeks) and an hour and a half for lunch. Barbara and I usually had lunch together, often not talking but companionably reading our books together. There was a splendidly varied selection of places which we patronised over the years.

In the early days at Lower Regent Street we had the rich variety of the Lyons Corner House: the noble white and gold self-service

(*Excellent Women*), the Vita-Sun (four small snack dishes for tenpence!), the Restful Tray (where we saw a nun eating a large steak one Ash Wednesday) or, on rare affluent occasions, the red-plush nostalgia of Old Vienna.

Later there was the basement self-service of the Lyons teashop in Fleet Street, where the large lady dishing out the food would flourish a ladle and say 'Gravy?' Or, to her 'regulars', '*More* gravy?' This place was rather spartan in its appointments but along two of the walls were upholstered banquettes. Occasionally, too, the menu would include liver and bacon, a great favourite. 'We don't ask much of life', Barbara would say. 'It takes so *little* to make us happy – just liver and bacon and a seat on the banquette.' And it was so.

The Kardomah in Fleet Street (*Less than Angels*) was a particular haven:

> They are altering the Kardomah and 'improving' the ground floor and soon the basement will be gone. Where now will we be able to read and write and brood? First the mosaic peacocks went, now this! What emotions are trapped in that basement.[16]

There was also the ABC teashop, later the Lite Bite (*A Glass of Blessings*, *An Unsuitable Attachment* and *No Fond Return of Love*), the health-food Oodles in Fetter Lane (*The Sweet Dove Died*), Hills in Fleet Street (where Digby and Mark once memorably took Esther Clovis and Gertrude Lydgate) and the Rendezvous in High Holborn (where the protagonists in *Quartet in Autumn* used Edwin's luncheon vouchers). They were all part of the world she inhabited, observed and reported upon, finding them of absorbing interest. A postcard I received from her once when I was on holiday began, 'Just had a jolly lunch at the Sizzle Bar in Ludgate Circus (20p).' Food was a great subject of conversation, and our first greeting in the morning, if one of us had been out to dinner the night before, was always 'What did you *have*?'

When we worked in Fetter Lane we sometimes went to the lunchtime book sales at Hodgsons, the auctioneers in Chancery Lane (now Sothebys): 'We did go into Hodgsons at lunchtime . . . but we were afraid we might find ourselves buying all those 40 vols of Angus [Wilson] and Iris [Murdoch] if we stayed, so we slunk out again and shall go on Monday.'[17] Or we might do a little shopping, either locally (at Gamages or in Leather Lane market) or, taking a bus up to Oxford Street, 'have a nice surge round Marks and Spencer'.

Some lunchtimes, in the years when she was unpublished, she personally delivered her unaccepted, apparently unacceptable novel to the various publishers' offices within reach of the Institute (to save postage) and, after a while, collected it again. She remained seemingly cheerful, though, as time went on, not hopeful, as she once again parcelled it up and took it on the rounds. Such moments were distressing to observe, the more so because she remained vulnerable to disappointment, though never bitter because of it.

> My novel has its umpteenth rejection (from Cassell). After lunch . . . at Oodles we go to Red Lion Square and I enter the portals of Cassell's to collect the nicely done-up MS. Where next? Up to Faber in Queen's Square?[18]

During the sixteen years when her novels were not published, the Institute gave a shape and purpose to Barbara's life for which she was grateful. But it was *not* enough to be the Assistant Editor of *Africa*. She had always thought of herself as a writer and she could no more stop writing than she could stop breathing. The notebook was always in her handbag and there was usually an idea for a novel over which she would be, as she used to say, brooding.

The Sweet Dove Died, born of her own emotional experiences at the time (1967), was completed, but there were also several false starts, ideas for novels that never really came to anything: an old professor living in the same village as his estranged wife, and a novel set in a redbrick university, based on an academic wrangle from the pages of *Africa*. But, as she herself approached retirement, so the idea evolved of our old people working in an office: 'Have thought of the idea for a novel based on our office move – all old crabby characters, petty and obsessive, bad-tempered – how easily one of them could have a false breast.'[19]

Even after ill health caused her to retire in 1974, Barbara continued to do some work for the Institute at home. This was partly because the small amount of money was useful (her Institute pension was infinitesimal) but mostly because she enjoyed still 'having something to do'.

When I got back to the office [after her illness she went back briefly, part-time] I found such a lot of different things happening (there is a new young Director in place of Professor Forde) that I was rather glad to be out of it all! I am still doing a little mild work e.g. the African tribal index . . . and the odd bibliography which I find quite a good discipline, so that I work for an hour or two in the morning.[20]

In her busy years at the Institute the only time she had for writing was early in the morning or at weekends. Now, when she had all the time in the world, no one seemed to want her novels. She duly noted the irony.

She had written novels before 1946 and she wrote one after 1974, but the mainstream of her work was done while she was at the Institute. She always said that she was glad that she had a job and that she was not just writing in a vacuum. She drew a great deal from that job – not simply raw material for her novels, characters and situations. But inhabiting a world with certain parameters gave a structure to her life, which, in its turn, gave her fictional world a solidity and cohesion.

Barbara gave the International African Institute splendid editorial service, but the Institute, in return, gave her a whole world to revel in.

4

Fellow Writers in a Cotswold Village

Gilbert Phelps

My first meeting with Barbara Pym had nothing to do with the fact that we both happened to be writers: it belonged to the small beer of social observances of the kind she so much appreciated and from which she could extract so much humour and unexpected significance. The news of the arrival of the two sisters who had bought Barn Cottage reached us by the village grapevine (just ahead of a postcard from a mutual acquaintance linking us up). After my wife (having already experienced the rigours of moving in to the small village of Finstock) collected milk and some newly-baked bread, we walked the few hundred yards from our own cottage to welcome the newcomers. Barbara's sister Hilary and I quickly discovered mutual ties, because she had recently retired from the BBC and I had myself worked there for sixteen years before leaving to become a full-time writer. But for some reason I had missed out on Barbara's novels of the 1950s and I knew almost nothing of her work, though as I was currently enjoying a modest success she knew something of mine. I shall never forget how very gently, indeed almost diffidently, she said, 'I, too, write novels', when, after all, she might well have been hurt by my ignorance. It was not long, of course, before I had remedied that: she lent me her earlier novels, showed me the admiring reviews they had received (and Bob Smith's more recent article 'How Pleasant to Know Miss Pym' in the journal *Ariel*), and told me the wretched story of her long years in the literary wilderness following the rejection of her seventh novel, *The Sweet Dove Died* – unaccountable to me as to so many others both because of its quality (I remember telling her that in my opinion it marked an advance in some ways, handling a very difficult subject with great

34

delicacy and deeper psychological insight), and because her earlier novels had achieved sales which should have been adequate enough to have encouraged her publisher to persist.

By now, in fact, I was as indignant as those who had long recognised the special nature of her work, and I tried to help by introducing her to fresh publishers and literary agents, only for her to receive the same response she had already encountered – that her kind of fiction was out of tune with the spirit of the times. 'But how can they *know*', she said, 'unless they try?', and as authors we sympathised with each other about what seemed to us the lack of enterprise and artistic commitment, and the subservience to the fads and fashions of the moment displayed by the vast majority of publishers.

We used to speculate, too, on the mysterious ups and downs of a writer's life, wondering what exactly it was that attracted even the most discriminating readers to some books and not to others equally good in our view; and why praise from the critics seemed so often to have little effect. We agreed that really there was nothing one could – or should – do about it: one could write only what one *could* write, and straining after effects that didn't come naturally, or seeking consciously to please the public or the critics, was disastrous to whatever talent one might possess. We tried to define what we as writers meant by success. Fundamentally, of course, it was a matter of satisfying the standards we had set ourselves, and I remember that on one occasion we spoke of the pangs of conscience that nagged at one's vitals if one knew that one had been faking. But we agreed that writers, more perhaps than some other artists, needed a public no matter how small, and that the admiration of personal friends alone was not sufficient to stimulate development and growth. As for success in purely commercial terms, we agreed that it was something 'added unto one'; it might happen or it might not, but it was a matter of sheer luck, like winning the football pools. Either way one had to keep on writing. It was easier for me, whose novels were still being published, to talk in this way (and Barbara was unaffectedly generous in her pleasure on my behalf) – not so easy for her, though she did so quite calmly and dispassionately. Not that passionate feeling wasn't there: there had been times, she admitted, when her failure to place her novels had filled her with anger and despair. She still had her job at the African Institute in London then, but it was first and foremost as a writer that she regarded herself, and during her years in Finstock she never stopped writing and revising her unpublished typescripts.

When I visited her after the mini-stroke which she suffered in March 1974 had caused an odd kind of dyslexia, her first words were 'What a thing to happen to a *writer!*' She was already making ferocious efforts to overcome her disability, sitting up in bed with a book in her hand (I think it was *Pride and Prejudice*) trying to force herself to make sense of the sequence of letters, though to begin with she found even reading very difficult, while her first attempts to write simple words and sentences of her own resulted in what she called 'Alice in Wonderland language'. She was fully aware of what was happening to her and perfectly coherent in her speech, and she immediately began a discussion about her condition – not in terms of its pathology but solely from the point of view of a writer. If she had been a painter, she wondered, would it have been her colour sense that would have been affected, or if a musician her command of tone and pitch? Was there some strange element of guilt and self-punishment about it? Or might it be, I suggested, a consequence of the strain imposed by the long years of neglect? She considered all these possibilities with her usual calm and ironic detachment – and I want to stress that though there had undoubtedly been strain she never in my experience revealed the slightest sign of self-pity: justified indignation in the cause of her creativity, yes, but none of the personal vanity or whining common enough with writers in a similar predicament.

Happily she soon recovered, and she was well enough to attend the dedication by the Bishop of Oxford, on 23 June 1974, of a plaque in our village church commemorating the baptism there of T. S. Eliot forty-seven years earlier and the party which my wife gave in our cottage beforehand. Both she and Hilary had given me generous support in the launching of the appeal – restricted at the request of Valerie Eliot to Oxfordshire (though Faber and Faber made a donation) – and in organising the occasion, and both of them were keenly appreciative of the readings from Eliot which the Bishop and my wife gave during the service. Soon after, on her doctor's advice, Barbara retired from her African Institute job and gave up her London flat. Now that she was settled in Finstock we saw a good deal more of each other. We discussed the pros and cons for a writer of living in a small, remote village, deciding that on the whole the advantages

far outweighed the disadvantages. We were quite certain that
ours was the right kind of village, not particularly attractive
(though in beautiful countryside), but still a real working village
with a genuine cross-section of English society – and certainly of
human nature – and a far healthier setting for a writer than some
of the 'prettified' places nearby, in which, in marked contrast, the
old indigenous inhabitants had largely been replaced by retired
people and weekenders. In any case we both really felt we had
the best of both worlds, with Oxford only some twenty minutes
away by car, and the train from nearby Charlbury to London
taking not much more than an hour.

From time to time Barbara would tell me of her progress with
Quartet in Autumn, which she had begun in 1973 and finished
three years later, though still without hope of publication.
Naturally in the inevitable breaks from our desks we often talked
about our books and the technical problems involved in writing
them. We each had preferences in each other's work and tried to
explain them. I was particularly attached at the time to *Less than
Angels*, and Barbara, in turn, gave me much food for thought
about my work: for example, she liked my novel *The Old Believer*
(*Mortal Flesh* in the American edition) but suggested, rightly I
suspect, that the vein of fantasy which I had explored in *The
Winter People* was my more natural one. It was not only as fellow
writers that we came together but also in the course of our mutual
involvement in church and village affairs. In these Barbara was
always helpful, patient and hugely tolerant. She was a sincere
and devout Christian, but she would have no truck with narrow-
minded gossip about people's sexual frailties and peccadilloes:
'There are far worse sins than those of the flesh,' she had
exclaimed with considerable passion on one occasion, 'such as
greed, selfishness and cruelty.' At the same time she could not
help herself regarding everything around her with her cool,
amused novelist's gaze – and when one was riding one of one's
hobby-horses it could be extremely disconcerting suddenly to
become aware of those grey, observant eyes.

We frequently laughed together over the complexities and
contretemps of church and village life, agreeing that it was all
'Barbara Pym territory'. But, quite apart from the fact that she was
too tactful and too kind, she was too much of an artist to need to
draw directly upon any actual person or occasion. I know she was
sometimes fascinated by one or other of our village personalities

and would say she was strongly tempted to 'put them in' one of her books as she expressed it. Personally, though, knowing the village so well myself, I could not identify any of them in *A Few Green Leaves*, her last novel (though not the last to be published), which she wrote entirely in Finstock and which, of course, has a country setting. On the other hand, she told me that the title of that novel – which seems to me a particularly poignant one, encapsulating Barbara Pym's central theme of destinies that are restricted by circumstance but which are lived with courage and dignity – was the result of an occasion when, one Saturday afternoon in winter, she and her sister were in church and overheard one of the 'flower ladies' (the volunteers who, week after week, decorate the church in readiness for the Sunday service) saying that the paucity of blossoms at that time of the year could always be offset by the use of 'a few green leaves'. In other words, the context in which we had our being *had* indirectly entered into her creative consciousness, to be transmuted by her art.

By the time Barbara came to write this novel (between 1977 and 1979) the tide of her literary fortunes had dramatically turned: she had been rediscovered, *Quartet in Autumn* earned worldwide acclaim, and publishers were now vying with each other to re-issue her earlier novels. Reporters, interviewers, camera crews and fans came flocking to quiet Finstock. The fame and success we had both talked about had come to her at last – she had, indeed, almost won the football pools! She enjoyed every moment of it, but she was quite unchanged, viewing it all with the same ironic detachment she brought to her writing. 'I can't deny it's all very nice,' she said to me, 'but what has *really* happened? I'm writing in exactly the same way now as I did before – and now there's all *this* going on!' She was, of course, deeply grateful to her long-time admirers Philip Larkin and Lord David Cecil for the part they had played in drawing attention so forcefully and skilfully to the virtues of her work, in *The Times Literary Supplement*'s survey of 'the most underrated authors of the century'; though she was still puzzled, angry about the years of neglect, and not a little cynical. Real quality, I pointed out, was bound to be recognised sooner or later. 'Yes, and it's often after one's dead!' she replied, 'so I have much to be thankful for.' We spent some time discussing the possible reasons for the enthusiasm with which her work was now being regarded, on both sides of the Atlantic. I suggested that it might be a symptom of a reaction, in America as well as in Britain, against the violence, social disintegration and full-frontal-nudity approach in the books and plays of the 1960s and 1970s, and she thought there might be something in that, as perhaps there is – a kind of reassertion of Classicism against the corrupted late-twentieth-century version of Romanticism.

At this stage we were also more closely involved professionally. We were, for instance, both elected Fellows of the Royal Society of Literature, and about the same time we became fellow judges for an award for fiction offered by Southern Arts (our regional branch of the British Arts Council). I found our collaboration delightful and stimulating: we seemed to go through exactly the same doubts and hesitancies, were at one in our appraisals and rejections, and had no difficulty in arriving at our final decision, and together we attended the prize-giving ceremony at the tiny theatre in nearby Chipping Norton. Tragically, as everyone knows, Barbara did not have long to enjoy her literary rehabilitation. When during her last illness we used to visit her, we always found her calm and cheerful, sitting up in bed and still working on her last novel. She endured the horrors of chemo-therapy with the utmost fortitude, but she made no pretence about her condition, and she was grateful when we somehow succeeded in matching her own calm and cheerfulness. Her overriding objective, of course, was to get the novel finished, but she was almost as concerned about the village and the church. 'I *must* hang on till after Christmas', she told us. 'It would cause *too* much confusion if I went before!' She died on 11 January 1980, and together with Hilary, her devoted sister, we celebrated the posthumous publication of *A Few Green Leaves* with a small party in our cottage, attended by some of her friends and admirers, including her new publisher, with a large photograph of Barbara propped up on a bookcase, one of her beloved cats cradled in her arms, gazing down at us quizzically but affectionately.

Part II
The Work

5

Barbara Pym's Novelistic Genius

Joyce Carol Oates

One of the most heartrending remarks in Barbara Pym's diary (entered in 1972, after *The Sweet Dove Died* was again rejected by a publisher) is 'What is the future of my kind of writing?'[1] It's a pity Barbara Pym can't be present today to see that the future – this fragment of the future at least – has vindicated, and acclaimed, her special novelistic genius. What we love in her work is, I think, *her* – an inimitable quality of personality that shines through the carefully wrought, understated prose, blossoming now and then in marvellous surprising perceptions. She is intelligent, witty, subtle, funny and serious at the same time; irreverent, yet always respectful of her characters (even as she exposes them in all their comic vanities and self-delusions – which are not so very different from our own, or one suspects, Barbara Pym's). Devotees of Pym always ask one another, 'Which book is your favourite?' – mine being *A Glass of Blessings*, followed closely by *Jane and Prudence*. Yet the autobiographical writings are perhaps as good. Who else but Barbara Pym would assure a friend that having a breast removed for cancer is really not *so* bad ('It was my first visit to hospital and apart from the first few days of discomfort . . . I rather enjoyed the experience. To have a lovely rest, to have flowers and grapes and books brought to you and to be a centre of interest is not at all unpleasant!'[2]); and who else would note, as Barbara Pym did on 8 October 1977, in what must have been a fragment of a yet-unrealised fiction,

She knew that she dared not pray for humility, to be granted the grace of humility, it being such a precious thing, but when others were decorating the church for Harvest Festival she

43

chose a humble, even humiliating task, emptying the cat's tray, bundling the soiled Katlitta into a newspaper. Yet had she even chosen it – it was just something that had to be done. Whatever thy hand findeth to do, do it with all thy might.[3]

As a consequence of Pym's gentle satirical humour, so frequently directed against organised religion (as against any sort of organised pretension), it is something of a shock to realise that she is, finally, a religious writer. *Whatever thy hand findeth to do, do it with all thy might.* And so Barbara Pym did.

6

The World of Barbara Pym

Penelope Lively

'Male and female created He them', thinks Tom Dagnall, the rector who is a central figure (heroes simply do not occur in a Pym novel) in *A Few Green Leaves*, observing neighbours through their window (p. 29). And that proposition is the crux of the story, as it is of the whole of Barbara Pym's work. Tom, widower – and, incidentally, the only clergyman in the oeuvre to receive relatively charitable authorial treatment (one thinks almost with nostalgia of Archdeacon Hoccleve) – and living with his sister, who walks out on him halfway through the book, is, like all Pym men, in search of feminine services of various kinds: culinary chiefly, parochial of course, and vaguely scholarly in connection with Tom's consuming interest, local history. 'A meek woman of retirement age could be of inestimable value', he thinks (p. 60), taking stock of a new arrival in the village – and we are right into familiar Pym country, the battle is on, restrained, structured, but a battle none the less. And if it were any other Pym novel we could be fairly certain that by the end the men would probably have won, at least in a technical sense of either having graciously given themselves in marriage, or, more probably, cunningly extracted themselves from emotional obligation. But the subtler, moral victory would be that of the women, that army of beady-eyed, vulnerable, frequently romantic, often exploited Pym women from Belinda Bede of *Some Tame Gazelle*, through Mildred Lathbury of *Excellent Women* and Jane Cleveland of *Jane and Prudence*, to Dulcie Mainwaring of *No Fond Return of Love* and now Emma Howick of *A Few Green Leaves*.

They have few illusions, these women: unlike the other brand of Pym heroine, the Prudences and the Harriets, who rush headlong into the sexual struggle, starry-eyed, doomed to humiliation, but ultimately the less susceptible, they are all too well aware of what is going on.

45

'We know that men are not like women', went on Miss
Doggett firmly. 'Men are very passionate', she said in a low
tone. . . .

'You mean that they only want one thing?' said Jane.

'Well, yes, that is it. We know what it is.'

'Typing a man's thesis, correcting proofs, putting sheets
sides-to-middle, bringing up children, balancing the house-
keeping budget . . . .'   (*Jane and Prudence*, p. 127)

But Jane, in fact, is thinking of her own role, rather than that
facing the agile Miss Morrow, down-trodden 'companion' who
has managed to carry off the eligible bachelor in *Jane and Prudence*.

A Few Green Leaves, though, ends on an optimistic note. It looks
as though Emma and Tom will marry, and might even live
happily afterwards. It is perhaps more tempered than the other
novels, the claws are retracted a little, the wit gentler – or is it, are
they? For one of the curious, and to the addict most compelling,
features of Barbara Pym's fiction is its quality of reticence. None
of the books gives itself up on first reading; it is on the second,
third and subsequent visits that some verbal felicity becomes
apparent, that a sequence of events falls into a pattern, and I
suspect that this may be particularly true of *A Few Green Leaves*.

On the face of it the territory is familiar: a cast of ten or so, two
or three leading figures through whose eyes we shall mainly
watch the unfolding of the tale, and a chorus of lesser
but significant characters who will provide both action and
commentary. Emma, a young anthropologist using her mother's
cottage in an Oxfordshire village while she writes up some notes,
is trifled with by an old flame who also settles himself in the
village (needing, of course, food rather than sex, which often
seems to come a long way down the servicing-priorities of Pym
men). She observes, with an amused and semi-professional eye,
the social structure of the village, in which the old villagers are
too well dressed to have any use for the discarded clothes at the
jumble sales arranged by the gentry, who appropriate them for
their own use. Fun is had at the expense of the new aristocracy:
the village's two doctors. There are other whiffs of the 1970s: a
pair of trendy young academics, a hunger lunch (' "Twenty-five
pence?" said the old doctor. "That would be five bob in proper
money, wouldn't it? That seems a bit steep for a slice of pappy
bread and a sliver of mousetrap" ' – p. 158), burgeoning

commitment to the local-history group. It seems in some ways a far cry from the early novels of the 1950s, and from the more dispersed London setting of *Quartet in Autumn* and *The Sweet Dove Died*.

And yet it isn't: the old flavour is there, and thank heaven for it. There is a curious sense in which Barbara Pym seemed to spring to life fully fledged as a novelist, thirty years ago, and what has happened since has been not so much the process of learning by mistakes through which most writers must go, as a deliberate reworking and extension of an already mastered formula. As Philip Larkin said in *The Times Literary Supplement* article that followed her 'rediscovery' in 1977, 'as novels they exhibit no "development"; the first is as practised as the last, the observation, the social comedy, the interplay of themes equally expert'.[1] Indeed, for me, the first, *Some Tame Gazelle*, remains in many ways the most masterly, the richest in understated humour, in devastating characterisation (the Archdeacon, oh the Archdeacon . . .), in narrative merry-go-round. It's a nice irony that *The Times Literary Supplement*, at the time, could only find that 'the book flows cheerfully on with little wit and much incident, and many readers will compare it unfavourably with the earlier novels of Mrs Thirkell'.[2] One sees a virtue of reviewing-anonymity: embarrassing, that would be, now.

But the 1950s novels attracted plenty of admiring comment: notably and always most perceptively from other writers – Antonia White, Olivia Manning, Pamela Hansford Johnson, John Betjeman, William Plomer. Looking back, though, it is possible to see how she suffered for being praised as much for what she was not as for what she was: 'this civilized and amusing novel makes a very nice change from the Brutalist school of contemporary fiction'; 'So many novels I pick up nowadays seem to deal with Saturday night in the back streets of Nottingham . . . far more fascinating than anything which could come from the one-track minded proles of Nottingham and Huddersfield.' It was such literary barbarities as this last that may have put off many potential readers who would have enjoyed her. She arrived, in a sense, at the wrong moment: in the roomier and more genial literary climate of the late 1970s (and, let's hope, the 1980s) that kind of critical nihilism is less often heard.

It was for social acerbity that she was praised ('students of the niceties of middle-class social quirks and mannerisms will derive quiet pleasure') both then and later. Well, yes, of course, up to a point – but that seems to miss the central, driving theme of the books, which is sexual conflict itself. Class doesn't really have a lot to do with it; what is going on is not tart observation of social manoeuvrings but a devastating, sublimely unfair, wonderfully funny and ultimately fatalistic analysis of the relations between men and women. Unfair because, while Pym men usually do, in the end, get their meals cooked for them, their indexes done, their bibliographies checked, their socks and pullovers knitted, they are also, finally, the victims: helpless but predatory, holding the ultimate weapon of choice (do women ever actually propose, wonders Belinda Bede, hopelessly loving the Archdeacon for twenty years, and consoles herself with the fantasy that his terrible wife Agatha must have done: there is no other explanation), but morally corrupt. It is a battle of gender rather than of sex: board comes a long way before bed, children are seldom evident. But love, or the need for love, is everywhere: 'Some tame gazelle, or some gentle dove: Something to love, oh, something to love!'

Out of comedy she creates a wry, moving commentary on what we all need, on what some of us will go to any lengths to get, on what some of us have to do without. 'Well, we can't expect to get everything we want', says a character in *A Few Green Leaves*. 'We know that life isn't like that' (p. 159). Deprivation is the central matter of the novels, making the best of things, living on the fringes, the observation of what often seems to be feckless lack of appreciation in others. But courage also, and stoicism and charity (in the proper, biblical sense of the word). Funny books which are also deeply serious; a cutting edge that is as clean as it is ruthless.

A Few Green Leaves is set in Oxfordshire; that is almost all we are told. Barbara Pym's style – economical, direct, never using a long word where a short one will do, relying above all on dialogue – has never included much by way of physical setting. If the reader pictures bosky vicarage gardens, sedate London offices (of anthropological societies), the suburbia of decayed expectations, it is all in the mind's eye – the author has not told us about it. Such descriptions as we get are a world of interiors: furnishings, clothes, above all what is eaten and drunk. The preciosity of Leonora's house in *The Sweet Dove Died*, the minute discussions between Belinda and Harriet Bede of what should properly be worn for which occasion, the carefully devised menus offered by woman to visiting man (food has a rich and subtle language of its own in the novels – chicken blanketed in white sauce, in the old days, for cherished curates; ham mousse, in the 1970s, for a former lover). And if at times this seems a shortcoming it is because we have come to expect a lot: the author has given us a particular and a total world and we want to relate it to the familiar and the general one. We want to specify the London landscapes obliquely hinted at, to set down Leonora and the characters of *Quartet in Autumn* in familiar streets and houses.

Quartet in Autumn seems, now, distinct from the rest and perhaps the finest achievement. More sombre than the others but with all their wit and accuracy; sadder, but shot with the same braveries, the same triumphs of humour over meanness and egotism. Four solitary poeple on the edge of retirement, making the best of things. Or not. Again, the real world impinges only in a shadowy way; if social change is hinted at in *A Few Green Leaves*, in *Quartet in Autumn* it is present only in the form of encroaching supermarkets and changed eating-places. For this is the other sense in which the Pym world is a particular and detached one: whatever is going on out there in the public world is of little or no concern to the story. Pym characters rarely read newspapers, hold political convictions or are perturbed by public events. The course of history is somewhere else, out there, irrelevant. And this, on reflection, is how it should be. The generalities of this particular fictional world are not the generalities of living in the 1950s, or the 1960s, or the 1970s, but the perennial problems of being man or woman, of being old or young, of being vulnerable or impervious, all of which may be tempered by the times but do not in the last resort have a lot to do with them. *A Few Green Leaves* gives us, again, a society complete in itself, constructed and peopled with all Barbara Pym's artistry: believable, moving, entertaining.

7

Where, Exactly, is the Pym World?

John Bayley

It used to be said of Raphael's paintings that they impress the viewer less at first in order to strike him more and more later on. Something of the kind is certainly true of a particular kind of art which may be as sublime as Raphael's, or much more simple and homely. Such art has clarity, joyfulness, absoluteness of being – a complete air of simplicity above all, which, as in the case of Raphael's paintings or Pushkin's poems, makes the achievement seem as effortless as it is open and uncomplicated.

These may seem portentous words with which to begin a discussion of the special qualities of Barbara Pym's novels. The fact is, however, that those novels belong to that category of art which offers something more each time we experience it, while at the same time they retain their air of openness and simplicity. Not many novels have this quality: indeed it would be true to say that the form as a whole – the word 'novel' itself suggests it – depends on a strong initial impact, securing the interest of the reader and keeping him enthralled while he reads. When he has finished and looks back over the story, its construction may strike him as artificial, in every sense, but by that time the artifice has done its work, the deception has succeeded, and the novel as a form is no longer concerned with what the reader thinks of it, just as the conjuror is satisfied to have kept his audience in a state of illusion during his act.

The finest flower of this process can be seen in Henry James's retrospective prefaces to the New York Edition of his novels, where it is taken for granted that a connoisseur of the form will be concerned above all, when he comes to appraise the novel, with the question of 'how it was done'. All critics base their verdicts, and the terms in which they express them, on the same kind of

50

summing-up, and not critics only. Virginia Woolf disliked the traditional arts of the novel, and criticised James's handling of the death of Millie Theale, in *The Wings of the Dove*, as if he were in fact a conjuror: 'There is a great flourishing of silk handkerchiefs and Millie disappears behind them.' A conjuror, or a comedian. Appreciative critics of Barbara Pym write of her subtle comic effects, of her world of 'high comedy', of the amusing arts with which she presents to her reader the small events of life. Perfectly just, and yet even such unexceptionable praise here seems wide of the mark. Criticism that would define the achievement of other novelists surprises the reader of her novels by its irrelevance to the experience they have actually had.

The reason seems to be that, however often we reread her novels (and they are among the most rereadable today), we can never fix our gaze on how she does it, on how she obtains her effects. Instead we are involved all over again in her world and what seems to be its indefinable simplicities. Each time we read her she seems more real. Each time we are more struck not by her 'art', or her 'comedy', but by the truth of what she says. Hence the apparent inability of ordinary critical praise words to convey an impression of what actually happens in reading her, and why we continue to read. Her first official critic, oddly enough, came closest, when the first review of *Some Tame Gazelle*, in 1950, described it as no more to be defined than some delicious smell or taste.

The difficulty of criticising them reflects, among other things, her novels' lack of pretension, for most distinctive and original novels inevitably have the air of having been designed to attract a particular sort of perception and praise. But perceptive praise, even by Philip Larkin or Lord David Cecil, seems, equally inevitably, to operate on a different plane from where her novels actually are. The gap between their unique selves and what can justly be said about them remains clear and palpable. It applies even to her own comments on her work in her diary, as when she describes herself as seeing something 'with the novelist's sardonic detachment'. Sardonic detachment? Well, well. Of course, like every other writer she could be intelligently self-conscious about what she was trying to do, as when she answered the charge of excessive reliance on very trivial things in her novels by saying, yes, she did think triviality was very important in life. And yet her comments join the comments of others on the other side of the line from where her novels are. In discussing them, let alone reading them aloud on radio or at a conference (which one can scarcely imagine her doing, although most modern novelists do it all the time), she can no longer *be* them.

That involuntary *being* determines, as in the context of a love relationship, our sense of her work. As in such a relation the person outside, who does not respond, might well comment on the infatuated reader who does, 'I don't know what he sees in her.' No wonder the friendliest critical comment appears superfluous. And no wonder she would never be taken up by intellectuals, for whom explanation and enjoyment are one and the same thing. No one could be proud of reading her, or think he *ought* to. She is not 'significant' or 'important'. The academic industry inevitably growing up around her will in practice find itself behaving more like the 'Janeites', in Kipling's story, than a sober and productive branch of scholarship.

The clue to the nature of her achievement does of course lie in her difference from other contemporary novelists, and in what that difference implies. The modern novel has become a totally self-conscious and hence wholly homogeneous work, in which the method, the purpose, technique, setting and author are all one and the same, and equally identified with what can be spoken and written about them. I quote at random from a review of a recent *succès d'éstime*: 'It is an exciting and demanding work by an author who remains laudably determined to make the novel *do something*.' Exactly. The novel is no longer an unconscious self, the loved object unaware of what makes it the loved object. It has become an instrument in the writer's hand, an extension of his eye, mind, wit.

The unconscious selfhood of a Pym novel is clear and open. It has its habits, its little ways, its lovable weaknesses, its jokes and high spirits, its underlying sense of the sadness of life, which is none the less (to quote from her own correspondence) 'not as bad as all that'. I now sound as wide of the mark as other critics, and more embarrassing, but I must plough on because I think the point I am getting at will at least show why and how she is different, and why (without in the least meaning to) she discredits and diminishes much of the outlook in novels today which are highly praised and considered important. The selfhood of her novels embodies a true sense of duality. It is a quality she, and they, are quite unconscious of. And it is truer to life than the appearances of living laboriously assembled in other modern novels. It is a rare possession, and the evidence of it strikes us more, and more deeply, with each rereading.

By 'truer to life' I mean that her novels take entirely for granted the fact that we live in two worlds, one of extreme triviality typified by the work situation, social exchange, irritations, small comforts of eating and drinking, planning clothes, perceiving others. On the other hand we live in a world of romance, aspiration, love-longing, loneliness, despair. Nothing would be easier than for a novelist to systematise this contrast and purposefully point it up. It would then become an artificial structure on which our sense of the reality of the work depended, and about which we would be fully conscious of the author's probable satiric or didactic purpose. T. S. Eliot's play *The Cocktail Party* is based on such a structural duality. In Barbara Pym's novels the two worlds completely coincide without losing their separate identity. Each is present, but neither can be demarcated or defined in relation to the other.

The duality could be expressed as that of body and soul, in today's art and fiction an exploded and outmoded concept, or else one that is kept artifically alive for special reasons. The world of fiction today is a world from which this kind of natural dualism has disappeared: all events, actions, thoughts and perceptions have the same place in it, and occur at the same level. A kind of equality of experience is *de rigueur*. Pym novels, without seeming to do so, reverse this process: the idea of body and soul is immanent in their outlook on life. It is the basic premise of her comedy, for dualism – the contrast between men and women, between Church and God, between how we live and how we feel – is the deepest source of human comedy.

The flat world of modern fiction is suited to black jokes and satire, not to comedy, and Pym novels contain no satire. Like Jane Austen's communities the churches in her novels exemplify human society and its needs. Most of those needs cannot be explained – they just happen. Ianthe, in *An Unsuitable Attachment*, gives herself up to being in love as if submitting thankfully to the fact that she has the 'flu. Barbara Pym has none of the modern compulsion to be exact; the first symptoms just give Ianthe 'a feeling she could not explain' (p. 75). Similarly, comedy itself is not a convention, or an artificial sustainment of gaiety, but simply the involuntary part of human life, manifesting itself in conversations heard on buses and in indefinable feelings felt by one person for another who is probably unaware of them. The unseen cartilage running through the tissue of each fiction is itself illustrative of what is indefinable in her novels, and resistant to conventional terms of praise. Our feeling for them, our addiction to them, is in the end as indefinable to ourselves as is the interest her heroines begin to take in one of the male characters. Catherine in *Less than Angels* begins to be more and more drawn to Alaric Lydgate; Wilmet in *A Glass of Blessings* to Piers Longridge; Mildred of *Excellent Women* to Everard Bone; most delicately noted of all is the feeling that Emma in the last novel, *A Few Green Leaves*, begins insensibly to entertain for Tom Dagnall the rector. Each is unaware of the movement of the soul, the movement of faith as it were, which is drawing them towards each other. Leonora, in *The Sweet Dove Died*, finds herself given over to a love feeling which she can *do nothing about*; and at the time she was writing the novel Barbara Pym commented in her notebook that this was the kind of love women instinctively preferred.

Certainly she did herself. And this kind of thing gives us the feeling that the author is not manipulating, is not in charge; that she gives herself up to the sensation of living, the mysterious prompting of the soul, as much as her characters do, living in them as they in her. This is itself remarkable, for in general such a surrender on the part of the author would be a sign of weakness, of an inferior type and genre of fiction. That it is so triumphantly not in the case of Barbara Pym is itself a sign of something inexplicable in the way her fiction works, of the way in which comedy with her is not cool and detached (as it predominantly is even with Jane Austen) but warm and open, completely vulnerable. The 'superior' modern novel has conditioned us to accept that its author is indeed 'determined to make the novel *do something*'; that its author is by assumption in charge not only of his characters and their situation but of his own feelings and emotions. It is part of the comedy of Barbara Pym's world that she seems to 'let go' as much as her heroines do.

This is another way of saying that her genius is in the art of being funny without being superior. The humorist, like the satirist, is immune from his own sense of humour, from the shafts he directs at others. With her this is not the case. She gives the impression of being amused by her own weaknesses, for example by her repetitive emphasis on jumble sales or on comforting moments – cups of tea, cakes and coffee. The easy-going novel is by tradition a source of comfort to its readers, with its happy endings, lovers' meetings – 'a feast of sugar-plums', as knowing Trollope sardonically put it. In a Pym novel this traditional comfort has been converted into actual substances, solids and liquids, and the reader is always gratified when a fairy cake, or the inevitable cup of Lapsang Souchong, is put to his lips. The author does not conceal the fact that she relies so much on these simple devices, but draws every attention to it, and is herself entertained by it.

At a deeper level there is humour in the fact that cups of tea become a sort of substitute for happy endings, and symbolic of their traditional role. Life has no happy endings, and its cups of tea do not always cheer, but in Pym novels they do, standing in for the fact that in her novels there are neither happy endings nor – as in the sort of novels that Prudence likes to read – 'satisfying[ly] unhappy' ones (*Jane and Prudence*, p. 47). Incidentally, it comes as a real shock to the reader when Prudence, on a lonely London Sunday with Fabian departed, cannot even find comfort in her cup of China tea, which seems to taste like disinfectant.

It is a touch of the unpredictable, which Barbara Pym became so good at. Ianthe finds Miss Grimes, whom she has cast in the role of grateful lonely spinster, a rather coarse old body, perfectly able to look after herself. *Quartet in Autumn* is full of such things, barely visible at first. They are connected with other Pym qualities – with the fact, for example, that the novels are so full of eating and drinking and thinking about clothes, activities which we are specifically enjoined in the Bible to 'take no thought' on. The central truth and comfort of the Church is not a bit eclipsed by the fact that its worshippers spend their time doing what it officially tells them not to do. In the same way trivial comforts live on the same plane and share the same identity with romance and infatuation, deprivation, and suffering that is 'permanent, obscure and dark'. Body and soul are not the same, but they live together and share the same fate and the same face.

The novels are indefinable in that they are neither satisfyingly happy nor 'satisfying[ly] unhappy'; they are just satisfying. Barbara Bird, the novelist whom Jane meets at a literary evening in *Jane and Prudence*, is a veteran novelist who has 'just finished my seventeenth'. Kidding on the level, she imagines a review of one of her novels which begins, 'Miss Bird's readers know what to expect now, and they will not be disappointed.' A younger woman whose name is not known to Jane or to Miss Bird bashfully gives the titles of her two novels, 'neither of which seemed familiar' (pp. 118–19). Barbara Pym had herself written two at the time, and no doubt it amused her to think of her own future as not unlike Barbara Bird's. Ironically, and sadly, it was not to be so, but, if it had been, Miss Bird's words would have come literally true. Barbara Pym's readers would have known what to expect, and they would not have been disappointed. Her novels would have been both predictable and indefinable.

More subtle than these humorous self-references are the comments on women's magazine stories, written for her livelihood by Catherine Oliphant in *Less than Angels*. From Wilmet and her mother-in-law in *A Glass of Blessings*, who glance at it at the hairdresser's, we learn that Catherine wrote a story based on her own experience in *Less than Angels*, when she sees her lover, who is to leave her, dining with another girl. Wilmet and her mother-in-law decide that 'Catherine Oliphant' is probably the pen name of some spinster living in Eastbourne who has herself had none of the experience she describes. The fact that they are wrong is less important than the implication both that the writer Barbara Pym *is* describing life from her own experience of it, and that even women's magazine stores may in fact be much 'truer to life' than their readers suppose. Barbara Pym is quite conscious that her art is converting the threadbare conventions of such stories back into life, as it were. Instead of pretending, as the magazine writers must do, that the formulae they work with are realistic and accurate accounts of experience, she deliberately emphasises the simplicities of those formulae in order to bring out the actual and daily consciousness of her characters, and their real pleasures and sorrows.

In a novel which emphasises its own definition of itself by ludic display – a novel of Nabokov's for example – this kind of thing not only would call attention to itself but would emphasise in doing so its own strictly fictional status. In the Pym world it enhances the indefinable nature of homely reality, which mixes in our ordinary consciousness with our sense of ourselves as taking part in a novel. The frequent references to characters from her previous novels, now leading uneventful and often married lives, work in the same way. They have as it were ceased to be characters in her novels, with all the potential for romance that implies, and been metamorphosed into the ordinary dull figures who might be acquaintances in our own daily existence.

The great conductor Sir Thomas Beecham used to say that good music gives us a sense 'of both wonder and contentment'. The Pym world shows a similar kind of quiet paradox, affording at the same time satisfaction and curiosity, in the same way that her reserve seems a natural aspect of her forthcomingness. People are fascinating, and to be found out about, and yet we know in another sense that they are perfectly ordinary. They stimulate curiosity in the novel in which they figure, and if they are mentioned in a later novel they have become just like everybody else. Among other things Pym novels make us realise how fundamentally unaesthetic are descriptions of sex in fiction. Physical consummation means fictional flatness. Did Prudence go to bed with Fabian? Jane longs to know, but knows also that she never will know, and this is the root of her feel for the richness of life. Barbara Pym does not know herself. Her imagination does not bother with the anticlimax of what happens in bed. It has its delightful or disappointing place in life no doubt, but not in this world of the novel, which depends upon our sense of 'something evermore about to be'.

Loving and longing, hopeless hoping, deprivation, romance, ecstasy – these are another matter, and Barbara Pym conveys them with unexampled accuracy, poignancy and humour. Her novels speak with the 'true voice of feeling', as Keats called poetry. Her admiration for Philip Larkin, and his for her, convey the manner in which both valued in art the simplicity of saying exactly what you think and feel. She noted in her diary that his personality was just like his poetry, and the same is true of her and her novels. What is aesthetically right and pleasing in her work is also that which most straightforwardly reflects her temperament. She gives it, and herself, away the whole time, and yet she is never defined by her novels. There is really no such thing as a 'Barbara Pym world'. That is the final paradox about her, and the final triumph of her art.

8

How Pleasant to Know Miss Pym

Robert Smith

Between 1950 and 1961 Barbara Pym published six novels. All enjoyed a mild success with reviewers and the public. But for nine years now no book by this writer has appeared, and the time seems suitable for a provisional assessment of her small but consistent body of work. Never commanding much attention, her books are becoming lost to sight amid the constant press of new novels of an outlook and genre very different from her own. Yet she has her enthusiasts, who each week read the reviews in the hope of finding that 'a new Barbara Pym' has been published and wonder who on earth can be brought to buy and read the often alarming and ill-mannered fiction of the present day. To these enthusiasts Barbara Pym has been a provider of the very best sort of 'books for a bad day'. This is to give a great deal of praise, but perhaps not quite enough.

Naturally there is great diversity among books chosen to solace a bad day (a day when, for example, one is feeling rather ill or the news is especially disturbing or troubles rend the household), but two characteristics distinguish all such books: they must take the reader into a different, pleasanter world, and they must make his escape easy. The present writer counts E. F. Benson's Mapp and Lucia books very high in this class, but, when an assessment of Miss Pym is to be embarked upon, a greater name is usually invoked (sometimes apologetically, but apparently irresistibly) – that of Jane Austen. Can Miss Pym be claimed as the Jane Austen of our times? In some ways, of course, this seems presumptuous, but in other ways it is too modest since, though her canvas is small, her range and scope are considerably wider than those of Jane Austen. But the comparison remains valid. There is the same woman's view, dealing sharply but on the whole good-humouredly with the closely observed minutiae of middle-class daily life, always enlivened by the needle of wit. Barbara Pym's novels are indeed, as a reviewer once wrote, 'small beer', but as the reviewer added, it is beer from an Oxford brewery.[1] It is unlikely that the taste for this has disappeared with the closing of Messrs Boots's admirable libraries, nor is this taste confined to the lady shoppers of provincial high streets.

Barbara Pym's world, and this is its charm, is a closed one: an enchanted world of small felicities and small mishaps. Yet it is also real and varied in theme and setting. In *Some Tame Gazelle* we are immersed in the society of a village or small provincial town; *Excellent Women* is set mainly in the inner residential parts of London – Pimlico, perhaps – and one form of middle-class society is confronted by another, the Bohemian–academic; much the same sort of confrontation occurs in *Jane and Prudence*, which combines London and the country; *Less than Angels* revolves around that academic life which goes on in the heart of London unsuspected by those who do not penetrate the mysteries of Bloomsbury or the Inns of Court; *A Glass of Blessings* is London and the country again; the last, *No Fond Return of Love*, observes with an anthropological eye the ways of a cheerful Thames-side suburb. The themes are universal: love thwarted or satisfied (even fashionable homosexuality is here, just under the surface in several of the books); worldly ambition, nearly always academic ambition, and the complications which ensue; the challenge of the daily routine – and Miss Pym was the first in the field in the preoccupation with the kitchen sink, over which her female characters so often come into their own. Here is the narrator in *Excellent Women* 'coping' with the kitchen of Helena Napier the anthropologist:

I noticed with distaste and disapproval that the breakfast things and what appeared to be dishes and glasses from an even earlier date were not washed up. The table by the window was also crowded; there were two bottles of milk, each half-full, an empty gin bottle, a dish of butter melting in the sun, and a plate full of cigarette stubs. I felt very spinsterish indeed as I stood there, holding the burnt saucepan in my hand.   (p. 153)

The delineation of character in these novels is as exact as the observation of life's small chores. Miss Pym's most notable creation is a new kind of heroine, the 'excellent woman': good aunt, good churchwoman, informed spinster, conscientious social worker, meticulous housekeeper. The catalogue of these virtues may sound dreary, and the type, as we all know, and as the novels show, too easily inclined to bossiness. But Miss Pym's heroines are redeemed by their modest and sensitive wit. To quote again from the narrator of *Excellent Women*, 'I was now put in my place as the kind of person who would have an oven cloth hanging on a nail by the side of the cooker' (p. 189), and again,

> There were offices on the ground floor and above them the two flats, not properly self-contained and without every convenience. 'I have to share a bathroom', I had so often murmured, almost with shame, as if I personally had been found unworthy of a bathroom of my own.   (p. 6)

These women, mending surplices, sewing on a manly button, disbursing small but effective charities, providing timely cups of tea, or just doing the washing-up, are foils to a host of others of different calibre – glamorous Prudence Bates in her tiny, fashionable flat, Helena Napier writing up her field notes on African tribes – but above all they are foils to the great (not monstrous, but half-caricatured) race of Men – bearably selfish, charmingly abstracted, unconsciously demanding, always calling for, and usually receiving from some woman somewhere, devotion and service. 'Of course, a man must have meat', pronounces Mrs Mayhew, the proprietor of the tea shop in *Jane and Prudence* (p. 30), and in the same novel an elderly spinster comments,

> 'They say, though, that men only want *one thing* – that's the truth of the matter.' Miss Doggett again looked puzzled; it was as if she had heard that men only wanted one thing, but had forgotten for the moment what it was.   (p. 70)

A passage in the last novel, *No Fond Return of Love*, illustrates neatly a difference between the sexes:

> 'Yes, after breakfast is an awkward time in a hotel', Dulcie said. 'One has no right to exist between the hours of half past nine and twelve. So much work is going on that it makes one feel guilty.'

'I suppose women – nice women – feel guilty. Men are only irritated', said Aylwin.   (p. 221)

In form and style these novels are equally well-bred. They are of unvaried classic proportions: some 70,000 words in length, arranged in twenty to twenty-five chapters, an arresting phrase or idea reserved for the beginning and end of each. The last sentence of *Some Tame Gazelle* is particularly rewarding: '"Oh, *come*, now", laughed the curate, and although his voice was rather weak as a result of his long illness, Belinda was overjoyed to hear that it had the authentic ring' (p. 252). The style seems at first flat and rather featureless, like a Midland landscape of tame hedgerows and copses which only on closer acquaintance reveals its subtle charm and interest. Occasionally there are lapses into the idiom of the Woman's Page (there are too many cosy 'It so happened that's), and references to foreign literature, philosophy and other esoteric matters are sometimes awkward. But, though Miss Pym is soon out of her depth, she quickly returns to the shallow, placid waters of which she is mistress.

Consider, for example, her treatment of religion. Her books are indubitably 'churchy', partly in the sense that church-going frequently occurs and clergymen are among her best characters, and partly from the tacit and unproselytizing assumption that the world divides into those who do and those who do not attend their parish church. The ethos is always decently Anglican, but this too is taken for granted and no hint of doctrinal or emotional problems is intruded upon the reader. Religion, for Miss Pym's characters, involves no anguish of conscience ('social' or personal), no dark night of the soul, but decisions about what vestments should be worn on Mid-Lent Sunday, what shall be served for luncheon on Fridays in the clergy-house, who is to query that enigmatic entry in the church accounts, and (in *Some Tame Gazelle*) 'that rather delicate affair of the altar brasses and the unpleasantness between Miss Jenner and Miss Beard' (p. 64). It would be priggish and silly to exalt one approach above the other, and neither Miss Pym nor her enthusiasts are this sort of prig or fool. Her treatment of religion suggests, in fact, a rather unusually strong, though reserved, religious sense. Similarly her treatment of love's troubles and delights seems to derive from a firm emotional base. Dulcie, in *No Fond Return of Love*, says, sadly but sensibly: 'People blame one for dwelling on trivialities . . . but life is made up of them. And if we've had one great sorrow or one great love, then who shall blame us if we only want the trivial things?' (p. 167).

The academic world is subjected by Miss Pym to the same detached dissection as the more familiar parts of the middle-class social field. There is a revealing account in *Less than Angels* of the writing of one of those vituperative reviews in which scholars sometimes vent their ill temper, and of its subsequent reception:

> He drew a heavy line on the paper, folded the sheets and put them into an envelope. In a day or two the editor of the journal, who was a gentle patient man, would set to work to improve the English and tone it down a little. 'It is a pity', he would say to himself, 'to have three consecutive paragraphs beginning "It is a pity".' He might even remember that Alaric Lydgate had once been refused a grant from the reputable institution whose limited funds had been squandered to no purpose. He might then go on to ask himself whether funds can be *squandered* to no purpose, whether indeed they can be squandered to *any* purpose. Certainly, as editor, he would feel none of the exhilaration which Alaric felt on finishing his review.   (p. 59)

Another passage in the same book deals with the distribution of that well-known dust-gatherer on bookshelves, the offprint of the scholarly article:

> It was thought by many to be 'good policy' to send an offprint to Esther Clovis, though it was not always known exactly why this should be. In most cases she had done nothing more than express a polite interest in the author's work, but in others the gift was prompted by a sort of undefined fear, as a primitive tribesman might leave propitiatory gifts of food before a deity or ancestral shrine in the hope of receiving some benefit.   (p. 63)

These novels are something more than simply books for bad days. Their acute observations of a limited social scene makes them a valuable record of their time, perhaps more valuable than anything an anthropological research team set to work in Surbiton could produce. As to art, Barbara Pym has evolved and remained close to a formula which has won her devoted readers, a small but select band, and she has made one area of life her own domain.

Her works are miniatures, exquisitely, nearly perfectly, done. But, beyond this, it is her wit and her sense of the ridiculous which make her books both delicious and distinguished. Above all, they must be ranked as comic novels, but the comedy is realistic and demonstrates again and again the happiness and merriment which can be found in the trivia of the daily round – that 'purchase of a sponge-cake' about which Jane Austen felt it proper to write to Cassandra. They can be read again and again, and at each rereading unnoticed felicities come to light. It is too soon to attempt any solemn judgement on this slender corpus, this 'sponge cake' of so delicate a taste. But, meanwhile, bad days come to us all, and we cannot anticipate their ever not coming. Let us hope that Miss Pym will begin again to help us deal with them.

9

Miss Pym and Miss Austen

A. L. Rowse

My description of Barbara Pym as 'the Jane Austen *de nos jours*' has been widely quoted, and I have been asked to elaborate on that theme. To deal with it fully is a job beyond me, and I have no wish to pose as a *literary* critic. So I propose to concentrate on one main aspect of their work: their relation to the society of their times, and their rendering of each.

Here there is a great contrast. Jane Austen's England – after Trafalgar and Waterloo – was the first, if not in Europe, then in the outside world; and she herself belonged to the most successful governing-class of her time. The aristocracy and country gentry, with their affiliations with middle-class industry and commerce – especially in London – ran the country, and it was a going concern.

Jane Austen belonged to this governing-class – her family was closely connected with the peerage, Navy and Church; she understood it thoroughly, shared its values – patriotism, duty, above all – and rendered it perfectly. I have heretofore corrected the frequent misapprehension that Jane Austen was only a miniaturist. Her work spans and depicts the essential elements of that society; she had a remarkably firm grasp of its hierarchical, articulated structure; she could assume it instinctively and naturally, without question, for it was solid and stable.

No such certainty or security in Miss Pym's world. The Georgian country houses – which were the glory of England, nuclei not only of government but of culture, art and taste – are everywhere being pulled down, emptied of their historic contents, turned into flats, institutions, offices. Through a gap in the trees, beyond a lake in the former park, one glimpses 'a great house now turned into a country club, with swimming pool and American bar, as the noticeboard proclaimed'. (What would Miss Austen think of such a transformation, such a society?)

Occasionally a former fossil from it, like Lady Beddoes in *Crampton Hodnet*, descends from her little mews-house or flat in Belgravia, where she has taken refuge, to open a church bazaar: nothing now to support her except her fossilised title and vague good manners, bewildered by the horrid world into which she has survived.

London itself is not what it was – indeed, semi-ruined after the devastation and bombings of the Second German War. The evidences of a squalid and seedy, deliquescent society are all too evident. 'The church had been badly bombed and only one aisle could be used. . . . We had made our way through the ruins where torn-down wall tablets and an occasional urn or cherub's head were stacked in heaps' (*Excellent Women*). In *Quartet in Autumn* a woman walks past 'the building in Bloomsbury' (how excellent those Bloomsbury squares once were) where she had worked in the 1930s: 'it had been on the first floor of a Georgian house – and found herself facing a concrete structure'.

In their village church 'there were bird-droppings on the altar and the vicar appealed for donations towards the repair of the roof. In 1970 the church was closed as redundant and . . . eventually pulled down'. At another church the door was locked: 'A pity, but that was the way things were now – it wasn't safe to leave a church open, what with thefts and vandalism'. All this offers an authentic picture of contemporary demotic society, with what were the lower classes out of hand, particularly an ungoverned younger generation that not only vandalises but burns churches and schools, and tears up gardens in public parks.

What indeed would Miss Austen make of such a deplorable society?

It offers some contrast with hers that exemplified the best model of social life that history records: a proper balance between the elegancies of urban society and the responsibilities of country life; that built such a city as Bath, and hundreds of country houses, threw round them their parks, planted the woods and planned the landscape. *Mansfield Park* shows us the care, the forethought and taste they put into it; the informed discussions that took place, the cult of the picturesque in which Jane Austen shared. It was the world of the finest architects, Adam, the Wyatts, Soane, Nash; and of the greatest painters, Gainsborough, Reynolds, Turner.

Miss Pym has nothing of that to support her: hers is a broken-down, tattered society, with only bits and pieces of a better order showing through. These are relics, still to be seen in the country and, to some extent – though questioned, and under threat – in country life. It is very brave of her – and she was stoical about life – to render it as comedy, though I don't suppose she altogether thought of it as such, any more than I do. She had an irrepressible sense of fun, and was determined to put the funny side of things and people in her work: in that sense less serious than Jane Austen, who came closer to the tragic, though neither of them wrote a tragic novel.

The phenomena and fauna of the hideous 1960s and 1970s – when Britain thoughtlessly imported a problem it did not have before – are faithfully portrayed.

> How had it come about that she, an English woman born in Malvern in 1914 of middle-class English parents, should find herself in this room in London surrounded by enthusiastic shouting, hymn-singing Nigerians? . . .
>
> 'I wonder if you could make a little less noise?' she asked. 'Some of us find it rather disturbing.'
>
> 'Christianity *is* disturbing', said Mr Olatunde. . . . 'You are a Christian lady?'
>
> Letty hesitated. Her first instinct had been to say 'yes', for of course one was a Christian lady, even if one would not have put it quite like that.

The situation is funny enough, though the effect is not wholly comic: it has ambivalent implications.

'Letty did her shopping on the way home' – for of course in this brave new world she has to work in an office all day – 'at a small self-service store run by Uganda Asians that stayed open till eight o'clock in the evening'. Her friend Marcia, waiting on a railway platform, 'noticed that somebody had scrawled in crude capital letters, KILL ASIAN SHIT!'. While in the Underground a woman slumped on a seat reared up, when someone attempted to help her, and 'shouted in a loud, dangerously uncontrolled voice, "Fuck off!"'.

What *would* Miss Austen think of such goings-on? Fairly certainly, that such people should be kept in their place – and quite properly. But the time for that is over in demotic society – and I know that people who have not achieved independence from it do not dare to say what they think of it, at least not out loud. The more apprehensive among us opt out of it, as courageous Miss Pym did not, but confronted it and turned it into comedy, if somewhat ruefully. The philosopher Hobbes sensibly left the country upon the idiocy of the Civil War.

The subject of most novels is that of heterosexual relations (except, refreshingly, for Proust). Here again there is a contrast between Miss Pym and Miss Austen that relates to their differing societies. Marriage is the crux in every novel of Jane Austen's, for that was the only career for women then. Not so in Pym's: careers are open to women. She herself had a job in an anthropological institute, where she learned about Africa and Africans; during the war she was a Wren, working with the Navy in Italy. These experiences are made use of in her novels, so naturally they offer more variety than Jane Austen's, who never went abroad.

And, with Miss Pym's wider experience in our mixed-up, messy society, there is more variety about sex, if indirectly and delicately handled. She understands about homosexual relations, and sees the comic side to them as about all sex – since sex makes fools of us all. We are given a recognisable pair of homosexual undergraduates in the novel about North Oxford, *Crampton Hodnet* – a sketch utterly real to a T, as they say. (Or to a tea party; for tea, Earl Grey or Lapsang, takes the place in Pym's novels that cigarettes and smoking do in Elizabeth Bowen's.)

This subtlefication of sex would have been beyond Jane Austen: she would have been shocked. Not so Miss Pym. Observing *every*thing as she did, she writes, 'Ned's scent, so much more powerful and exotic than the discreetly British "after-shave" lotion which was all that James had ever used, seemed to fill the room'. It is a subtle touch, but also quite real and convincing, that the woman in the book wants the ambivalent man rather than the more masculine type. Evidently Miss Pym did not care for crude, pipe-smoking, tobacco-smelling brutes; though the charity of women may be inexhaustible, they seem to put up with it to keep their menfolk quiet. It is an amusing give-away that Miss Pym thinks that women can 'manipulate' heterosexual men (she did not find this so in her own experience, for all that it is an instinctive conviction with women) – they do not find it so easy with homosexuals.

Love, rather than marriage, is the crux of Barbara Pym's novels. In one of them she says that everyone has the desire to feel needed. Is this so? I should say that this is particularly a woman's view; and of course hers, like Jane Austen's, is an essentially feminine world. In life Miss Pym – see her diaries in *A Very Private Eye* – had an immense desire to be loved. Not much satisfied, it would appear. Jane Austen at least had a good offer of marriage, which she declined because she did not love the man. Miss Pym never succeeded in fixing hers – and I think I know why.

Paradoxically, I first fell for her on account of her comic, understanding, forbearing, forgiving view of menfolk. It made me laugh, it was so true. It is the fate, or vocation, of women to forgive, she tells us. Men are such selfish creatures, always putting themselves and their preoccupations first; leaving the women to do the washing-up (why not? I think, with masculine assurance), taking the last chocolate biscuit on the plate, not noticing things, etc. Miss Pym noticed too much – it makes life difficult, puts men off; *one* reason for her failure in practice with them. She certainly got her own back in the novels, but engagingly, endearingly, convincingly – with none of the boring exaggeration of Women's Lib. She was above all that, far more subtle, and never for a moment vulgar. She was a gentlewoman, as Jane Austen was – though middle class, where Jane was upper class.

Another thing I deeply admire about both: though both were ladies, they knew the *facts of life* all right, and within the context of their art expressed them, by suggestion or implication, without raising their voices. Neither woman was a prude, they had no humbug or illusions. Actually, Jane Austen's correspondence with her sister Cassandra was bowdlerised by the Victorians; not so Barbara Pym's diaries, or not much. The subtlety and decorum of their work is all the more effective. The violence and horrors of so many contemporary novels are counter-productive with their mugging and thugging and drugging, their rapes and murders: the more they pile it on, one ceases to react, one is just bored. All those 900-page over-advertised monsters that fill Fifth Avenue bookstores will be forgotten five minutes after their authors leave the scene. Not so these two women, neither of them fully or properly appreciated in their day; both of them now more discriminatingly and highly thought of than ever, for only good art defeats the erosion of time.

I love them too for their stoical refusal to subscribe to illusions about life. These women – like Edith Wharton, Willa Cather, Flannery O'Connor – have an adult view of life, unlike the adolescent views of a Hemingway or Scott Fitzgerald. Jane Austen and Barbara Pym had the wisdom to come to terms with life. Though love, and the relations between the sexes, were the central feature in their work – and especially in Barbara Pym's life – they knew that these affairs often work out not satisfactorily, were reasonable about it and continued to do their duty in life, not throw it up in a gesture of despair, suicide or alcoholism. Women are apt to be wiser than men.

Love meant everything to Miss Pym (except for religion and duty), and yet she was disappointed – I think her expectations were too high, one couldn't come up to her standards. In *Crampton Hodnet* Miss Morrow stands for Miss Pym in her disappointment.

She had somehow expected something less ordinary. And yet one must be reasonable and remember that falling in love is never ordinary to the people who indulge in it. Indeed, it is perhaps the only thing that is being done all over the world every day that is still unique.

'You don't seem to realise that one can learn to care', said Mr Latimer pompously.

'No, I don't', said Miss Morrow firmly. 'Learning to care always seems to me to be one of the most difficult lessons that can be imagined.'

In *Less than Angels* a friend reflects, 'Minnie is too full of what is known as *simple* goodness, and goodness is so much better when it is not simple'. This might have been said by Miss Compton-Burnett, a recognisable influence in Pym's early novels, pointed but without the acerbity. In the end it seems that Miss Pym settled for the smaller consolations – always excepting the greatest of all, her art.

The small things of life were often so much bigger than the great things, she decided, wondering how many writers and philosophers had said this before her, the trivial pleasures like cooking, one's home, little poems especially sad ones, solitary walks, funny things seen and overheard.

The funny things prevail over the sad in her work: indeed its surface is a continual ripple of amusement, like the sparkle of sun on water, not the hard crystal glitter of Compton-Burnett's *mots*. All the same, I love Miss Pym for her sharp touches: '"I wonder if your regard for truth will be helpful to you in your business career", said Digby sarcastically. "It might even be a hindrance"'. 'It occurred to me that he [Father Bode] might well be the kind of person who would prefer tinned salmon, though I was ashamed of the unworthy thought for I knew him to be a good man'. Miss Pym knew all about good food and good wine, which did not much interest Jane Austen, and even more about clothes. She was also better educated and more widely read, as an Oxford girl: 'the pathos of anyone not knowing French – I mean, not at all!'. She knew Italian too, and even German.

'Over lunch at his club, the high, querulous voice of a Bishop complaining because there was no more Camembert left made him smile'. Miss Pym's observant eye on men's feeding-habits often made her smile – we can imagine her smiling as she wrote, as we know Jane Austen would smile as she wrote amid the chatter in the drawing-room. Jane Austen's family was distinctly clerical, her father a parson of the Church of England, an organ of government essential to keeping order in the nursery. Miss Pym was a devoted churchwoman, familiar with all its endearing rites and habits, even to the absurd Imposition of Ashes on Ash Wednesday (for she was High Church). She was so fond of it and its jokes that it was always good for a laugh, its characters made for fun.

At one point a memorial requiem is to be held in the University Church for a well-known agnostic; anyone who knows Oxford knows that that was good form. One could not think of going to Chapel, of course: that would be bad form, and indeed Nonconformity hardly makes an appearance in the novels. The Roman Catholic church is admitted, though one does not wish to endure the ministrations of peasant priests not up to one's intelligence. The forlorn activity of 'going over to Rome' is at one point mentioned in the same breath as 'a fate worse than death' (whatever that may be). The books are full of clergy of every hue and description – rectors, vicars and especially curates, in whom unmarried ladies like Miss Doggett take such an interest. She is a very recognisable dragon of North Oxford, and so appropriately named – Miss Pym had a peculiar gift for names. I only wish that this bullying, interfering female could have received her come-uppance as Lady Catherine de Bourgh did in *Pride and Prejudice*. Perhaps a suitable fate would have been to marry her off to an overblown Archdeacon, pompous Archdeacon Hoccleve.

The historian realises that the Church of England – in its breadth, imprecision and tolerance – carries and expresses the character of the English people in the way that neither Rome nor Nonconformity does. At one point, after a discussion of pros and cons, a character concludes, 'Perhaps the Anglican way was the best of all'. Both Barbara Pym and Jane Austen are linked to the central spine of English life and tradition, and give an authentic and faithful depiction of it in the way that no dissenter on the Left or Right could; neither D. H. Lawrence, nor Evelyn Waugh and Graham Greene. In the literal sense they are eccentric to it, more powerful, but distorted, exaggerated, their portrayal of it less just and true.

The serious side to the fun on the surface – think again of Jane Austen's dunderhead of a clergyman in Mr Collins – is that neither woman says anything about the inner spirit of religion: too serious a matter for comedy, a private concern between themselves and God. A witness of her life has told us that Jane Austen was 'thoroughly religious and devout; fearful of giving offence to God, and incapable of feeling it towards any fellow creature'.

We may be sure that this holds good for Barbara Pym too. She only once says something about prayer, and then behind the screen of one of her characters: 'One or two people were kneeling in the church, and I knelt down too and began to say one of those indefinite prayers which come to us if we are at all used to praying, and which can impose themselves above our other thoughts, so often totally unconnected with spiritual matters'.

Barbara Pym and Jane Austen are well worthy of each other; they were both moral perfectionists, both perfect artists. And only art redeems mankind from the slime.

10

Love and Marriage in the Novels*

Mary Strauss-Noll

Barbara Pym once received a warm fan letter which concluded,

> I do hope you will marry, because you would make such an understanding wife; you would expect your husband to be more or less helpless, though loveable, and you would not be disappointed. . . . On the other hand, perhaps if you were married you would have no time for writing, so I do not really know what to wish.[1]

In a letter to a friend, Barbara Pym wrote a playful little dialogue about the same subject:

> 'Mrs Minshall seems to want us all to be either dead or married', said Mrs Pym to her daughter as they drove home in the car.
> 'Well, I do not see what else we can be,' said Barbara in a thoughtful tone. 'I suppose we all come to one state or the other eventually. I do not know which I would rather be in.' (*A Very Private Eye*, p. 80)

Such ambivalence toward the married state is also found in Barbara Pym's fiction. In fact, marriage in her novels is often like the banquet in Emily Dickinson's poem that concludes, 'Hunger – was a way / Of Persons outside Windows – / The Entering – takes away'.[2] Like the persona in Dickinson's poem, many of Pym's

---

* I wish to thank Hazel Holt, Hilary Walton, Robert Smith and Honor Wyatt Ellidge for generously sharing their insights and anecdotes. In addition, I am most grateful to Timothy Rogers, Colin Harris and their staff at the Bodleian Library for their extraordinarily efficient and friendly assistance.

characters yearn for the day when they 'trembling drew the table near', but once they are married they become quickly disenchanted with their husbands, realising that 'Perhaps nothing could be quite so sweet as the *imagined* evenings with their flow of sparkling conversation' (*Jane and Prudence*, pp. 101–2, emphasis added).

There is a curious mixture of romance and cynicism in the attitude of most of Pym's single women. Many of them seek marriage (or at least yearn for it) while realising that it has drawbacks. They are aware that most of the men in their lives are not exactly prizes; indeed, some of them are self-centred dullards unworthy of the splendid–excellent women. Despite this fact, it is taken for granted that marriage should be women's goal, and they are considered failures if they do not achieve it.

The ambivalence of the single women and the disillusionment of the married women occur throughout all Pym's writings. These attitudes, however, are best illustrated within the contexts of the four novels in which matchmaking is most central: *Some Tame Gazelle*, *Excellent Women*, *Jane and Prudence* and *No Fond Return of Love*. When we also examine the final novel, *A Few Green Leaves*, as well as some of her unpublished works, we see that ironically the ideal state in Pym's fiction appears to be widowhood. Widows such as Beatrice Howick enjoy the successful status of having married, but they are not troubled by the inconveniences associated with a husband. They can both have their cake and eat it.

Belinda Bede, the protagonist of Pym's first novel, *Some Tame Gazelle*, is not a widow, but she is so content with her unrequited love for her married Archdeacon that, in a sense, she does both have her cake and eat it. Having been loyally devoted to Henry Hoccleve for thirty years, Belinda reflects that 'she was now a contented spinster and her love was like a warm, comfortable garment, bedsocks, perhaps' (pp. 157–8). There is nothing negative about this metaphor. Like its American equivalent 'old shoe', Belinda's 'warm bedsocks' suggests cosiness, habit, familiarity – something she has lived with for a long time, something that fits comfortably.

Content to worship the Archdeacon at a distance, Belinda believes that there is 'a certain pleasure in not doing something; it was impossible that one's high expectations should be disappointed by the reality' (p. 89). Belinda has every reason to fear that marriage to Henry would be disappointing: she has had ample opportunity to observe his behaviour. She has seen him leaning out of an upper window of the rectory loudly berating his wife because moths had got into his suit. She knows that he always sleeps late, sometimes sits on the floor of his study playing patience, and then complains bitterly of overwork. When her sister Harriet complains about Henry's sermons, which are often no more than long passages of 'depressing' and 'horrid' poems (p. 20), Belinda loyally defends him but remarks to herself, 'Of course the real truth of the matter was that poor Henry was too lazy to write sermons of his own and somehow one didn't think of him as being clever in a theological kind of way' (p. 21).

Henry treats Belinda very insensitively. For example, one evening while his wife is out of town, Belinda indulges his fancy for reading aloud by drowsily listening to him read the *Faerie Queene*, a 'soothing poem. It just went on and on' (p. 149). When he comes up for air, Hoccleve asks Belinda if the evening reminds her of the 'old days' when he used to read to her. 'Belinda was speechless, as she considered this proof of man's oddness. Whatever did he imagine that it reminded her of?' (p. 150).

When Agatha Hoccleve returns from her trip looking exceptionally well, Belinda is 'shocked to find herself wondering whether a month's absence from her husband could have anything to do with it' (p. 163).

Despite her realisation that Henry can be selfish, lazy and insensitive, Belinda cherishes him and loyally defends him against his detractors. Her comments, however, make it clear that she realises it is easier to indulge someone you are not married to; it is easier to get along with a self-centred man (or a spoiled child) if you do not live with him. As she herself points out, 'I love him even more than Agatha does, but my feeling may be the stronger for not having married him' (p. 161).

Belinda does have an opportunity to marry. In one of the funniest scenes Pym ever wrote, the comically insufferable Bishop Theodore Grote proposes to Belinda, who hastily assures him that she does not love him. For her, marriage without love is out of the question, and she never could love the sheep-faced Grote, who pompously assures her that she is 'equal to being the wife of a bishop' (p. 224).

What is important to both Belinda and her sister Harriet is that they have something to love, some tame gazelle or some gentle dove, an Archdeacon Hoccleve or (in Harriet's case) a pale young curate. Marriage might spoil everything.

Occasionally Barbara Pym presents a character such as Connie Aspinall who marries just for the sake of being married. Bishop Grote accidentally encounters her in the Army and Navy store, takes her to tea and proposes. Connie accepts him after he has assured her that she is 'quite equal to being a bishop's wife' (p. 240). She is different from such readers of the greater English poets as Belinda, whose romanticism prompts her to avoid marriage so as not to be disappointed.

Some Tame Gazelle is the most autobiographical of Barbara Pym's novels. Belinda and Harriet represent Barbara herself and her sister Hilary, as the young author imagined they would be in middle age. Archdeacon Hoccleve is Henry Harvey, the first of several men for whom Pym felt unrequited love. In fact, her friend Robert Liddell once wrote of her, 'She knew all about disappointment and frustration – had she been in *Who's Who* she might have put "unrequited love" down as her recreation.'[3]

In a letter dated July 1938 to Henry Harvey's wife Elsie, Barbara Pym wrote, 'It is known that every woman wants the love of a husband, but it is also known that some women have to be content with other kinds of love' (*A Very Private Eye*, p. 84). Belinda Bede in *Some Tame Gazelle* is one of these women, but her story is told with such humour that she is not at all pathetic or lonely. She and her bouncy sister Harriet lead a cosy and contented life; they have a comfortable home, pleasant friends and many enjoyable interests. We may smile at them, but we certainly are not meant to pity them.

When we read *Excellent Women*, there are many occasions to smile, but there are also moments when we pity Mildred Lathbury, for, unlike Belinda Bede, she has no tame gazelle nor is she content to love from afar. Mildred wants what most human beings crave: to love and be loved in return. She feels acutely the pain of being 'not really first in anybody's life' (p. 39). Like all of Pym's single women, she is considered by others to have inferior status and must suffer the often patronising and sometimes cruel treatment of married women.

Mildred *wants* to marry. When she contemplates a spinster life with her friend Dora, she complains, 'I saw us in twenty or thirty years' time, perhaps living together, bickering about silly trifles. It was a depressing picture' (p. 105). After she and Dora attend a reunion at their school, they both feel like failures: 'We had not made particularly brilliant careers for ourselves, and, most important of all, we had neither of us married. That was really it. It was the ring on the left hand that people at the Old Girls' Reunion looked for' (p. 112). Mildred cynically realises that most of the husbands of her former classmates are 'dim', but at the same time she romantically imagines them to be far more interesting than they probably are (p. 112). No doubt many of them are as comically eccentric as Dora's brother William Caldicott – who objects to his new office because 'different pigeons come to the windows' (p. 71).

In her extreme diffidence Mildred believes that 'It was not the excellent women [such as she] who got married but people like Allegra Gray, who was no good at sewing, and Helena Napier, who left all the washing up' (p. 170). When the dashing Rocky Napier exclaims that he cannot imagine anything he would like less than the love of an excellent woman, Mildred compares the declaration of such a love to having a large 'white rabbit thrust suddenly into your arms' (p. 235). She had previously used the same image to describe Everard Bone's dismay when Helena declared her love for him. In both contexts, the rabbit metaphor is startling: Everard is shocked by it and asks Mildred to explain herself, but she tells him that if he doesn't see, she can't explain (p. 145). Rocky thinks that a white rabbit might be 'charming', but Mildred hastily assures him that 'after a while you wouldn't know what to do with it' (p. 235). Her use of the same image to describe both Helena's love and an excellent woman's love suggests that Mildred views them as equally undesirable. Yet, as Rocky points out, there is something appealing about a white rabbit. Mildred's rabbit image by no means suggests the unalloyed pleasure of Belinda's warm bedsocks, but neither is it entirely negative. With its ambiguous overtones, the image serves as a fitting metaphor for Mildred's mixed feelings for the anthropologist Everard Bone.

When Everard invites Mildred to have dinner with him at his flat, she sees herself putting the meat into the oven and preparing vegetables: 'I could feel my aching back bending over the sink' (p. 218). But after she declines his invitation she starts worrying about whether she was the first person he had telephoned that evening. Either she is beginning to like him, or her need to be 'first' with someone is prompting her to show an interest in Everard. When he invites her a second time, she accepts. During the course of the evening, Everard asks her, ever so hesitantly, of course, if she will help him read the proofs and make the index of the book he is writing. Mildred's reaction is completely devoid of all romance:

> before long I should be certain to find myself at his sink peeling potatoes and washing up; that would be a nice change when both proofreading and indexing began to pall. Was any man worth this burden? Probably not, but one shouldered it bravely and cheerfully and in the end it might turn out to be not so heavy after all. (p. 255)

Excellent Women concludes on this optimistic note, as Mildred looks forward to what Helena Napier had called 'a full life' (p. 256). Mildred has few illusions about men; she has observed that they 'did not usually do things unless they liked doing them' (p. 9), that they often behaved childishly, and that 'most of them don't seem to mind speaking frankly and making people unhappy' (p. 145). Despite this awareness, Mildred prefers a life of reading proofs and washing dishes for Everard Bone to her present state as 'chief of the rejected ones' (p. 170).

Mildred Lathbury's attitude toward spinsterhood is not unique in literature. In Charlotte Brontë's *The Professor*, when Cremsworth asks his wife Frances how she would have 'liked celibacy', she answers, 'Not much, certainly. An old maid's life must doubtless be void and vapid – her heart strained and empty. I should have probably failed, and died weary and disappointed, despised and of no account, like other single women.'[4] In Pym's unpublished 'Finnish novel', a young woman reflects on the phrase used to describe an old spinster: 'She never married. Oh, the quiet finality of those words! It's like the shutting of a door. The very sound of them conjures up the whole of that woman's life.'[5]

In a letter to Barbara Pym, Philip Larkin described *Excellent Women* as

> a study of the pain of being single, the unconscious hurt the world regards as this state's natural clothing . . . time and again one senses not only that Mildred is suffering, but that nobody can see why she shouldn't suffer, like a Victorian cabhorse.[6]

Mildred Lathbury escapes this unhappy fate described so

eloquently by Brontë, Larkin and Pym herself. It is not at all
uncommon for a heroine to shun spinsterhood and seek marriage.
What is uncommon is Mildred's air of cheerful resignation.
Marriage to Everard Bone, as Mildred well knows, would be a
mixed blessing. Once married, her attitude might resemble that of
the speaker in Emily Dickinson's ambiguous poem:

> I'm 'wife' – I've finished that –
> That other state –
> I'm Czar – I'm 'Woman' now –
> It's safer so –[7]

Belinda Bede compared love to warm bedsocks; Mildred
Lathbury described it as a large white rabbit; Prudence Bates in
Jane and Prudence describes her unrequited love for Arthur
Grampian as 'a constant companion or a pain like a rheumatic
twinge in the knee' (p. 37). Who wants rheumatic twinges?
Apparently Prudence does. 'She had got into the way of preferring
unsatisfactory love affairs to any others' (p. 9).
  Her married friend Jane Cleveland finds Prudence's romanticism
incomprehensible. When Jane asks about Prudence's trip to Spain
with Geoffrey Manifold, her latest love interest, Prudence says
'seriously', 'Everything would be spoilt if anything came of it. . . .
That's almost the best thing about it' (p. 216).
  Prudence does not envy her married friends; she sees them as
dull and disappointed: 'Jane had retained her independence more
than most of her married friends. And yet even she seemed to
have missed something in life' (p. 83). Jane's husband Nicholas
used to be so attractive, Prudence thought, but being a husband
had done its 'worst for him, rubbed off the bloom' (p. 80).
Prudence's envy is aimed rather at Jane's and Nicholas's daughter:
'To be eighteen again and starting out on a long series of love
affairs of varying degrees of intensity seemed to her entirely
enviable' (pp. 158–9).
  There is, however, another side to Prudence's situation. In the
very first scene of the novel Pym writes, 'Prudence Bates was
twenty-nine, an age that is often rather desperate for a woman
who has not yet married' (p. 7). Prudence enjoys her love affairs,
obviously, but she has to live in a society that expects women to
marry (or to at least want to). She has to put up with patronising
and inane comments about her job from her former teachers and

from married women. Her mother's friends badger her about why she is not married, and even her single friends criticise her for not wanting to settle down. Although she dislikes herself for doing so, Prudence refers to Jane as '"my friend", almost as if she hoped to give the impression that she had been lunching with a man' (p. 76).

Jane is determined to see Prudence married and does all in her power to help her find a suitable husband. There is, however, some degree of ambivalence in Jane's attitude toward marriage. Like so many wives in Barbara Pym's fiction, Jane Cleveland's romantic expectations of marriage were disappointed. Gazing fondly at her husband one day, Jane reflects:

> this was what it all came to in the end. The passion of those early days, the fragments of Donne and Marvell and Jane's obscurer seventeenth-century poets . . . all these faded away into mild, kindly looks and spectacles. There came a day when one didn't quote poetry to one's husband any more.   (p. 48)

Jane might not quote poetry to Nicholas any more, but they are, relatively speaking, one of the happier married couples in the novels of Barbara Pym. They are most unlike Agatha and Henry Hoccleve. Both as a husband and as a clergyman, Nicholas is a cut above men such as Hoccleve, Grote and Fabian Driver. And yet one feels that Jane wants more – at least for her daughter Flora and for her friend Prudence. It's too late for Jane. One gloomy evening, washing dishes by the light of 'a dim but unshaded bulb [that] added a kind of desolation to the whole scene, with its chicken bones and scattered crockery', Jane suddenly turns to Prudence and tells her that she 'must make a fine thing' of her married life (p. 161). She hopes that her friend will escape the 'dimness' that characterises most marriages (p. 193).

Taken out of context, some passages from *Jane and Prudence* might suggest that there is a grim (or at least melancholy) view of marriage presented in the novel. Not so. The ambivalent attitude toward marriage is presented in a humorous fashion. As Rosemary Dinnage points out,

> It is typical of a Pym novel that all the teasing is benign, and if there is any hostility toward men for their insensitivity, it vanishes on the breeze of the gentlest ridicule. Women do adore these creatures, is her attitude; isn't it a splendid joke?[8]

Barbara Pym commented directly on this issue herself:

> after *Jane and Prudence* somebody said to me 'You don't think
> much of men, do you', but that isn't really my attitude at all. To
> quote a joke phrase, some of my best friends are – have been –
> men! Certainly I've observed and studied men and their
> behaviour very closely, perhaps because I used to work with
> anthropologists and so got used to analysing people's
> behaviour.[9]

Barbara Pym looked on marriage like an anthropologist with a
good sense of humour. She was neither a man-hater nor a
frustrated old maid, nor was she opposed to marriage in principle.
Like many women, married or single, she saw advantages and
disadvantages in both states. In an ironical journal entry (1963)
after lunching alone in a restaurant, she asked herself about the
woman at the next table: 'Would her attitude towards me change
if she knew I were unmarried or would she envy me?'[10]

Dulcie Mainwaring does not have to get married herself to
realise that marriage is, at best, a mixed blessing. Although at the
end of her story romanticism wins out, throughout *No Fond
Return of Love* Dulcie fluctuates between romantic and cynical
attitudes toward love and marriage.

The title of her story is itself most romantic and refers to
Dulcie's love for Maurice, her former fiancé who has broken off
their engagement because Dulcie was 'too good' for him. Maurice,
says Dulcie, is one of 'the people from whom one asks no return
of love. . . . Just to be allowed to love them is enough' (p. 75).
Her attitude here is reminiscent of Belinda Bede's devotion to
Henry Hoccleve; however, in describing what marriage to Maurice
would have been like, Dulcie displays a curiously mixed attitude:

> Theirs would have been one of those rather dreadful marriages,
> with the wife a little older and a little taller and a great deal
> more intelligent than the husband. Yet . . . there was a small
> ache in her heart as she remembered him. Perhaps it is sadder
> to have loved somebody 'unworthy', and the end of it is the
> death of such a very little thing, like a child's coffin, she
> thought confusedly.   (p. 54)

A 'child's coffin' is truly a cryptic image, for, while it is, indeed, a 'small thing', it is ever so much more heart-rending than the adult-sized object.

Dulcie feels an immediate romantic attraction for Aylwin Forbes, the handsome, conceited writer–editor she meets at a conference of bibliographers. From their first acquaintance, the sight of Aylwin gave her a 'fluttery disturbed feeling in the pit of her stomach' (p. 39).

On the one hand, Dulcie would like to marry. She agrees with the woman who humorously describes celibacy as an unnatural state that 'sticks out a mile' (p. 149). She considers herself on a lower 'plane' than women who have husbands, and like Wilmet Forsyth in *A Glass of Blessings* Dulcie frequently comments on women's need to be needed. When her aunt objects to the engagement of Dulcie's friend Viola, Dulcie impatiently declares that Viola 'should take this chance of happiness even if it *does* seem to be a rather incongruous match in some ways' (p. 238).

On the other hand, Dulcie is given to making rather negative (or at least disillusioned) comments about marriage. When Viola says that Aylwin Forbes is married 'in a sense', Dulcie cynically agrees that 'People usually were married, and how often it *was* "in a sense"' (p. 16). She feels sad to learn that her own sister, 'an apparently happily married woman should confess to a secret hankering' for romantic escape. And yet, observing her brother-in-law, 'she could appreciate that perhaps a desire for escape was not so surprising. Many wives must experience it from time to time . . . especially those whose husbands smoked old pipes that made peculiar noises' (p. 115). Suitable marriages between people with 'interests in common', according to Dulcie, are simultaneously both 'satisfactory and depressing, just the kind of "suitable" marriage she had advised Aylwin Forbes to make and which he obviously never would' (p. 239).

But there she is wrong. At the novel's end, when he is free (his estranged wife Marjorie having run off with a man she met on a train), Aylwin is on his way to propose marriage to Dulcie, the most 'suitable' woman imaginable for him. Ironically, Aylwin is taking this step for the most *romantic* of reasons; having suddenly and unaccountably fallen in love with Dulcie, he compares himself to Edmund falling in love with Fanny at the conclusion of *Mansfield Park*.

Pym does not tell us how Dulcie's marriage to Aylwin turns out, but we cannot help wondering. Pym's characters are so vividly rendered that we find ourselves making conjectures about them as though they were real people. We hope that, on the inevitable day when Aylwin's romantic passion fades away into 'mild, kindly looks and spectacles, Dulcie will love him enough to respond as Jane Cleveland did and make the best of her situation.

Love and marriage are as central to Pym's final novel as they are to her first. Emma Howick has two love interests in the course of *A Few Green Leaves*: Graham Pettifer, a fellow anthropologist, and Tom Dagnall, rector of the local church. The first man dallies with her briefly, then returns to his estranged wife; the second becomes the object of Emma's matrimonial hopes. Typical of Barbara Pym, there is a good deal of ambivalence involved in these relationships.

For Emma, Graham was once 'the one. . . . But it didn't come to anything and then he married somebody else' (p. 196). After losing contact with him for many years, she happens to see him on a television talk show, and impulsively writes him a note inviting him to visit her if he is in the neighbourhood. Not only does he come to visit, but, separated from his wife, he also moves into a cottage in the nearby woods to finish writing his book. When she sees him again after such a long time, Emma's reaction to Graham is ambivalent and amusing. She realises that he is not as tall as she is and wonders if it had 'always been like that or had he shrunk, diminished, in some way?' (p. 87). The first time she sees him at work in the garden of the rented cottage, 'the perfect picture of an academic working on a book in rural surroundings', there is something self-consciously 'comic' about him that makes Emma smile and ask herself if she really had once loved this man (pp. 130–1).

Earlier, when Graham had written Emma a very brief note to 'warn' her that he planned to rent a cottage in her district, she wished that he had indicated something of his feelings so as to 'help her to clarify her own, for she was not sure whether she wanted him or not' (p. 120). After she has seen a lot of him, she still does not know if she wants him. It is no wonder. Graham does not treat her very well. Like many Pym men, he uses women. He takes it as his due that Emma will arrange to have the larder stocked before he moves into his cottage and that she will merrily carry casseroles through the woods to him. Once, when he is inclined to show her some affection, he enjoys kissing her while lying in the grass, remarking that he deserves 'a break' from his work (p. 148). At other times he treats her coolly; she never knows where she stands with him.

Finally there comes an evening in his company when the conversation strikes her as 'arid academic chat', and she even wonders if he has invited the other guests to his cottage so as to avoid being alone with her (p. 174). 'Unbearably irritated by the whole situation', Emma insists on going home, and she sees little of Graham after that (p. 175). Having finished his book, he is leaving the cottage to be reunited with his wife, who has been decorating a new house for them to live in. He bids Emma goodbye most affectionately, assuring her that they will soon meet again. Emma wryly says to herself, 'the three of us' (p. 191), for she knows that his wife is waiting in the new house.

Emma has met Claudia Pettifer, Graham's wife. '*Sent*' (p. 151) by her husband to represent him at Esther Clovis's funeral (he did not want to interrupt his work), Claudia asked Emma to lunch with her after the service. On that occasion Claudia asked Emma if she were 'wise', and Emma answered, 'I haven't married, so you can draw your own conclusion' (p. 153). This scene is reminiscent of the luncheon Mildred Lathbury suffers through with Allegra Gray in *Excellent Women*. Mrs Gray is even more patronising to Mildred than Claudia is to Emma, causing Mildred to respond with similar ambiguity: 'I haven't been married, so perhaps that's one source of happiness or unhappiness removed straight away' (p. 125).

There is no ambiguity, however, in Emma's feelings during the Christmas Eve church service. Sitting between her mother and her mother's friend, Emma

> found herself wishing that she had a man with her, though the idea of the man being Graham did not appeal to her. Some nebulous, comfortable – even handsome – figure suggested itself, which made her realise that even the most cynical and sophisticated woman is not, at times, altogether out of sympathy with the ideas of the romantic novelist.   (p. 239)

She does not have far to look for him: the man she seeks is at the altar conducting the service. Up to this point in the story Emma's attitude toward Tom Dagnall has been rather ambivalent. On the one hand, she views him as 'good-looking', 'nice', 'agreeable', 'sympathetic', perhaps a potential husband for her friend Ianthe Potts. On the other hand, Emma, like some of the other people in the village, finds Tom's fascination for local history eccentric and excessive. Emma is simultaneously amused by and sympathetic to his plaintive letter in the parish magazine asking to be invited to share a 'simple family meal' (p. 145).

The turning-point in her feeling for him is the evening he comes to dinner at her cottage. Tom strikes her as pleasant and companionable. A short time later she is very moved by his appearance and manner when he conducts a funeral service for one of his parishioners. In the last scene of the novel, while conversing with him at the historical-society meeting, Emma realises that with Tom she can 'embark on a love affair which need not necessarily be an unhappy one' (p. 250). Like Dulcie with her Aylwin, Emma would need all the love and patience she could muster in order to survive marriage with a self-absorbed man whose overriding concerns are the location of the deserted medieval village and obscure 'burial in wool' laws. Like Mildred with her Everard, Emma accepts Tom good-naturedly, warts and all.

Unaware that her daughter has decided to set her cap at Tom, Mrs Howick is bustling about at the historical-society meeting scheming how best to bring them together. Even though Mrs Howick thinks that Tom Dagnall is boring and 'ineffectual', she is determined to do everything in her power to see him wed Emma. Beatrix Howick has always felt that a woman should marry and she is most especially anxious that her daughter should do so:

> it seemed suitable – though she did not herself set all that much store by the status. Her own husband . . . had been killed in the war, and having, as it were, fulfilled herself as a woman Beatrix had been able to return to her academic studies with a clear conscience.   (p. 8)

A widow, Beatrix Howick has the best of both worlds.

Mrs Wyatt, in the unpublished novel *Beatrice Wyatt* or *The Lumber Room*, has a similar attitude. She likes being a widow. It is a very 'comfortable and socially-accepted state'. One has fulfilled one's function, especially if there are children. When her daughter asks why widows are considered 'rather noble beings', a friend replies, 'It is because they are clever enough to have the status of married women without the bother of having husbands.'[11]

In Pym's delightful (unpublished) story 'Back to St Petersburg', Laura Kennicote goes off to St Petersburg for an illicit weekend with the son of her foreign employer. When her home-town minister and his wife turn up at the same hotel, Laura introduces her lover as her husband. Some time later when she wishes to return to her home town, she avoids scandal by following the recommendation of an elderly friend: Laura pretends to be a widow and lives happily ever after.[12]

The comments on widowhood as a sort of ideal state provide the most striking examples of ambivalence toward marriage in the fiction of Barbara Pym. Widows such as Beatrix Howick and Letty Crowe's cousin (in *Quartet in Autumn*) are content, perhaps even a little smug. Certainly they are better off than the Agatha Hoccleves in Pym's novels. They have their children (and sometimes their grandchildren), so they are not lonely. They have had husbands, so they are not considered failures. Best of all, they have their freedom, so they do not have to put up with Henry Hoccleves and Fabian Drivers.

Of her own life and writing, Barbara Pym said,

I had a quiet but enjoyable life and I believe that this is reflected in some of my novels. I prefer to write about the kind of things I have experienced and to put into my novels the kind of details that amuse me in the hope that others will share in this. I like to think that what I write gives pleasure and makes my readers smile, even laugh. But my novels are by no means only comedies as I try to reflect life as I see it.[13]

Barbara Pym did, indeed, write about the kinds of things which she had experienced. Her unrequited love for Henry Harvey is the basis for Belinda Bede's devotion for Henry Hoccleve. Her affection for a man younger than she is reflected in Ianthe Broome's relationship with John Challow. Pym's affection for a young homosexual is reflected in Wilmet Forsyth's experience with Piers Longridge and in Leonora Eyre's relationship with James Boyce. Like Dulcie Mainwaring, Barbara Pym enjoyed 'investigating' people. Like Marcia Ivory, the author also had a mastectomy. Like Emma Howick, Barbara Pym lived in a cosy

cottage, attended meetings of the local historical society and wrote
books. Like so many of her women characters, Barbara Pym
enjoyed attractive clothes and good food, gardening and domestic
pleasures. Like so many of her excellent women, Barbara Pym
thought that 'Perhaps to be loved is the most cosy thing in life
and yet many people, women I suppose I mean, know only the
uncertainties of loving' (*A Very Private Eye*, p. 192).

Despite the fact that many of the personality traits of her female
characters are similar to her own, Barbara Pym did not allow
personal feelings to dominate her novels. She too suffered the
pangs of unrequited love and the patronising comments of
insensitive acquaintances. But her books are not the 'spontaneous
overflow of powerful feelings': to quote some of her favourite
lines from Wordsworth, her stories present 'emotion recollected
in tranquillity'; they are written apparently with 'calm of mind, all
passion spent'. There is a sharp contrast in tone between
descriptions of real-life events in her journals and fictional
accounts of similar situations in the novels. In her fiction Barbara
Pym's tone is ironic, amused, detached. According to her close
friend Hazel Holt, such detachment did not come easily because
Barbara was so deeply involved in life.

In reminiscing about Pym on a recent BBC radio programme,
her good friend Honor Ellidge said that Barbara was an 'extremely
romantic' person who took love affairs seriously: 'She seems to
have been very unlucky . . . when she got serious – she seemed
to back away. . . . I don't think anyone knew quite what
happened, ever.'[14] Mrs Ellidge's description of Barbara Pym is
quite similar to one that the author herself wrote about Leonora
Eyre in *The Sweet Dove Died*: seeking romatic love, Leonora had
'gone about in eager anticipation of such an experience but when
she seemed to be on the threshold of it she had always drawn
back; something had invariably been not quite right' (p. 195).

After parting with Gordon Glover, Barbara Pym reflected in her
journal, 'One feels so without a chap especially when *one* has had
one. A nice lump of misery which goes everywhere like a dog' (*A
Very Private Eye*, p. 138). Happily for us, this dog-like lump of
misery was transformed by Barbara Pym's imagination into
Belinda's warm bedsocks, Mildred's white rabbit and Prudence's
rheumatic twinge in the knee. These metaphors do not have jolly
connotations, to be sure, but neither do they have tragic ones.
Like the attitudes toward love and marriage which they symbolise,

they are ambivalent. Together or separately, love and marriage are usually considered mixed blessings in the novels of Barbara Pym.

11

Barbara Pym and the War of the Sexes

John Halperin

Perhaps the time will come when one may be permitted to do research into the lives of ordinary people. . . .

(*No Fond Return of Love*, p. 18)

'What a good thing there is no marriage or giving in marriage in the after-life', remarks Jane Cleveland in *Jane and Prudence* (1953); 'it will certainly help to smooth things out' (p. 214). The war of the sexes goes on continually in Barbara Pym's novels, with men apparently winning it at some moments, women at others. 'As an anthropologist', Rupert Stonebird in *An Unsuitable Attachment* (1982) knows 'that men and women may observe each other as warily as wild animals hidden in long grass' (p. 13, opening paragraph).

Pym has sometimes, unfairly, been compared to Jane Austen, and readers coming to her for the first time have been heard to proclaim their disappointment upon finding out that her work is not at all like Austen's. Of course this is not Pym's fault; indeed, given her own reverence for Austen, she would have been the first to find the comparison inappropriate. Like the books of all great novelists, hers are unique: no one is like her, she is like no one else. A convenient comparison one could make – and that by way of a sort of thematic shortcut only – might be to say that her novels resemble Henry James's in containing amongst them virtually no relationship between the sexes which is entirely satisfactory. In the works of both authors – and in the works of each the balance of power keeps shifting – we see men victimised or taken advantage of by women, and women victimised or taken advantage of by men. What has been called James's 'vampire' theme – one human being living off and gaining sustenance from

88

another, and depriving him or her of life in the process – is ubiquitous in Pym's novels as well.

The present discussion will focus on four of Pym's novels: *Jane and Prudence*, *Less than Angels* (1955), *A Glass of Blessings* (1958) and *The Sweet Dove Died* (1978, written in the 1960s). But brief reference to several other sources may help to set the scene of conflict under scrutiny here. Pym's closest friend and literary executrix, Hazel Holt, has observed, 'Do you remember, in *A Very Private Eye* she says: "With the years men get more bumbling and vague, but women get sharper." There is no doubt that she thought women the stronger sex.'[1] In *A Very Private Eye: An Autobiography in Diaries and Letters* (1984) we find her remarking in a letter to Philip Larkin in 1977 that her 'treatment of men characters suggested [to some readers] that I had a low opinion of the sex' (p. 303) – a suggestion with which she disagreed but which, by her own admission, she found herself unable to refute. Mildred and Mrs Morris in *Excellent Women* (1952), 'a couple of women against the whole race of men' (pp. 23–4), are among dozens of female characters in Pym's novels who sometimes see themselves as fighting a lonely battle against superior odds – the power, the impregnability and the callousness to the other sex of men.

Equally to the point are two other passages in *A Very Private Eye*. 'Women have never been more terrifying than they are now', Pym wrote in her diary in 1955; 'no wonder men turn to other men sometimes' (p. 197). And in 1963, corresponding with her friend Bob Smith, Pym inquired, 'Why is it that *men* find my books so sad? Women don't particularly' (p. 223). If men find her books 'sad', perhaps it is because, in them, men are so often portrayed as, on the one hand, overbearing and egotistical, and, on the other, weak and incompetent, dependent for their survival from day to day upon the unselfish and untiring support of exhausted and harassed – and, yes, 'excellent' – women.

There is a battle going on all right in Pym's novels, but the most interesting thing about it is that no one is winning.

Jane and Prudence, arguably Pym's best novel, depicts women as victims of men, of their selfishness and brutality. Some nastiness on the distaff side is also visible, but *Jane and Prudence* remains the most sustained attack on men among Pym's novels.

The small case against women here may be quickly summarised.

The novel argues that men evade marriage when they can, but often are trapped into it by women; the latter take 'precedence' in it, and 'husbands [exist] only in relation to them' (p. 8). A husband, Jane observes, is 'someone to tell one's silly jokes to, to carry suitcases and do the tipping at hotels' (pp. 10–11). Jessie Morrow, the intrepid husband-hunter in *Jane and Prudence*, declares that 'women are very powerful – perhaps they are always triumphant in the end' (p. 110): she means in their relationships with men. We have seen that Pym believed this herself. In *Jane and Prudence* Jessie overpowers the elusive widower Fabian Driver and makes him marry her. Driver's first wife, Jessie learns, had typed his manuscripts for him: 'Oh, then he had to marry her . . . that kind of devotion is worse than blackmail – a man has no escape from that' (p. 126) – and she formulates her matrimonial plans accordingly. For Fabian, finally, 'it was as if a net had closed round him' (p. 199); the wild animal hidden in the long grass is brought down by the huntress. Jane remarks that women 'are getting so much bigger and taller and men are getting smaller' (p. 161) – and, since 'Victorian times', the relation between the sexes has been reversed. The women are in charge now; the men are exhausted (p. 172). Jane looks upon the first sex with pity: 'men are such children in many ways' (p. 150).

But the primary animus in *Jane and Prudence* is against men; and if male readers do find Pym's books sad, this novel is certainly one of the saddest. What Pym dwells on here, perhaps more single-mindedly than anywhere else, is the *heartlessness* of men. On two occasions Fabian is said to be *eating* hearts – both times *en casserole* (pp. 33, 46). Indeed, the eating-habits of men are a sort of moral index here. 'A man must have meat', declares Mrs Mayhew (p. 30). 'A man needs eggs!', says Mrs Crampton (p. 51). 'A man needs a cooked breakfast', observes Miss Doggett (p. 90). 'Man needs bird', Jane thinks: 'Just the very best, that is what man needs' (p. 52). While Arthur Grampian, Prudence Bates's boss, eats smoked salmon for dinner at his club, Prudence, we learn, has to choose between shepherd's pie and stuffed marrow in a restaurant (p. 41). When Jane and her husband lunch at Mrs Crampton's restaurant, Jane is given bacon, one egg, and some potatoes, while Nicholas is presented 'with *two* eggs and rather more potatoes . . . Nicholas accepted his two eggs and bacon [with] the implication that his needs were more important than his wife's with a certain amount of complacency' (p. 51). In this novel men are consumers, women providers.

In Jane's words, men 'expect women to do quite everything for them' (p. 189). They expect in fact to rule, while the women seem resigned and reduced to serving them. This carries over into the arena of interpersonal relations. Thus Grampian is pleased to see that Prudence is in love with him, though he has no plans to do anything about it: 'the tears in Miss Bates's eyes proved that he still retained his old power over women', he reflects with satisfaction (p. 197). The death of Fabian's wife, we learn, 'came as a great shock to him – he had almost forgotten her existence'; he retaliates for this selfish act of his late wife by carrying to her grave flowers said to be not 'her favourites' (p. 28).

> He had been unprepared for her death and outraged by it, for it had happened suddenly, without a long illness to prepare him, when he had been deeply involved in one of the little romantic affairs which he seemed to need, either to bolster up his self-respect or for some more obvious reason.   (p. 57)

And, on the relationship of Grampian and his wife:

> it was splendid the things women were doing for men all the time. . . . Making them feel, perhaps sometimes by no more than a causal glance, that [men] were loved and admired and desired when they were worthy of none of these things – enabling them to preen themselves and puff out their plumage like birds and bask in the sunshine of love, real or imagined, it didn't matter which.   (p. 75)

The operative clause here is 'when they were worthy of none of these things'.

Both Jane and Prudence are asked again and again to prop men up in various ways, to massage their egos – and without much reward, for the men in the novel are clammily selfish. Thus the relation of the sexes in *Jane and Prudence*. Men, it is said, require love and attention, while it is left to women to type their theses, correct their proofs, put their sheets sides-to-middle, bring up their children and balance their housekeeping budgets (p. 127). 'Oh, the strange and wonderful things that men could make women do!' Jane thinks (p. 158). When Prudence loses Fabian to Jessie, she (Prudence) observes that men prefer 'restful and neutral' women (p. 193) to those less passive; men need to dominate. Inconstant and promiscuous themselves, men require steady women waiting at home (p. 213). In the war of the sexes 'husbands [take] friends away' from their wives (p. 83), ridicule and soon dispose of women's views (p. 134), and, by withholding their 'sympathy' for women, reduce them to dependence on 'the sympathy of other women' (p. 200). Men think women should be satisfied with their own company (p. 205), while inducing in their wives 'the blankness and boredom of indifference': thus do women 'suffer' for their attachment to men (p. 198).

The truth, *Jane and Prudence* suggests, is that men are more 'limited' than women (p. 165). A woman's love can transform a man; without a woman's love a man would be a cipher. Having lost Fabian, Prudence finds herself stuck with the colourless Geoffrey. 'What object could Fate possibly have', Prudence wonders at the end of the novel. 'But of course, she remembered, that was why women were so wonderful: it was their love and imagination that transformed these unremarkable beings. For most men . . . were undistinguished to look at, if not positively ugly' (p. 217).

So much for men.

Less than Angels is more even-handed in its approach to the sexes – perhaps because its central subject lies elsewhere. Still, in it one gets glimpses of Pym's characteristic views on the differences between men and women.

Again we see here women victimised in various ways by men.

Some of them had been fortunate enough to win the love of devoted women – women who might one day become their wives, but who, if they were thrown aside, would accept their fate cheerfully and without bitterness. They had learned early in life what it is to bear love's burdens, listening patiently to their men's troubles and ever ready at their typewriters.   (p.49)

Tom Mallow, meeting Deirdre Swan, 'in her eyes . . . had read the unspoken question, that was so often in women's eyes, "When shall I see you again?" His first impulse had been to ask

"Are you any good at typing?"' (p. 67). The novel refers to 'the universal concern of women for men' (p. 196), but not to any reciprocal feeling on the part of men. In one of the most moving sections of *Less than Angels*, Elaine, Tom's first and now forgotten love, remembers Anne Elliot's famous words in *Persuasion* on the nature and the quality of feminine and masculine feelings:

> We certainly do not forget you so soon as you forget us. It is, perhaps, our fate rather than our merit. We cannot help ourselves. We live at home, quiet, confined, and our feelings prey upon us. You are forced on exertion. You have always business of some sort or other to take you back into the world immediately, and continual occupation and change soon weaken impressions.   (p. 186)

That word 'fate' keeps cropping up in Pym's novels – whether used by herself or quoted from elsewhere. She seems to have shared with Jane Austen a deep sympathy for the hapless fate of the undowried, unmarried woman. This theme is articulated everywhere in Pym's novels. Women are stronger than men, yes; but by needing women and playing on their sympathies, men *use* them to their advantage: it is their *fate* to be used. Thus, at the end of *Less than Angels*, Alaric Lydgate needs Catherine Oliphant, discarded by Tom, to put his life in order: 'Like so many men, he needed a woman stronger than himself' (p. 242).

But the novel also gives the other side of the case. 'What seems wrong with so many relationships now', Catherine observes, is 'the women feeling that *they* are the strong ones and that men couldn't get on without them' (pp. 113–14). It may be true, but it is tactless and self-destructive of women to operate openly on this basis, which so many do. (In *Northanger Abbey*, we may recall, Jane Austen observes that a woman, should she wish to marry, must never let a man see how clever she is.) 'Women do think the worst of each other, perhaps because only they can know what they are capable of. Men are regarded as being not quite responsible for their actions' (p. 135), Pym's Catherine observes. In *Less than Angels* women take advantage of men by 'intimidating' them and 'often [leading] them captive in marriage' (p. 40). The stronger of the animals in the long grass is the female, but she does not always exercise her power with discretion and gentleness. Catherine sometimes employs analogies similar to Rupert

Stonebird's memorable one in *An Unsuitable Attachment*. We catch her, in *Less than Angels*, thinking this:

> Men appeared to be so unsubtle, but perhaps it was only by contrast with the tortuous delicacy of women, who smothered their men under a cloud of sentimental associations – *our* song, *our* poem, *our* restaurant – till at last they struggled to break free, like birds trapped under the heavy black meshes of the strawberry net.   (p. 110)

Being the stronger sex does not necessarily make women happy; Catherine feels 'the general uselessness of women if they cannot understand or reverence a man's work, or even if they can' (p. 105).

The unwinnable war goes on in *A Glass of Blessings*. As in *Jane and Prudence*, men are given an especially low valuation here.

In the opening chapter we are presented with an account of a woman civil servant 'discovered preparing Brussels sprouts behind a filing cabinet' in her office – 'poor thing, I suppose she felt it would save a precious ten minutes when she got home' (p. 11), as Sybil, Wilmet Forsyth's mother-in-law, puts it. A woman cowering behind a filing-cabinet while she gets a head start on her husband's dinner is appropriately emblematic of the story *A Glass of Blessings* tells. The ladies discussing this event agree that when it comes to food men look upon every 'meal as no more than was due to them . . . "Women are prepared to take trouble . . . whereas men . . . hardly think it worth while"' (pp. 13–14). Wilmet's friend Rowena Talbot, a good cook who would like to experiment at home with unusual menus, is prevented from doing so by the 'tyranny' of her husband and children (p. 37). Rowena's husband Rodney 'complacently' agrees that his wife 'does have a good deal to put up with' (p. 138), but has no plans to alter his pleasant life. So it is not surprising to find that Rowena envies 'really *wicked* women, or even despised spinsters' – because, as she says, they may continue to 'have their dreams', whereas the married woman knows 'that there's absolutely no hope of their coming true . . . the despised spinster', at least, is *'free!'* (p. 149).

In fact in *Crampton Hodnet*, the novel Pym put aside in 1939, only recently published (1985), we come face to face with just such a person – a 'despised spinster' who appears to be *'free!'* – or so it seems to another unhappy wife who notices, while lunching out, that her neighbour's hands are 'ringless'.

> Then, presumably, she hadn't got a husband. She was a comfortable spinster with nobody but herself to consider. Living in a tidy house not far from London, making nice little supper dishes for one, a place for everything and everything in its place, no husband hanging resentfully round the sitting-room, no husband one moment [paring] gooseberries and the next declaring that he had fallen in love with a young woman. [She] sighed a sigh of envy. No husband.   (p. 172)

Here are enumerated by Barbara Pym some of the advantages of spouselessness apparent to an independent-minded Oxford graduate in her early twenties. There is relief as well as 'envy' in the resounding refrain of this passage: 'no husband'. Pym's failure to marry became more galling to her in later life, as some of the subsequent novels demonstrate quite plainly.

But in *A Glass of Blessings* marriage is still portrayed as a dead end. Wilmet, who believes that her clerical friend Father Thames 'went about cajoling or bullying women into being the answer to prayer' (p. 27), is also unhappily married. She falls in love with Piers Longridge, who turns out to be living with a male model. Wilmet's husband James, we discover late in the novel, is having an affair with our old friend Prudence Bates. And so it goes – the women in *A Glass of Blessings* are cabined, cribbed and confined, their morale 'tottering' (p. 151), while the men do what they please. 'Men are so narrow-minded and catty' (p. 215), Rowena complains.

But the 'tyranny' of men is perceived here, once again, as unnatural, since they remain the essentially weaker vessels. While Wilmet admits that 'women especially . . . want to be needed', she also observes that 'our advice and strength' are 'sometimes greater than theirs' (p. 165). Despite Rodney's career at public school and university, in the war and in the Civil Service, Wilmet sees 'that I with my sheltered life was in some ways more fitted to deal with certain things' than her best friend's husband (p. 201). Men are like bees seeking a queen: when they find her 'they will follow her to the hive' (p. 233).

This queenliness is criticised broadly in *A Glass of Blessings*. 'Women are so terrifying these days and seem to expect so much, really far more than one could possibly give', the homosexual Piers declares (p. 9). We may recall Pym's 1955 diary entry (*A Glass of Blessings* was written in 1955–6): 'Women have never been more terrifying than they are now . . . no wonder men turn to other men sometimes' (*A Very Private Eye*, p. 197). In *A Glass of Blessings* the men wear themselves out in work, the women remain unchanged – and thus, ultimately, stronger. 'Women nearly always outlive men', as Sybil remarks (p. 118). When Wilmet and her friend Mary Beamish go out to lunch one day, they observe in their midst 'a rather uncomfortable-looking husband with his wife's parcels piled on his knee. "That poor man looks so miserable" [Mary comments]. At that moment a young clergyman with an elderly woman, presumably his mother, came in. The two men looked at each other as specimens in a zoo might, each commiserating with the other in his unhappy situation.' Wilmet merely observes that many men 'let themselves be led by their women', and the subject is dropped (pp. 81–2). But the image of the two caged specimens – once, perhaps, wild animals hidden in the long grass, but now definitively captured – lingers on. 'One never knows what men are *feeling*', Wilmet muses (p. 213), but in the restaurant scene it is clear that they are feeling caught.

A final observation on *A Glass of Blessings*. In it the relation of the sexes seems to bring out in some women a modest sadism. The usually sensible Wilmet agrees that refusing a man's offer of marriage brings with it 'a kind of triumph' (p. 24). And her mother-in-law declares that 'Women like to see men doing domestic things, especially if they are not done very well – if the tea is too weak or too strong, or the toast burnt' (p. 188). The perverse pleasure of seeing men founder outweighs the inconvenience of bad tea or burnt toast.

The Sweet Dove Died is perhaps Pym's most complex treatment of the war of the sexes. In addition to the struggle between men and women for control of their lives, this novel tells the story of a battle between a middle-aged woman (Leonora) and a younger man (Ned) for the heart, soul and body of another young man

(James). Peripherally, there is the abbreviated contest between uncle (Humphrey) and nephew (James) for Leonora, and that (equally abbreviated) between Leonora and Phoebe for James. *The Sweet Dove Died* may be the most even-handed among this group in its account of the foibles, the strengths and the weaknesses, of both sexes. Though no one is winning it, the battle rages on in this novel with a ferocity unmatched in its predecessors.

The very first sentence serves notice that again Pym's view of men will not be complimentary: '"The sale room is no place for a woman", declared Humphrey Boyce' (p. 7). He thinks of women as hopelessly ignorant when it comes to the buying and selling of antique books. Humphrey's further thoughts on the matter are given to us:

A *book* sale was certainly no place for a woman; had it been a sale of pictures or porcelain, fetching the sort of inflated prices that made headline news, or an evening sale – perhaps being televised – to which a woman could be escorted after being suitably wined and dined – that might have been another matter altogether.   (pp. 8–9)

Women are pronounced satisfactory cooks for men, and indeed spend much of their time trying (for the most part unsuccessfully) to capture them with culinary temptations, having, it seems, few other weapons at their disposal. But the many meals Leonora serves up to James and Humphrey and others gain her little ground (she forgets which of them likes chocolate mousse).

Ned sees his defeat of Leonora in his contest for the possession of James as reducing her to 'a wounded animal crawling away to die' (p. 159) – another extension of the metaphor of the wild animal hidden in the long grass – and comments complacently, 'Life is cruel and we do *terrible things* to each other' (p. 160). Here he is the zookeeper with the net. Women's chief function and virtue, according to Ned, is to forgive men: 'That was what women should do and even did, in his experience; they overlooked things, they took people back, above all they forgave' (p. 199). Not all women in this novel are so malleable, however. Leonora's friend Liz 'now loved cats more than people' because her husband had 'behaved so appallingly' that forgiveness is out of the question (p. 26). Women's susceptibilities to handsome men are used cunningly by Humphrey in his antique business: 'James's good looks and pleasing manners were a definite advantage in attracting customers to the shop and persuading difficult American women to buy' (p. 11).

On the other hand, women in this novel (especially Leonora) are described in predatory terms: they wish to entrap, capture, imprison men. Leonora ejects an old lady from her lodgings in order to move James into them; once there he feels as trapped as any animal in any zoo, and his departure from Leonora's house to join Ned is described as a sort of prison break-out. Leonora tries to recapture James; Pym's language is significant: 'wooing James' back is compared to 'an animal being enticed back into its cage' (p. 207). Again the wild animal in the long grass is overtaken by the hunter, the would-be zookeeper. It is no coincidence that in *The Sweet Dove Died* there is a visit to a cat show during which James finds himself identifying sympathetically with the confined animals:

> They had stopped in front of a cage where a cat-like shape shrouded in a cloth lay fast asleep. How much wiser to contract out altogether, James felt, as this creature had evidently done. Or to sit stolidly in one's earth tray, unmoved by the comments of passers-by. Yet too often, like some of the more exotic breeds, one prowled uneasily round one's cage uttering loud plaintive cries. (p. 68)

The word 'one' signals the movement from the animal to the human world.

That women wish to 'trap' men is made clear again and again in *The Sweet Dove Died*. 'Just when you think they're close they suddenly go off', complains Miss Culver (p. 118). Leonora 'did sometimes feel slightly uneasy when James was out of her sight' (p. 119). No wonder James, in Pym's words, fancies himself 'fenced in' (p. 129) by Leonora. His response once again is that of the wild animal with its route to freedom cut off. 'He had a sudden impulse to run down and bury himself in . . . leaves, covering over his head and body in an extravagant gesture of concealment . . . There was no escape. . . . [Leonora] would arrange or adapt him to her satisfaction' (p. 149).

As in the other books, battles for the affections of men are described in terms of triumph and defeat: thus Leonora thinks of James's former mistress Phoebe 'as her vanquished rival' (p. 126). The women in this novel treat each other badly in their contest to become the one Eve to present 'Adam with the apple' (p. 39). 'Leonora had little use for . . . women friends, but regarded them rather as a foil for herself, particularly if . . . they were less attractive and elegant than she was' (p. 53). Nor does she want a man to be conscious for a second of other women when he is with her. When Humphrey takes Leonora out to tea and remarks that he and his late wife sometimes used to meet in the very café they are sitting in, Leonora responds in a 'tone reverent to conceal her boredom. She considered it a slight error of taste that he should be able to think of another woman, even one long dead, when he was with her' (p. 38).

Pym's verdict here is that women are more petty than men. 'Only a woman could think of a trivial thing like stopping the milk when one was in the middle of an affair', we are told (p. 171). It is indicative that Leonora 'had always cared as much for inanimate objects as for people' (p. 182). Like Gilbert Osmond and Madame Merle in James's *The Portrait of a Lady*, Leonora has a great regard for *things*, and collects people largely to supplement the inventory of her possessions.

Hazel Holt has remarked that Barbara Pym 'saw all the faults and weaknesses [of men] very clearly, but with the eye of love . . . she always [had] great affection, even for those who had hurt her'.[2] *A Very Private Eye*, along with other testimony, suggests that Pym, who (like Jane Austen) wished to marry but never did – owing to a long series of near-misses and absurd anticlimaxes – regarded men with affection, yes, but also with wariness, cynicism and some contempt. Their selfish treatment of women in her novels may have in part a biographical source. Like her character Dulcie Mainwaring in *No Fond Return of Love* (1961), Pym for many years at the International African Institute found herself, instead of getting an early start behind a filing-cabinet on the family dinner, 'making indexes and doing little bits of research for people' (*A Very Private Eye*, p. 50). She would have preferred to work on the Brussels sprouts. Certainly many of the men she knew disappointed her in one way or another. And yet Pym understood her own gender well enough to know that the war of the sexes was not entirely of man's making, as no war can be fought without an opponent – thus the long line of 'terrifying' females in her books. Her women are not always 'excellent'. Indeed, they are often overbearing, vindictive, trivial – and sometimes cruel. They do not use their superior strength magnanimously. Men, though potentially tyrannical by nature, forcing women to become slaves or ignoring them, do not always win the war of the sexes, because they too misuse the superiority of their status, or because, when they come home at the end of the day, they are subject to a tyranny and tenacity superior to their worn-out wills. And so the sexes remain at knife-edge, with neither gaining a clear victory; it is something like the deadly stalemate in France during the First World War, with each side making sorties from time to time and then returning to its trenches to lick wounds and plan the next campaign. As Barbara Brothers has written, Pym's fiction carefully avoids 'portraying an idealized version of love . . . While Pym . . . mocks women's naivety and their romantic susceptibilities', she also 'exposes male pretentiousness, men's pompous acceptance of their own importance, and their vain belief in the myth they have created'.[3] Perhaps the only peaceful solution to this impossible situation, thinks one of the characters in *Crampton Hodnet*, is platonic love – 'the most beautiful relationship between a man and a woman was one in which they were in perfect *spiritual* harmony' (p. 186). In any case, 'beautiful' relationships of other kinds do not work in Barbara Pym's novels.

Though hers is primarily a comic genre, her comedy, like all great comedy, is essentially serious, focusing as it does on psychological aberration, especially that of mental cruelty. Those who regard her work as trivial or light or cosy have perhaps failed to perceive the hard edge of the laughter in it. The protagonist of Anita Brookner's *Hotel du Lac* (1984) comments that she knows women too well to regard them complacently, and the same may be said of Barbara Pym. She knows that one partner in a relationship may be weaker than the other, but that, as in many of James's stories, strength is often defeated by weakness. Such unnatural relations give her comedies of manners tragic overtones. Her books are funny, but no one in them is very happy.

All conflict is potentially tragic. Pym's novels deserve to be read with greater attention paid to their tragic theme: the powerlessness of love, and the pathos, the ultimate failure, of human relations.

12

The Novelist as Anthropologist

Muriel Schulz

Her work with the International African Institute provided Barbara Pym with comic material both for her own amusement and for her novels. She delighted in recording from anthropological tracts and working into her novels such ludicrous phrases as (in *Less than Angels*) 'The hyaenas have stolen the beer-strainers of the bad sons of the good women' (p. 243). In her fiction she speculated – sometimes wickedly – on possible relationships between anthropologists and their subjects. Has studying the Pygmies perhaps made Tyrell Todd petty and small-minded? Is it coincidental that Professor Fairfax, who has studied a tribe engaged in head-shrinking in *Less than Angels*, should himself have 'a rather shrunken-looking head'? (p. 8). Is it inevitable that Tom Mallow, raised by his mother and her brother, should study the role of the mother's brother in an African tribe? In the novels she could make jokes about anthropologists which would have been considered tactless at the Institute. 'I wonder if the study of societies where polygamy is a commonplace encourages immorality?' Rockingham Napier says in *Excellent Women*. 'Do anthropologists tend to have many wives at the same time?' he asks his wife and Everard Bone, who are not amused (p. 97). Pym enjoyed the comic similarities between practices in primitive societies and those in English culture. Everard Bone's mother, who detests birds, eats as many as possible, remarking in *Excellent Women*, 'At least we can eat our enemies. Everard, dear, which was that tribe in Africa which were cannibals?' (pp. 149–50). In *Less than Angels* Tom Mallow's uncle sits imprisoned in a darkened room all day like 'a sacrifice laid before the altar of the television set which demanded a constant tribute of victims' (p. 181). Pym also had a droll appreciation for primitive elements in her own

101

culture. In *Excellent Women* Rocky Napier conjectures that members of the Learned Society will prove themselves to be 'little better than primitive peoples' when food is served at a party. An anthropologist agrees: 'The so-called primitive peoples have an elaborate order and precedence in eating but I'm afraid that when we get started it's every man for himself' (p. 87). In the same novel Helena Napier apologises for the lack of soap and towel in the Ladies, explaining, 'We are at our most primitive here' (p. 95).

Work at the International African Institute also provided Barbara Pym with raw material for her fiction. Hazel Holt recalls in *A Very Private Eye* how Pym used the little she knew about the authors published by the journal *Africa* to create a fantasy world around them. 'I couldn't ask W. if his Mother was better because I couldn't remember if we'd invented her' (p. 183). Anthropologists appear as central characters in several of her novels and often reappear as shadowy figures in others. Pym encountered two generations of anthropologists during her years at the Institute, and both are represented in her fiction. The older ones were often amateurs, colonial officers and missionaries who as a matter of interest recorded information on the tribes to whom they were assigned. The younger generation were professionally trained social scientists ('depressingly scientific', according to Rocky Napier in *Excellent Women* – p. 88). In her novels the older ones may be a little mad, with 'bees in [their] bonnet[s]' and 'a wild Ancient Mariner gleam in the eye' – *Less than Angels*, (pp. 148, 22), but Pym treats them affectionately as people who are amusing and pleasant to be with. At the marvellous Institute party in *Excellent Women* she draws a contrast between the older generation – with whom the outsiders, Rocky and Mildred Lathbury, share tea and carry on a friendly banter – and the younger generation, whose papers and conversation are completely unintelligible to the novice. The older generation enjoy the party, as does the President of the Learned Society, a mild, kindly man with bits of meringue clinging to his beard. The younger ones – those called by Helena Napier and Everard Bone 'the really worthwhile people' – appear to take no pleasure at all in the tea (p. 89). They stand aloof and wait instead for the learned discussions to begin.

Pym's opinion of those discussions and of the manuscripts she edited for *Africa* is suggested in the Bishop of Mbawawa's complaint in *Some Tame Gazelle* about the debasement undergone by anthropology since Frazer's day to 'a mere matter of

genealogies, meaningless definitions and jargon' (p. 206). The
books by older anthropologists had been interesting and personal.
The titles often referred to the author (*Five Years with the Congo
Cannibals* or *With Camera and Pen in Northern Nigeria*, in *Excellent
Women*, p. 88), and many included photographs of the author
with his native friends. The new anthropologists were unlikely to
develop such friendships, since they studied social and political
systems, not people. The titles and contents of their books were
expected to be objective and impersonal, like Tom Mallow's thesis
(in *Less than Angels*), which, Professor Mainwaring promises, will
typify the new anthropology: 'it will be a model of dullness, *quite
unreadable*' (p. 124). Mainwaring displays more cheerfulness than
Pym was able to summon up while trying to put a collection of
seminar papers into a published volume. 'How nice it would be if
the publication of such papers were to be forbidden by law!' she
wrote in a letter to Bob Smith (*A Very Private Eye*, p. 273).

At the Institute Barbara Pym had ample opportunity to observe
the weaknesses of anthropology, as well. A major problem – the
difficulty of 'getting it right' – resulted from the anthropologist's
insistence upon studying unfamiliar cultures.[1] If one must work
with strange and exotic tribes, how does one go about
understanding the meaning to the native of cultural phenomena?
Some of the difficulties encountered by the stranger in an alien
culture are illustrated in *No Fond Return of Love* by the Brazilian
visitor to England, Senhor MacBride-Pereira. He delights in
observing the culture around him, but he is hopelessly confused
by what he sees. Consequently he is forever intrigued by the
commonplace ('A young English girl with a pot plant – what
could be more charming' – p. 70), and confused by the ordinary
(watching the young lovers kiss before entering their respective
houses, he asks himself, 'Orpheus and Eurydice? . . . Now what
have I seen – an end or a beginning? Romeo and Juliet, Paolo and
Francesca, or just two young lovers of today, a suburban idyll?' –
p. 166). The unusual utterly mystifies him; seeing the middle-
aged and not very attractive Viola Dace getting out of a taxi and
having her hand kissed, he thinks lamely, 'The things I see! . . .
Who knows what it might not be!' (p. 167). In fact, the last lines
of the novel focus on the difficulty the outsider has in interpreting
another culture. When Aylwin Forbes arrives by taxi, Senhor
Pereira, looking away for a moment to choose a sugared almond,
fails to see who gets out. 'He took a mauve sugared almond out of

a bag and sucked it thoughtfully, wondering what, if anything, he had missed' (p. 254). What he has missed is the culminating action of all that he has observed. Aylwin Forbes is coming to court Dulcie Mainwaring. However intrigued and observant he may be, the untrained observer from another culture often misses the significance of what he observes and is reduced to recording interesting but meaningless facts.

The trained anthropologist, observing an alien society, is not much better at interpreting cultural phenomena than is the amateur. Neither training nor detachment guarantees the accuracy of their observations. Long before the publication of Derek Freeman's charge of bias in Margaret Meade's Samoan studies (1983),[2] social scientists were aware that it is impossible to conduct a totally value-free study of human institutions. Inevitably the outsider brings biased assumptions to the study of alien cultures and, as a consequence, no two sets of observations will be alike; the expectations of two different anthropologists will seriously skew the observations of each. In *Less than Angels* Barbara Pym dramatises the biases and consequent obtuseness of anthropologists in her portrayal of the French anthropologist Jean-Pierre le Rossignol, who is in London to study the English. Jean-Pierre brings to his study the condescension of a Frenchman toward other cultures, an attitude that nicely parallels the patronising stance of anthropologists toward their African tribes. When someone wonders why English women do not marry, Jean-Pierre glances around the room and inquires, 'Do you need to ask?' (p. 19). In response to Deirdre's remark that parties are interesting if one can be detached, he replies, 'Oh, but one must be detached about so many things! Otherwise how could a Frenchman endure the English Sunday?' (p. 22). And, when he completes his study, he returns 'thankfully' home to France (p. 166).

On Sundays he visits churches, as a means of passing the day and of studying the English at prayer, a study which presents the reader with an opportunity to analyse the methodology of the anthropologist in the field. First of all, Jean-Pierre is insensitive to the feelings of those he studies. His detached interest in English churches offends Deirdre Swan, who sees his study as a frivolous approach to behaviour which in her family is considered to be a serious matter. In addition, his mere presence upsets the ecology of some of the social gatherings he studies. In Deirdre's church the congregation are conscious of his presence – he has dressed inappropriately in a grey suit and yellow gloves – and, as a result, things are not exactly what they would have been if he had not been there. In addition, he sits in an unmarked family pew, one that has been occupied by the same family for forty years. Ironically enough, he fails to observe the consequences of his mistake – the consternation and fluster which are evident to everyone else in the church; he has sat too far forward to be able to observe what is going on around him. His comments on the service are inappropriate ('I found it enchanting') and ethnocentric ('I felt almost at home, though there were some interesting differences' – p. 82), quite in contrast to Deirdre's mother's rather thorough analysis of the early-morning service. Although he could learn much about the church from Deirdre and her family, he asks no questions about it.

Rossignol's most serious drawback as an observer, however, results from his anthropological bias. In his determination to isolate patterns of culture, he imposes them upon the data before him. Ever eager to generalise upon the behaviour of 'the English', he incorrectly translates individual behaviour into societal norms. For example, when he wishes to say goodbye to Deirdre's mother and aunt, he is told that they are in the kitchen washing up.

> 'I see; the older female relatives work in the kitchen when there are no servants. The mother and the father's sister?'
>
> 'No, Aunt Rhoda is my mother's sister.'
>
> 'Ah, yes, I understand. Women more closely linked would work better together – they would not fight.'   (p. 84)

As it happens, Deirdre's mother and aunt do not work well together; they are locked in a combat involving daily skirmishes. Since there is no place in Jean-Pierre's anthropology for exceptional behaviour, he does not discover this bit of information about the two women. Perhaps it would make no difference if he had. Jean-Pierre does not appear to refine his assumptions when they are falsified by evidence before him. He remains confirmed in his belief that the English invariably nap after eating their Sunday lunchtime joint of meat, despite Deirdre's repeated explanation that only older people nap in the middle of the day (pp. 73, 84). Before returning to France, he visits Bournemouth to study 'the English' on holiday, apparently blind to the easily observable fact that only a small subset of English men and women holiday in such places.

A second weakness of anthropology derives from the detachment and objectivity so highly valued among the younger generation of scholars. The fact that scientific detachment has led social scientists to dehumanise the people they study, turning them into mere objects, has become a common criticism of anthropology. Indeed, scientific detachment has created a new anthropology, with practitioners who are less inclined to consider the social and political implications of their work than were the older ones. Unlike either the colonial administrators, who took responsibility for the political fortunes of their constituencies, or the clergy, who took responsibility for their souls, the new anthropologists, in refusing to identify with the interests of 'their' tribes, create a paternalism devoid of humanistic or ethical concern for the problems of their subjects. Nor do they ask themselves whether their work helps perpetuate the poverty or exploitation of the natives. They do not talk about the political consequences of their work; they see themselves as theoretical scientists, concerned with constructing models which will illuminate their knowledge of humankind. To identify with the interests of their tribes would compromise their scientific objectivity. The people they study serve merely as so much data supporting anthropological abstractions and theories.

In *Less than Angels* Barbara Pym presents a definition of anthropology that casts significant light on her views of the field and on themes occurring in her own work:

> They went out to remote places and studied the customs and languages of the peoples living there. Then they came back and wrote books and articles about what they had observed and taught others how to do the same thing. It was as simple as that. And it was a very good thing that these languages and customs should be known, firstly because they were interesting in themselves and in danger of being forgotten, and secondly because it was helpful to missionaries and government officials to know as much as possible about the people they sought to evangelise or govern.   (p. 15)

There appears to be a great deal of irony in the definition. It suggests, first of all, a judgement, evident in her portrayal of the

field in her novels, that anthropology has gradually become
a sterile, self-perpetuating discipline producing unreadable
documents of little or no value except as they provide models for
the training of future anthropologists. Tom's thesis is, as Professor
Mainwaring has predicted it would be, dull and unreadable, like
other anthropological treatises that Tom has recommended to
Catherine. Mainwaring has given all of his own anthropology
texts to the Foresight Centre (an ironic name for an institute
devoted to preserving worthless records of the past). 'They are
not the kind of reading to see me into my grave', he explains to
his young students (p. 209). Early in her retirement, Letty Crowe
discovers the same thing in *Quartet in Autumn*, when she
innocently selects a sociology book to read for pleasure. Finding
herself 'frozen with boredom, baffled and bogged down by
incomprehensible jargon', she turns instead to novels (p. 117).
Even the works by the older generation of anthropologists gather
dust on the Institute's shelves. In *Excellent Women* Rocky Napier
reads off the titles of books by earlier anthropologists – books that
he suggests have some charm and personality – but he notes that
they are currently 'the books that nobody reads' (p. 88).

A second aspect of the definition is its explanation that
anthropologists study remote societies. Why, Pym asks in her
novels, must one study exotic, unfamiliar societies? One's own is
just as interesting and strange. In *No Fond Return of Love* Dulcie
Mainwaring speaks for the value of doing research on one's own
culture: 'Perhaps the time will come when one may be permitted
to do research into the lives of ordinary people, . . . people who
have no claim to fame whatsoever.' 'Ah, that'll be the day!' laughs
the librarian of a learned institution (p. 18). Dulcie remains
confirmed in her belief that everyday objects and customs are
worthy of study; hearing a discussion of Proust's relics, she
insists, 'I think the relics of any woman could be just as interesting.
. . . Particularly if she had been unhappy, and who hasn't, and if
she had kept things' (p. 124).

A third aspect of Pym's definition of anthropology is its
implication that cultures are dying out only in remote parts of the
world. In the novels, as in her notebooks, Pym stresses quite the
contrary. England, too, is suffering losses as a result of change
and decay. She notes with dismay that her church has become
'redundant'; wreckers are pulling down buildings between Fleet
Street and Aldwych (to be replaced, she presumes, by 'shoe-box

buildings'); Gamage's is closing; the Institute has moved, its earlier quarters to be demolished; even the *Church Times* has diminished ('no Answers to Correspondents', *A Very Private Eye* – p. 266). The novels, too, lament the changes England is undergoing. Tom Mallow (in *Less than Angels*) perceives the irony that anthropologists are ignoring the decay of their own cultures. Standing outside the debutante dance he has refused to attend, he asks himself, 'If we lamented the decay of the great civilizations of the past, . . . should we not also regret the dreary levelling down of our own?' (p. 163).

Who is to preserve the memory of England's institutions and customs? If not the anthropologist, the novelist. During her years at the Institute, Pym was exploring in her works the possibility that the novelist is a kind of anthropologist of her own culture. To Philip Larkin she explained that, although she had no degree in anthropology, she had mastered its esoteric terminology. She recognised, as well, that the two professions were alike in their goals: in *Less than Angels* the anthropologist attempts to show the nature of the human condition by 'laying bare the structure of society'; the novelist, 'by covering it up' (pp. 194–5).

As she worked with anthropological papers for the journal *Africa*, Barbara Pym apparently became aware, as well, that the novelist's methods are in many ways like those of the anthropologist. Hazel Holt remarks in *A Very Private Eye* that 'Her natural curiosity, her detective work, her "research into the lives of ordinary people" continued, to become (especially in her notebooks) what the keeping of field notes is to an anthropologist' (p. xv).

In *No Fond Return of Love* Pym provides the reader with an opportunity to observe the methods used by the novelist in doing field work. Dulcie is not a writer; she indexes and reads proofs for others. Nevertheless, she observes life with a novelist's eye. As she watches a woman walking a dog, she notices the colour of the woman's coat, the colour and fabric of her gloves, and the fact that the woman is carrying two books. 'What is the use of noticing such details?' she wonders. 'It isn't as if I were a novelist or a private detective' (p. 60).

Watching Dulcie follow the spur of Aylwin Forbes, we see the novelist at work. Her sources of information are the Public Record Office, public libraries and churches. Her reference books include street maps, telephone directories, *Who's Who*, *Crockford's* and Kelly's Directories. She follows strangers around, studying their behaviour. She inspects the titles of books on other people's shelves. She notices minute details about people and guesses at the implications of all that she observes ('She noticed that he had been carrying an *Evening Standard*, and it gave her an insight into his character to see that he was the kind of person who bought an evening paper at lunch-time, thus spoiling his evening's pleasure' – p. 39). Dulcie's methods are Pym's own. Hazel Holt recalls in *A Very Private Eye*, 'She infected me, too, with the fascination of finding out about people, and lunchtimes were often spent in public libraries, searching for clues in Crockford's, Kelly's Directories or street maps' (p. xiv). Most of all, novelists observe others. In doing this kind of research, they have an advantage over anthropologists. Since there is nothing identifying them as being outsiders (even at home in England, Tom Mallow's haircut marks his detribalisation), they can observe people's activities without disturbing the ecology of the society they are describing. Thus, in *No Fond Return of Love*, Pym shows us the novelist at dinner in a West Country hotel observing other patrons: 'They ate their stewed plums and custard and drank their thimble-sized cups of coffee, quite unconscious that they were being observed' (p. 176).

In *Less than Angels* Pym specifically compares the scientific anthropologist (Tom Mallow) with the writer (Catherine Oliphant), and it is clear that Catherine has many of the traits necessary to the social scientist. Like Tom she is capable of detachment, but with a significant difference. Tom's training has detribalised him; he has lost his sense of belonging to English society. He refuses to attend his cousins' debutante party, going instead to watch it from the outside and theorise about its sociological significance. Walking in a romantic setting with Deirdre Swan, he thinks, as an anthropologist might, 'This is the place where the young men and women walk at night and are allowed a certain amount of licence' (p. 151), but he does not act. It is she who must kiss him. When Tom returns home, it is clear that his mother expects no display of affection from him. Both she and Elaine, his childhood sweetheart, have trained themselves to suppress their longing for Tom's affection, since he has none to give. Scientific detachment has dehumanised him, removing from him the capability of feeling. Before returning to Africa, Tom becomes aware that he has ceased to experience love and pain. Unable to rekindle his love for Elaine, his first sweetheart, he feels a fleeting regret at the loss of the young man who once quoted poetry in moments of intense feeling. Much as he would like to find that part of himself again, he is incapable of overcoming the distance between the detached anthropologist who no longer experiences intense feeling and the sensitive young man he mourns. Confused by his inability to respond to the affection offered him at home, Tom returns to London and, shortly afterward, to Africa. There he falls victim to the anthropologist's mistaken belief that the problems of 'his' tribe need be no concern of his. Tom is killed during 'a political riot, in which he had become involved more out of curiosity than passionate conviction' (p. 231).

Catherine, too, is capable of detachment, but she does not lose the capacity to feel emotion. Watching Tom and Deirdre holding hands in a restaurant, Catherine is 'horrified at the sardonic detachment with which she had been watching them' (p. 107). How, she wonders, can she notice their moussaka getting cold just at that moment when she realises that she has lost Tom? Although she is shocked and unhappy, her dispassionate interest in other people's lives provides her with some refuge from that pain. Going into a nearby restaurant, she loses herself in a writer's fascination with the conversations going on around her, and afterwards she becomes so absorbed in her own writing that she forgets, for a while, her unhappiness at losing Tom. Nevertheless, she experiences the pain of the 'heart's banishment', and she grieves during the months that follow.

Catherine retains, too, an ability to empathise with others. Pym's interest in and affection for the society in which she lived made her an inspired witness of her own culture, and she gave the traits of curiosity and empathy to Catherine. As Tom Mallow more than once remarks to himself, Catherine is a far better observer of behaviour than he ('He imagined how Catherine would have enjoyed it, her bright eyes darting here and there, missing no detail' – p. 180). A consequence of his detribalisation is that he often fails to see what is going on around him in England; one wonders whether he is any *more* observant in Africa. Diane Lewis has suggested that insensitivity to one's own culture is a general defect of trained anthropologists, having serious consequences for the discipline:

It has been suggested that lack of fieldwork in the anthropologist's own society is a measure of the anthropologist's 'disassociation' from his own culture and has probably led to distortion in his abilities to grasp another culture. . . . We do not know the extent the anthropologist's lack of understanding of, and involvement in, his own culture has affected the development of theory and method in the discipline, but it may turn out that this social ignorance has seriously skewed perspective on other cultures.[3]

Pym recognised that anthropologists' training diminishes their curiosity about and interest in the world around them. Pym's books abound with keen observers who are *not* anthropologists. Although fascinated by the routine of English life, they lack the insight or training that would enable them to draw generalisations from what they see. Mabel Swan and Rhoda Wellcome in *Less than Angels* are said to observe their neighbours 'from a distance, . . . as the anthropologists did' (p. 256); in fact, they observe far more than does Mabel's daughter, Deirdre, who is training as an anthropologist. In *Excellent Women* Mildred Lathbury, who has a 'talent for observation' (p. 70), goes with Rocky Napier to the Institute party to observe the anthropologists: 'They study mankind and we will study them', he suggests (p. 36). Senhor MacBride-Pereira, in *No Fond Return of Love*, spends a great deal of time at his window observing his English neighbours; and, in the same novel, Dulcie Mainwaring is so compulsive an observer of others that she wonders what use she can make of the minute details she notices. Ironically enough, the one anthropologist who is observant of English society – Emma, in *A Few Green Leaves* – believes that it might have been better if she had been a novelist: she fears that much of what she observes is too commonplace to be useful in sociological surveys.

The ablest observer of all is Catherine, the writer, in *Less than Angels*. She not only sees more details than others: she can also see into the hearts of people. Thus the impersonal and insensitive nature of Tom's thesis shocks and dismays her:

'It would, *however, be dangerous at this stage to embark on any extensive analysis* . . .' she read. 'Oh, what cowards scholars are! When you think how poets and novelists rush in with *their* analyses of the human heart and mind and soul of which they often have far less knowledge than darling Tom has of his tribe.' (p. 167)

Catherine's empathy enables her to analyse the people and the behaviour she observes. In the same way that anthropologists interpret alien cultures, writers interpret their own. Thus the anthropologists see Alaric Lydgate simply as just an irascible man who chooses to write savage scholarly reviews. Catherine sees quite well that he is a sad and lonely man, and that his impersonal reviews ('It is a pity . . . that the author did not . . .' – p. 58), which squash the authors like so many bugs, serve simply to mask his inability to write up his own anthropological notes (Xavier Albo, in reply to Diane Lewis, has commented that, to the people studied, anthropologists look very much like entomologists rather than ethnologists!). Because she is sympathetic, as well as understanding, Catherine involves herself in Lydgate's problems and is able to help him. By revealing to Lydgate the truth about his work, she is able to free him from the alienation which he has suffered.

During Pym's days at the Institute, anthropologists deplored any kind of involvement in the lives of their subjects (Miss Clovis attacks Catherine for encouraging the burning of the African notes, rather than Lydgate for electing to destroy them). The impersonal stance of the researcher and the sterile circularity of the profession led to a widely spread crisis of conscience in anthropology during the 1960s and 1970s, one voiced in *Less than Angels* by Tom Mallow, lamenting his loss of faith in his work:

> But I just wonder sometimes what's the use of it all. Who will benefit from my work, what exactly is the *point* of my researches? Are my people out there going to be any happier because I happen to have found out that they have a double descent system? Who will be any better off for my having discovered new facts about the importance of the mother's brother? (p. 105)

It is clear, at the end, that his work is of no importance at all. His notes are as useless to other anthropologists as Alaric Lydgate's were to Tom: after Tom's death, the notes are packed up and shipped to his mother in Shropshire, rather than to the Institute in London.

Catherine's writing, too, is ephemeral: her articles and romantic fiction appear in magazines having a one-month life span. However, the kind of writing she does has benefits for others: it either provides information that they seek to have or else gives them pleasure, not unlike the pleasure that she finds in quoting to herself and others the words of great writers.

Writers can give comfort to others because they are able to put into words what the less gifted can only feel. Much has changed in the Shropshire community where Tom grew up. Mallow Park is 'almost engulfed by later "improvements" ' (p. 177). Tom's mother, a member of one of the town's leading families, no longer has the leisure to take the train into London. She regularly sells vegetables at a stall in the local market. Despite the differences that he notes, Tom's visit ends with a reminder that the human condition is as unchanging across time as it is across cultures. After Tom leaves for Africa, and Elaine is left alone again, Pym quotes an extended passage from *Persuasion*, in which Anne Elliot muses about the loneliness of the woman left behind, expressed in words that Elaine might have addressed to Tom:

> We certainly do not forget you so soon as you forget us. It is, perhaps, our fate rather than our merit. We cannot help ourselves. We live at home, quiet, confined, and our feelings prey upon us. You are forced on exertion. You have always business of some sort or other to take you back into the world immediately, and continual occupation and change soon weaken impressions. (*Less than Angels*, p. 186)

Since Elaine is not a reader, she will miss 'the consolation and pain of coming upon her feelings expressed for her in such moving words' (ibid.).

It is that enduring truth of human nature that Barbara Pym records in her novels, truth more evident in the everyday world of the novelist than in the exotic world of the anthropologist. Once the similarities between the novelist and the anthropologist had appealed to her imagination, it was perhaps inevitable that she should document in her novels rituals and customs typical of her own culture. Consequently several of her novels constitute an anthropology of the middle-class England of her own time. *Less than Angels* provides a rather sly anthropology of anthropology. Pym explains the forms of address used at the Institute: those of high status address each other by their Christian names ('Felix',

'Gervase'), while according to those of lower status (the students) the more formal style of address ('Mr Fox', 'Mr Penfold'). A seminar paper is information culled from books by others and, ideally, presented with the author's own interpretation. A thesis, in order to preclude the kind of careful reading by examiners that might lead them to reject it, should be long and boring. The sending and receiving of offprints has great significance among social scientists. These facts are slipped into the novel almost as baldly as they might have been recorded in an anthropologist's field notes.

More general information about English culture is provided in *No Fond Return of Love*. We are introduced to the learned conference, at which papers are read touching on the problems of an editor, the problems of indexing and the terrors of doing a proper bibliography. Pym presents us with rather contrived explanations of a variety of customs: a lay reader's duties and limitations – information which bores Viola Dace (p. 13); the ritual for ordering tea at a jumble sale – Dulcie already knows how to do so and responds with a thoughtful commentary (p. 79); the intricacies of making marmalade – Viola has never cared for marmalade (p. 167); and the patrons and setting of the tea room – where 'a novelist or a sociologist might have felt very near the heart of reality' (p. 141).

The most anthropological of her novels, however, is *A Few Green Leaves*. The heroine, Emma Howick, is an anthropologist writing up research on attitudes she has studied in one of the new English towns. As she completes her work, she considers the possibility of doing a study of the village in which she lives. Toward this end she amasses, during the course of the novel, research notes on a variety of topics, recorded against a future when she might be ready to do something with them, notes which are included as part of the novel. Inquiring about the holding of surgeries on Mondays and Thursdays, Emma's question displays an obtuseness toward her own culture typical of anthropologists:

'Are people in the village ill then?' Emma asked in her innocence.

Mrs Bland seemed nonplussed, almost indignant, at the question, so Emma did not press it. Of course people were ill, always and everywhere. . . .

[R]emembering her role as an anthropologist and observer – the necessity of being on the outside looking in – she crept away, meditating on what she had observed. There was obviously material for a note here.   (pp. 19–20)

Emma gathers many notes during her stay in the village. She begins by entitling her research, 'Some Observations on the Social Pressures of a West Oxfordshire Village', but decides, in rephrasing it, to exchange the word 'village' for the sociological jargon 'community' (p. 38). Much that is included in the novel would fall appropriately under the second title that Emma proposes for her study: 'The Role of Women in a West Oxfordshire Community'. As in her other novels, Pym explores here chiefly the cultural customs that are the province of women. We learn that men would not be asked 'to fetch or carry jumble, unless it was . . . particularly heavy' (p. 43); men 'don't go blackberrying' (p. 162); men are less satisfactory as medical patients – and they are less likely to be found sitting in the doctor's waiting-rooms – than women (p. 209). The novel provides a description of many of the rituals conducted by the women of the village: the jumble sale, with notes on its jargon ('the things one wore were known as clothing or garments rather than just clothes' – p. 43) and a catalogue of items for sale (p. 45); the hunger lunch for people starving in the Third World; 'drinks parties' designed to 'sort out in a social way sheep from goats' and to identify people who will help out in staging the village festivals (p. 59); funerals (Emma worries uncertainly about the etiquette of taking flowers and hopes that by attending she might find 'something for noting in her paper "Funeral Customs in a Rural Community" ' – p. 232). When the village women hold a bring-and-buy sale, Emma speculates about the possibility of doing 'a serious sociological study . . . of this important feature of village life' and toward that end collects a set of notes 'under headings, almost as if she were indeed preparing a paper for a learned society' (p. 69). Under the heading 'Participants', she writes, 'Men. None' (p. 70). Learning who is and who is not allowed to arrange flowers at the flower festival, she considers recording it as a note on village status (p. 77). Emma initiates with two other anthropologists a discussion about the impact of the flower festival upon members of the community. The male dismisses the notion that such customs express cultural values, insisting that celebrations such as the flower festival can have nothing in common with African festivals or European peasant fiestas. However, his wife, also an anthropologist, concedes that the festival may indeed have an impact on the lives of the middle-class women in the village.

Anthropologists expect to find their important truths in male rituals (their journal in *Excellent Women* is entitled simply *Man*). Like Dulcie, Pym insists that the world of women is just as significant to a culture. However, her anthropology is not one-sided: she does not restrict herself to the world of women. She describes behaviour in the local pub of a small village ('the old men sitting like some group of primitive sculpture' – p. 86). Talk is suspended when an unknown couple enter, as everyone watches them. The couple attempt to integrate themselves by engaging the natives in conversation. The tension finally relaxes when another couple, known to both groups, enter and begin a conversation with the newcomers. The latter no longer constitute an alien element upsetting the ecology of the room.

The most significant sociological topic created in *A Few Green Leaves*, however, is the passing of the gentry as an influence on local lives. Here is exactly the sort of cultural decay that anthropologists use to justify their work to themselves and to others. In considering an anthropology of the village, Emma realises that in her notes she has not mentioned the gentry. They should have been first on her list, but she has learned little about them.

Pym does, in the course of the novel, provide a great deal of information about what the gentry have meant to the village and how it copes without them. The novel opens with the villagers exercising their right, on one Sunday each year, to roam the grounds of the manor once owned by Sir Hubert de Tankerville in order to collect firewood – ' "faggots", as the ancient edict has it' (p. 2). The former retainers of the manor have been resettled in council housing outside the village, so few of the present inhabitants have any direct knowledge of the de Tankervilles. Later in the novel a group of villagers tour the manor, accompanied by Miss Lee, the local historian, 'who had "known the family" and was, as always, very ready to point out ways in which things were different from the old days' (p. 165). Miss Lee remembers what kinds of books the family read in Sir Hubert's time; she can recall who did the flowers and what the arrangements were like; she knows the tastes and habits of the family – even to when and where they said family prayers. She is the village's living link with the past.

During a discussion of the patronage practised in the days of the de Tankervilles, one villager complains that, with the passing of the gentry, the village has lost its centre. Emma speculates that there really is a centre to the present village: the clergy and the doctors have taken the place of the gentry, a possibility explored by the novel itself. The rector, Tom Dagnall, and the two physicians, Martin Shrubsole and Luke Gellibrand, minister to the physical and spiritual needs of the people, with roles that often overlap. Actually medicine has largely supplanted religion as a personal centre for people living in this village, the consultation having replaced the confessional. On Mondays the surgery is especially full, since people who did not go to church on Sunday seek out the doctors to receive solace and prescriptions. So important has medicine become that patients are abandoning the older Dr Gellibrand, who dispenses advice which denies the presence of illness ('go and buy yourself a new hat, my dear' – p. 15), in order to see Dr Shrubsole, who generally includes the important prescription for medicine, a validating 'ritual scrap of paper', with his suggestions to patients (p. 13). The importance of the doctors surprises Emma, who believes that the rector should have replaced the lord of the manor as the leading citizen of the village. But Tom Dagnall is ineffectual as a spiritual force in the village, and his services are poorly attended. Many of those managing the upkeep of his church are non-members and non-believers; even the organist is an agnostic. Indeed, the church figures more prominently in the social life of the village than in its spiritual life, and Tom's interest in history creates a more devoted following than does his ministry.

The rector comes into his own only on holy days (although even some of these are being secularised) or when someone dies. Toward the end of the novel, Miss Vereker, who served as governess to Sir Hubert de Tankerville's children, returns to the village to see for one last time the manor, the church, the mausoleum and old friends. However, so much has changed and her own memory has become so dim that she becomes disoriented and, finally, hopelessly lost in the woods near the manor, where Emma and Avice Shrubsole find her sleeping. She decides against a visit to the manor, or to the church, or even to her former friends. After spending a night in the home of the new leading citizen of the village, the young physician Martin Shrubsole, she decides to visit the mausoleum instead: 'That was always the same' (p. 228).

When Dr Gellibrand notifies Tom that Miss Vereker has been found wandering in the woods, Tom wonders what concern it can be of his. She may need a doctor to treat her bronchitis or a psychiatrist to treat her mental disorientation, but she is not yet ready for the rector. When Miss Lickerish dies, Tom observes that some situations can be handled only by the rector. If Miss Vereker had been beyond the comfort of physicians and psychiatrists – if, in fact, she had been beyond comforting – then she would have been passed on to him. Secularisation has much diminished the role of the clergy.

Barbara Pym does not put her work forward as anthropology, but it is clear that she saw it as related. She writes a different kind of anthropology, perhaps a better one, but she was under no illusions about the willingness of anthropologists to take seriously the work of the novelist. In *A Few Green Leaves*, while Graham Pettifer is chatting with Emma Howick and two other anthropologists, the question of doing anthropology in an English village comes up:

> 'I've often thought one could do a study of this village', said Tamsin innocently. 'But I suppose it's such a well-worked field that there'd be nothing new to say.'
>
> 'Emma would find something new', said Graham. . . . 'Even if she had to make it up.'
>
> 'Well, one can't really do that', said Robbie. 'After all, we're not novelists', he added, smiling in a superior way into his beard.
>
> Suddenly Emma felt unbearably irritated by the whole situation and got up to go.   (p. 175)

Reading through Pym's works, one wonders which is closer to the truth: the anthropologist's objective record or the novelist's fictional account? Certainly the world she created had a remarkable degree of reality to her. In the novels the reader keeps hearing bits of information about characters from earlier novels, rather as one might hear of an anthropologist who has gone off to the field. In later novels we learn through gossip, for instance, that Mildred Lathbury (*Excellent Women*) has married Everard Bone, that Deirdre

Swan and Digby Fox (*Less than Angels*) have married and are
about to become parents, and that Digby has given the address at
the funeral of Esther Clovis (*Excellent Women* and *Less than Angels*).
Wilmet Forsyth, Piers Longridge and Keith (*A Glass of Blessings*)
are touring the same castle as Dulcie in *No Fond Return of Love*
(p. 193). Miss Lee's Christian guesthouse in *A Few Green Leaves* is
the Anchorage, the West Country Hotel owned by Aylwin
Forbes's mother in *No Fond Return of Love*. And Pym's own novel
Some Tame Gazelle is among the books on the shelf in Dulcie
Mainwaring's guestroom in *No Fond Return of Love* (p. 73).

Philip Larkin apparently warned Pym that this sort of thing
could be overdone, but, she told him, she saw the reappearance
of characters as 'a kind of superstition or a charm' (*A Very Private
Eye*, p. 203). Not only that. Her characters were neither fanciful
creations nor representative abstractions. Drawn from life, they
embody a truth about the originals that it is the gift of the writer
to be able to divine. In *A Very Private Eye* Hazel Holt recalls Pym's
discussion of her characters at the Institute:

> In the endless afternoons of office life and in our free time, we
> talked about her books and the characters she had created
> (what happened *after* Mildred had married Everard, what the
> original of Rocky had really been like) so that the world of the
> novels soon became as much a part of our lives as the real
> world. (pp. xiv–xv).

Pym's characters had for her a deep reality which she might have
characterised as being very near the heart of things – a favourite
phrase used to express her belief that the nature of the human
condition is revealed most clearly in the common everyday world.
It is ironic that those who are immersed in the culture lack the
training and insight necessary to interpret it, and those who are
trained to interpret cultural behaviour are committed to the study
of the unfamiliar and the unusual. It is the novelist who combines
the qualities needed to explain the culture in which she is
immersed. Claude Lévi-Strauss has said that, if natives study
themselves, they produce either history or philology – not
anthropology.[4] Barbara Pym's novels demonstrate that they
produce literature as well – literature embodying an interpretation
of the culture that an anthropologist might well envy.

13
Literary Allusions in the Novels

Lotus Snow

'But these little remembered scraps of culture had a way of coming out unexpectedly.' Thus Belinda Bede of *Some Tame Gazelle* apologises to herself for having quoted unsuitably. A friend's plan for a pond of goldfish and water lilies has brought to her lips lines from 'The Fish, the Man and the Spirit'. 'Leigh Hunt writes rather charmingly about a fish', she says. *'Legless, unloving, infamously chaste'* (p. 59). True to her modesty as her disclaimer is, it is false to her remarkable knowledge of English poetry. As Archdeacon Hoccleve reflects, 'She often wasted her time reading things that nobody else would dream of reading' (p. 55). Across the novel she ranges in thought and speech from the anonymous *Sawles Warde*, written in the twelfth or thirteenth century, through the poetry of intervening centuries to that of Sir John Betjeman. Indeed, her lifetime love for Henry Hoccleve is in part based upon his equal devotion to the English poets. His sermons are studded with quotations from the poets of the seventeenth and eighteenth centuries; his conversation abounds in passages from Gray's 'Elegy' and Young's *Night Thoughts*; and he enjoys nothing so much as listening to himself reading aloud to Belinda from *The Faerie Queene, Samson Agonistes* or *The Prelude*.

Belinda, Archdeacon Hoccleve and Jane, a former tutor of seventeenth-century literature in *Jane and Prudence*, are undoubtedly the greatest votaries of English poetry in Barbara Pym's eleven novels. Yet, in all the novels but one, characters find solace in poetry. To the single exception Jeremy Treglown offers his snarling approval: 'One of the good things about *Quartet in Autumn* is that Barbara Pym's characters don't spend much time casting about for appropriate literary quotations.'[1] Conceivably he has overlooked the obvious reason for this: whereas the characters of the other novels are persons of culture, the foursome in *Quartet in Autumn* are office workers of average education.

In the other ten novels the characters, men and women alike, give the effect of artlessness in their instant recall of the quotation appropriate to the experience at hand. The men, clergymen and scholars for the most part, may be assumed to be familiar with the English poets. And the women, generally spinsters keenly observant of their genteel milieux and wryly humorous about their disappointments in love, find in poetry a form of communication with themselves. As Deborah Wilde, heroine of an unfinished draft of a novel entitled *Something to Remember*, writes, 'He took away himself and left with me the great English poets instead, and after a while they began to be a consolation, as they always had been. For at the time there's no consolation, none whatever.'[2]

A survey of the allusions in Barbara Pym's novels shows her range of knowledge and her preferences among the English poets and novelists. Lines from the seventeenth-century poets, both the great and the obscure, are often quoted, and, from the great, most frequently John Donne's love poetry. 'The Relique',

> When my grave is broke up again
> Some second guest to entertain

and 'The Good-Morrow',

> For love, all love of other sights controls,
> And makes one little room an everywhere

are favourites of hers, the former quoted in *Excellent Women*, *Jane and Prudence* and *No Fond Return of Love*; the latter, in *Less than Angels*, *Quartet in Autumn*, *The Sweet Dove Died* and *Crampton Hodnet*. Elegies XVI, 'On his Mistress', and XIX, 'To his Mistress Going to Bed', are commonplaces of Jane and Prudence's conversation. In *A Glass of Blessings* Piers Longridge faithlessly promises Wilmet, 'We'll build in sonnets pretty rooms', quoting 'The Canonisation'; and his sister recalls with shame the letter she had once written Rocky Napier, quoting 'The Broken Heart':

> My rags of heart can like, wish, and adore,
> But after one such love, can love no more.

Young Penelope of *An Unsuitable Attachment*, speculating what Rupert Stonebird's relation to Ianthe is, picks up a volume of Donne, which falls open at 'The Curse':

> Whoever guesses, thinks, or dreams he knows
> Who is my mistress, wither by this curse.

Andrew Marvell's love poems, specifically 'To his Coy Mistress', with its witty urgency, and 'The Definition of Love', in its passionate despair, are well known to the heroines of *Jane and Prudence*, *A Glass of Blessings* and *No Fond Return of Love*. And, since most of Barbara Pym's women, spinsters and wives alike, have not found romantic love, it is not surprising that they find comfort in the love poems of lesser seventeenth-century poets – Campion, Crashaw, the Earl of Rochester, Lovelace, Cowley. For example, Belinda thinks how much more one appreciates great literature if one loves, especially if the love is unrequited, and quotes to herself lines from Thomas Carew's 'Eternity of Love Protested':

> My very ashes in their urn
> Shall like a hallowed lamp forever burn.

And Helena Napier, Rocky's wife, imagines that, should she and Everard Bone meet ten years hence, they will be like the pair in Michael Drayton's Sonnet IV:

> Be it not seen in either of our brows
> That we one jot of former love retain.

Nor, perhaps, is it surprising that Belinda and Jane should take delight in the tortuous conceits of John Cleveland. Belinda likes his description of a lady's hand, 'tender as 'twere a jellied glove' from 'Fuscara, or the Bee Errant'; and Jane is haunted by lines from 'To Julia, to Expedite her Promise':

> What doth my she-advowson fly
> Incumbency?

and

Not one of all these ravenous hours
But thee devours.

Francis Cleveland of *Crampton Hodnet* also recalls a couplet of his
ancestor's when his student suggests a purely Platonic relation
with him:

Love that's in contemplation placed
Is Venus drawn but to the waist.

Reared in a country rectory, Mildred of *Excellent Women* is
familiar with Tobias Hume's 'Fain Would I Change that Note',
which was often sung by curates at village concerts. Cherishing
her secret love for Rocky Napier, she suddenly bursts out to an
astonished friend with two lines from the poem,

Oh Love they wrong thee much
That say thy sweet is bitter.

Jane neatly puts her finger on the addiction of Miss Pym's
women to these love poems: the seventeenth-century poets
'realise[d] the importance of the body' (p. 59).

They also realised the importance of the spirit, certainly, but the
religious poetry of the century is less akin to the needs of the
heroines. After the sudden death of her lover, Tom, Catherine of
Less than Angels meditates upon the sixth stanza of Henry
Vaughan's 'They are all gone into the world of light':

He that hath found some fledg'd bird's nest may know
    At first sight, if the bird be flown;
But what fair well or grove he sings in now,
    That is to him unknown.

Six lines of Thomas Flatman's poem on Judgement Day are part
of Archdeacon Hoccleve's most memorable sermon. But it is
Milton and George Herbert who are most often quoted or
mentioned. Adam's assumption of his superiority to Eve is
amusedly referred to twice in *Some Tame Gazelle* and once in *Jane
and Prudence*, and the magnificence of *Paradise Lost* is referred to
twice in the latter novel. Basil Branche, the young curate in *An
Unsuitable Attachment*, quotes cynically from the epic at the

wedding-reception of the 'unsuitable' pair Ianthe Broome and John Challow: 'Imparadised in one another's arms, as Milton put it. . . . Or encasseroled, perhaps – the bay leaf resting on the *boeuf bourgignon'* (p. 252).

During their undergraduate days Henry Hoccleve had read aloud to Belinda from *Samson Agonistes*, and, middle-aged and ill, she dreams of his reading the poem to her on her deathbed. Jane quotes from it, and even Leonora of *The Sweet Dove Died* can jumble it and the Preface to the *Lyrical Ballads* in choosing to think of her life as 'calm of mind, all passion spent' or as 'emotion recollected in tranquillity'. *Comus* is alluded to in *Some Tame Gazelle* and *Less than Angels*; the sonnet 'When I consider how my light is spent' in *Excellent Women*; and Milton's metrical version of Psalm 136, 'Let us with a gladsome mind' in *Jane and Prudence*. Yet, although the references to Milton are almost as numerous as those to Donne, the reader feels with Jane, and perhaps with Barbara Pym, that 'In many ways one dislikes Milton, of course; his treatment of women was not all that it should have been' (p. 30).

In truth, Milton fares less well in Barbara Pym's novels than George Herbert, for Milton is alluded to and Herbert is quoted. In *Some Tame Gazelle* Archdeacon Hoccleve chides his pedantic wife by quoting the fifth stanza of 'The Elixir':

> A servant with this clause
> Makes drudgery divine,
> Who sweeps a room as for Thy Laws,
> Makes that and the action fine.

One more romance shattered, Prudence reads, without comfort, Herbert's poem 'Hope':

> I gave to Hope a watch of mine; but he
>   An anchor gave to me.
> Then an old Prayer-book I did present;
>   And he an optic sent.
> With that I gave a vial full of tears;
>   But he, a few green ears;
> Ah, loiterer! I'll no more, no more I'll bring;
>   I did expect a ring.

Herbert supplies the title for *A Glass of Blessings* from his 'The Pulley'. At the close of the novel, Mary Beamish, now a bride, exclaims that life is perfect, like a glass of blessings; Wilmet identifies the poem by quoting the first two lines; and the bridegroom, Father Marius Lovejoy Ransom, just inducted as a vicar, adds, 'But don't forget that other line, . . . How, when all the other blessings had been bestowed, rest lay in the bottom of the glass. That's so very appropriate for a harassed suburban vicar' (p. 253). And, last, at Miss Lickerish's funeral in *A Few Green Leaves*, Herbert's adaptation of Psalm 23, 'The God of love my shepherd is', is sung.

Following the seventeenth-century poets, the Romantics, major and minor, are the most frequently quoted by Miss Pym's characters. The sixth stanza of Wordsworth's 'The Tables Turned',

> One impulse from a vernal wood
> May teach you more of man,
> Of moral evil and good,
> Than all the sages can

is quoted in full in *Less than Angels* and *Quartet in Autumn* and alluded to in *No Fond Return of Love*. 'We are Seven' appears in *Jane and Prudence*; 'A slumber did my spirit seal' in *A Glass of Blessings*; 'She dwelt among the untrodden ways' and 'Elegiac Stanzas Suggested by a Picture of Peele Castle in a Storm' in *No Fond Return of Love*; and 'Daffodils' in *A Few Green Leaves*. Lines from the second of the Lucy Poems and from 'Tintern Abbey' are quoted in *An Unsuitable Attachment*.

Coleridge is not quoted, but his most famous poem is referred to twice in both *Less than Angels* and *A Glass of Blessings*. In the earlier novel the glittering eye of the Ancient Mariner characterises the appearance of anthropologists who have been to Africa, and in *A Glass of Blessings* it connotes the feverish look of Wilmet's would-be conquest, Piers, who has been drinking. Another possible reference to Coleridge lies in the name of Dr Gellibrand's formidable wife in *A Few Green Leaves*, Christabel.

Byron is recalled twice in *Some Tame Gazelle*, first by Archdeacon Hoccleve, who quotes lines from *Childe Harold's Pilgrimage* (IV.i) to forestall another guest at a dinner party, an Italian count, from bursting into Dante to describe the glories of Italy; and again by Belinda, who wonders what Bishop Grote's reference to Byron can be as she cheerfully rejects him. Can it possibly be 'When we two parted / In silence and tears'? Writing of an infatuated young man in *Crampton Hodnet*, Pym quotes *Don Juan*: 'Man's love is of man's life a thing apart'.

Shelley is represented in *Less than Angels* beginning 'Rarely, rarely, comest thou, / Spirit of Delight!', lines quoted by two of the women who love Tom Mallow; and in *A Few Green Leaves* and *An Unsuitable Attachment* by 'The Question'. In *A Few Green Leaves* a retired headmistress awakens in the night remembering the last line, 'That I might there present it! Oh! To whom!', and in *An Unsuitable Attachment* the anthropologist Rupert Stonebird considers the same line with respect to ordering reprints of his article 'Some Aspects of Extra-Marital Relations among the Ngumu'.

Keats is more extensively read by Barbara Pym's characters than either Byron or Shelley. Archdeacon Hoccleve reads *Hyperion* to his dinner guests, and after his fine performance Belinda dares to announce that she likes *Isabella* better. Receiving her pastor's apology for having chosen another woman, not herself, Mildred of *Excellent Women* is jarred by his quoting from 'Ode to a Nightingale' '*I cannot see what flowers are at my feet*', and snaps, 'I always think *Nor What Soft Incense* would be a splendid title for a novel' (p. 212). Bored with the squabbling of the Parochial Church Council, Jane sees how much of the Ode she can remember:

> Fade far away, dissolve, and quite forget
> What thou among the leaves hast never known,
> The weariness, the fever and the fret
> Here, where men sit and hear each other groan.

The young curate of *Crampton Hodnet* quotes from another stanza of the same poem and Miss Morrow of the same novel cites *Endymion*.

Jane's protégé Prudence, dining with her current lover, is accosted by a fellow diner, warning, 'Oh, it is such an *anxious* moment, . . . that first glance at the menu, will there be *anything at all* that one can eat? *Then felt I like some watcher of the skies*, on first looking into Chapman's Homer, you know. . . . I always feel that if I can do *anything* for my fellow diners' (pp. 204–5). One of Keats's minor poems lends Pym's eighth novel, *The Sweet Dove Died*, both its title and its theme; and, visiting Keats's house in

Hampstead on a rainy day, Leonora, who had imagined a golden afternoon for the visit with James and Ned, recalls the opening line of 'To Autumn': 'Season of mists and mellow fruitfulness' (p. 154).

Among the lesser poets of the era, Keats's friend Leigh Hunt is twice quoted in *Some Tame Gazelle* (about the uncharming fish) and once in *A Few Green Leaves* (from 'The Story of Rimini'). In *Some Tame Gazelle* other poems alluded to are John Keble's 'Now every morning is the love'; Thomas Moore's 'Believe me if all those endearing young charms'; Hartley Coleridge's 'She is not fair to outward view'; Charles Lamb's 'Old familiar faces'; and, of course, Thomas Haynes Bayly's

> Some tame gazelle, or some gentle dove;
> Something to love, oh, something to love!

Jane recites a stanza from George Darley's 'The Siren Chorus', and in *Quartet in Autumn* one of the four compliments another by paraphrasing Walter Savage Landor's 'Finis': 'Nature she loved and next to Nature, Art'. In addition, Landor's Ianthe Poems are alluded to three times in *An Unsuitable Attachment*.

More Victorian than Romantic poets are alluded to in the novels, though overall the allusions to the former are fewer. Tennyson is quoted four times, first by Catherine Oliphant, the writer of short stories in *Less than Angels*. Absently she types '*Dear as remembered kisses after death*' and then wonders whether her hero would have read *The Princess* (pp. 27–8). Similarly, Dulcie Mainwaring of *No Fond Return of Love* cuts short her reference to *In Memoriam* as she comforts her cleaning-woman, 'life is often cruel in small ways, isn't it. Not exactly nature red in tooth and claw, though one does sometimes feel' (p. 88). In the same work, the Reverend Mr Latimer reads at random to his landlady, Miss Doggett. And, on their first meeting, the common John Challow boldly reads to the proper Ianthe these lines from 'Now sleeps the crimson petal, now the white':

> Now lies the earth all Danäe to the stars
> And all my heart lies open unto thee.

Browning is more summarily treated. Leonora of *The Sweet Dove Died* reads to James, her dove, 'The Lost Mistress', and James,

later seeing a vine covered with woolly grey buds, remembers the
second stanza for his clandestine lover, Phoebe:

> And the leaf-buds on the wine are woolly,
>   I noticed that, today;
> One day more bursts them open fully
>   – You know the red turns grey.

Matthew Arnold, perhaps Barbara Pym's favourite Victorian,
since he too was a specialist in loneliness and isolation, is
remembered more fully than Tennyson or Browning. In *Excellent
Women* Rocky Napier reads Mildred the first four lines of 'To
Marguerite Continued',

> Yea! In the sea of life enisled,
> With echoing straits between us thrown,
> Dotting the shoreless watery world,
> We mortal millions live *alone*

and, also quoting these lines, Aylwin Forbes of *No Fond Return of
Love* reflects, 'Well, one knew that anyway. The years either
brought people nearer together or drove them further apart'
(p. 211) and adds the last three lines of the fourth stanza:

> A God, a God their severance ruled!
> And bade betwixt their shores to be
> The unplumb'd, salt, estranging sea.

In *Less than Angels* Catherine tries to comfort her lover, Tom
Mallow, who feels that his research has no value, by quoting to
him the last lines of 'Dover Beach':

> Ah, love, let us be true
> To one another! for the world, which seems
> To lie before us like a land of dreams,
> So various, so beautiful, so new,
> Hath really neither joy, nor love, nor light,
> Nor certitude, nor peace, nor help for pain;
> And we are here as on a darkling plain
> Swept with confused alarms of struggle and flight,
> Where ignorant armies clash by night.

A few evenings later she sees Tom in earnest conversation with his new love at a café she and Tom used to frequent and thinks, 'He is telling her about his lost faith. . . . How awful if she too is quoting *Dover Beach* – Tom will think all women are alike. But did girls of nineteen know Matthew Arnold – was he much read nowadays?' (p. 107).

Again, in *An Unsuitable Attachment*, Rupert Stonebird tries to explain to Ianthe in what sense Sophia Ainger, a clergyman's wife, 'know[s] about life. . . . Perhaps I was thinking of Matthew Arnold. . . . I think she sometimes feels that there really is neither joy nor love nor light' (p. 216).

A line from Christina Rossetti's 'A Birthday' flashes through Belinda's mind as she learns from her seamstress that her beloved Henry's wife does not keep as good a table as she does: '[My] heart [is] like a singing bird' (p. 52). Barbara Bird of *Crampton Hodnet* thrills to the same line after tea with her tutor, Francis Cleveland. Again, Barbara wishes she had quoted lines from Christina Rossetti's 'Remember' in her farewell note to Francis:

> Better by far you should forget and smile
> Than that you should remember and be sad.

Mildred of *Excellent Women* also thinks of these lines, first with reference to her pastor's sister, who has never known a lover, and later with reference to herself in her unrequited love for Rocky Napier. Again, thinking of both Winifred and herself, she remembers another Rossetti song, also published in 1862, 'When I am dead, my dearest', and pauses to ask herself 'when there had perhaps never been a dearest. Weren't we all a little like that?' (p. 64). And in *Quartet in Autumn* Marcia rejoices that her mastectomy 'had been a success and she had *not* died', and recalls a line from Christina Rossetti's 'Twice': 'I shall not die but live' (p. 20).

As she falls in love with Tom Mallow, nineteen-year-old Deirdre Swan reads Dante Gabriel Rossetti's sonnet 'Lovesight': 'When do I see thee most, beloved one?'

Prudence of *Jane and Prudence* cherishes a similar schoolgirl passion for the poems of another Victorian, Coventry Patmore, particularly 'Saint Valentine's Day' and 'Tired Memory'. Other minor Victorians, quoted once each, are Thomas Edward Brown ('My Garden', in *Excellent Women*), Elizabeth Barrett Browning ('A

Musical Instrument', in *Less than Angels*), Walter de la Mare ('Autumn', in *A Glass of Blessings*), Swinburne ('Atlanta in Calydon', in *No Fond Return of Love*), Cecil Francis Alexander ('All things bright and beautiful', also in *No Fond Return*), and Ernest Dowson (*'Non sum qualis eram bonae sub regne Cynara'*, in *Some Tame Gazelle*, and *'Vitae summa brevis spem nos vitae incohare longam'*, in *Crampton Hodnet*).

A couplet written by a Victorian who was not a poet obviously charmed Barbara Pym. She copied it into her commonplace book on 29 May 1932, while at Oxford; then gave it to heroines of early, unpublished novels to quote; and finally anchored it with Belinda of *Some Tame Gazelle*. The couplet,

> Ah! had she been more beauteous or less kind,
> She might have found me of another mind

was written by Samuel Butler, author of *Erewhon*, to Eliza Mary Ann Savage, the original of Ernest Pontifex's kindly aunt in his posthumous novel *The Way of All Flesh*. Barbara Pym did not use all the lines she copied from the poor sonnet Butler wrote to poor Miss Savage:

> Hard though I tried to love I tried in vain,
> But she was plain and lame and fat and short,
> Forty and over-kind. Hence it befell
> That though I loved her in a certain sort,
> Yet did I love too wisely but not well.
> Ah! had she been more beauteous and less kind,
> She might have found me of another mind.

Among sixteenth-century poets, Shakespeare, of course, is more often part of the memories of Miss Pym's characters than other Elizabethan poets, and frequently is cited without quotation marks. For example, in *Some Tame Gazelle* a librarian who regards the married state as 'tiresome' incorporates Sonnet 116 into his counsel: 'Of course I never advise anyone to enter into that state without long and careful thought, . . . but I should be the last to admit impediments to the marriage of true minds' (p. 145). Similarly, *Twelfth Night* occurs to Mildred in *Excellent Women* as she thinks of the Wren officers in love with Rocky Napier ('But perhaps they had been wise enough not to tell their love' – p. 172), and to Miss Morrow of *Crampton Hodnet* as she thinks of the atmosphere of the past in the British Museum ('Youth's a stuff will not endure' – p. 124, citing one of Feste's songs). Again, Jane in *Jane and Prudence* is reminded of 'one of those rather tedious comic scenes in Shakespeare – Dogberry and Verges, perhaps [from *Much Ado about Nothing*]' as she listens to the maunderings of the Parochial Church Council (p. 115). A fourth instance is the application of Othello's pleas to Piers Longridge's homosexuality. In *A Glass of Blessings* Wilmet's mother-in-law, Sybil, remarks, 'I see now the clue to Piers's lack of success in this world. I believe that he has loved not wisely but too well' (p. 220). And Tom, the rector in *A Few Green Leaves*, regards abstemiousness in wine-drinking as 'an excellent thing in women' – a use of the tribute to Cordelia, Pym hastens to add, not 'quite what Lear or Shakespeare meant when they coined the phrase' (pp. 186–7).

Just as frequently, allusions to Shakespeare are acknowledged by the use of quotation marks. Told by movers that Rocky Napier's desk is riddled with worm holes, Mildred in *Excellent Women* neatly combines lines from *Hamlet* and *As You Like It*: '*Something is rotten in the state of Denmark. . . . Men have died and worms have eaten them, but not for love*' (pp. 173–4). Seeing a row of houses whose gateposts are ornamented with stone lions, Catherine of *Less than Angels* strokes their heads and bodies and exclaims to Tom, 'You know my *favourite* Shakespeare sonnet, don't you? *Devouring time, blunt thou the lion's paws* . . . do you think *he* could have seen a worn stone lion and that gave him the idea?' (p. 87). Perhaps one of Barbara Pym's favourite sonnets was number 34, for in both *No Fond Return of Love* (p. 222) and *A Few Green Leaves* (p. 81) characters quote the first two lines:

> Why didst thou promise such a beauteous day
> And let me travel forth without my cloak?

In the eleven novels Edmund Spenser appears to be read only by Archdeacon Hoccleve. Belinda enjoys his reading the *Faerie Queene* aloud to her – '[It] was such a soothing poem. It just went on and on' (p. 149) – and his quoting lines from 'A Hymn in Honour of Beauty' at the wedding-reception of his curate,

something about love being a celestial harmony of likely hearts

Which join together in sweet sympathy,
To work each others' joy and true content.

(p. 250)

Christopher Marlowe is also quoted, from *Hero and Leander*, in *Some Tame Gazelle*, as Harriet refuses Mr Mold's proposal:

Harriet was not the kind of person to believe with Marlowe that

Where both deliberate, the love is slight
Whoever loved, that loved not at first sight?

(p. 136)

Lines from *Dr Faustus* appear in *No Fond Return of Love* as Aylwin Forbes reads in *The Times* the obituary of a contemporary:

Cut is the branch that might have grown full straight,
And burned is Apollo's laurel bough.

(p. 209)

Aylwin himself quotes from Thomas Wyatt's 'Remembrance' as he recalls his romantic courtship of his estranged wife: 'Thanked be fortune, it hath been otherwise / Twenty times better' (p. 67).

Two other Elizabethan poets are briefly quoted: George Peele from 'A Farewell to Arms' ('His golden locks Time hath to silver turned', in *No Fond Return of Love* – p. 136), and Samuel Daniel ('Pity is sworn servant unto Love', in *A Few Green Leaves* – p. 165).

But the couplet from John Heywood's *Proverbes* is integral to the portrait of Wilmet in *A Glass of Blessings*. At Christmas time she receives an anonymous gift, a heart-shaped little box, either Regency or Victorian, inscribed with the couplet

If you will not when you may,
When you will you shall have nay.

Of course she imagines it is from Piers and, accordingly, is extravagantly disappointed when she discovers that the present was sent by her friend Rowena's husband. Much later, when Piers coolly tells her that she is a snob, she puts the little box away. Perhaps, she thinks, there is a grain of truth in the inscription.

As with Edmund Spenser's poetry, allusions to the eighteenth-century poets occur most frequently in *Some Tame Gazelle*. True, Professor Mainwaring of *Less than Angels* chides his students in anthropology because a younger generation no longer reads Wharton, Blair and Young (p. 209). But both Edward Young's *Night Thoughts* and Thomas Gray's 'Elegy' are staples of Belinda Bede and Henry Hoccleve's conversation, to say nothing of his sermons. In his extraordinary sermon on the topic of Judgement Day, he quotes extensively from Belinda's favourite, the *Night Thoughts*, as well as six lines from Robert Blair's *The Grave*. His concluding admonition to his congregation, from Young, is indeed dramatic:

> Say dreamers of gay dreams,
> How will you weather an eternal night,
> Where such expedients fail?
>
> (p. 112)

Quotations from the 'Elegy' are a requisite for his affectation of eighteenth-century melancholy, regarding himself as he does as fearfully overworked, even though his sermons are a tissue of quotations. Phrases from the 'Elegy' also appear without quotation marks in later novels, as, for example, 'far from the madding crowd's ignoble strife' in *Less than Angels* and 'the short and simple annals of the poor' in *A Few Green Leaves*. The lines 'Alas, regardless of their doom, / The little victims play' from Gray's 'On a Distant Prospect of Eton College' are quoted in *Crampton Hodnet* by one of Francis Cleveland's students.

Although Belinda sings 'the spacious firmament on high' from Addison's 'Ode', published in the *Spectator* in 1712, her favourite hymn is 'Light Shining out of Darkness' from William Cowper's Olney Hymns. Her sister Harriet, given over to romance rather than reflection, quotes a line from Goldsmith's 'Song' in *The Vicar of Wakefield*, 'when lovely woman stoops to folly', and attributes it to Shakespeare. Absently Belinda corrects her, 'I have an idea it may be Pope' (p. 142). Leonora of *The Sweet Dove Died* also quotes the line, identifying herself as lovely woman and James as folly (p. 103).

Lines from Pope are quoted in *Excellent Women* and *Less than Angels*, the latter deriving its title from the *Essay on Man* (I.vi). Mildred of the earlier novel quotes from the *Essay on Criticism* the familiar lines

A little learning is a dangerous thing,
Drink deep, or taste not the Pierian Spring

and paraphrases another line, 'where angels fear to tread' (p. 221). She also quotes from a minor eighteenth-century poet, Isaac Watts. Looking at the clerks, students, typists and eccentrics in a self-service cafeteria and feeling hopeless at the divine command to love them all, she thinks of Watt's version of Psalm 90:

Time, like an ever-rolling stream,
Bears all its sons away.

These lines are jokingly paraphrased by the head librarian in *An Unsuitable Attachment*, as Miss Grimes, who is not qualified for her library post, approaches retirement: 'Time like an ever-rolling stream . . . bears even Miss Grimes away' (p. 28).

The title of Miss Pym's sixth novel, *No Fond Return of Love*, seems to be a paraphrase of the first line of a stanza from a little-known eighteenth-century poet, Fanny Greville:

I ask no kind return of love,
No tempting charm to please;
Far from the heart these gifts remove,
That sighs for peace and ease.

References to Middle (and older) English poetry are few and are confined to *Some Tame Gazelle*, with a single exception. For the village fête Archdeacon Hoccleve wishes the children to recite lyrics or passages from Gower or Chaucer. He does succeed in forcing one child to recite

In dingles deep and mountains hoar
They combatted the tusky boar

so that he can explain to a bored audience the derivation of the word 'dingle' from a twelfth- or thirteenth-century work entitled *Sawles Warde*. With equal ostentation he gives at dinner a short dissertation on the beast fable in the Middle Ages. When the Bishop of Mbawawa visits from Africa, he wickedly places on his night table for bedtime reading a copy of *Beowulf*.

Though Belinda is amused by these antics of her dear Henry,

she is intimidated by his wife, Agatha. Not only does Agatha know all about *Piers Plowman*, but she also possesses a niece who is doing excellent research at the university on certain disputed readings in *The Owl and the Nightingale*, a twelfth-century poem attributed to Nicholas of Guildford. Indeed, *The Owl and the Nightingale* is alluded to five times, inasmuch as the curate, Mr Donne, becomes engaged to Agatha's niece, Olivia Berridge. At their wedding Olivia's Professor of Middle English gives her away, and at the reception he makes 'an unintelligible but obviously clever little speech about *The Owl and the Nightingale*, embellished with quotations from that poem' (p. 250).

The one allusion to Middle English verse outside *Some Tame Gazelle* occurs in *Excellent Women*. Finding herself falling in love with Everard Bone, Mildred reminds herself that she will see him at the lunchtime service at St Ermin's during Lent. A poem which begins 'Lenten is come with love to town' crosses her mind and she hastens to *The Oxford Book of English Verse*. The Middle English given there,

> Deowes donketh the dounes,
> Deores with huere dernes rounes
> Domes forte deme

fails to comfort her.

Twentieth-century poets are but sparsely represented in the novels, but not, it appears, because Barbara Pym did not read them. Sorting his wife's books for a widower, Jane wonders whether she read poetry secretly.

> People do seem to be ashamed of admitting that they read poetry, . . . unless they have a degree in English – it is permissible then. . . . I wonder what [Constance] made of Mr Auden and Mr MacNeice? Perhaps the seventeenth century was more to her taste, as it is to mine. (*Jane and Prudence*, p. 109)

The same sentiment is implicit in Jessie Morrow's flippant comment (in *Crampton Hodnet*) that Auden and MacNeice might have been equal to an obscure poem entitled 'Conversation in a Tool Shed' (p. 114).

Auden and MacNeice are not quoted. T. S. Eliot is only

paraphrased in *A Glass of Blessings* as Wilmet describes the coming of spring: 'We had a hard winter that year. February and March were cruel months – not in the poet's way perhaps, but bad enough for most of us. . . . April was balmy and delicious, and cruel in the way the poet did mean, mingling memory and desire' (p. 148).

Belinda, the Archdeacon and Jane do, however, make incidental reflections upon Eliot and the modern poets. Distressed at her seamstress's failure to eat the lunch of cauliflower cheese she has prepared for her, Belinda glances at Miss Prior's tray: 'And then, in a flash, she realised what it was. It was almost a relief to know, to see it there, the long, greyish caterpillar. Dead now, of course, but unmistakable. It needed a modern poet to put this into words. Eliot, perhaps' (*Some Tame Gazelle*, pp. 50–1). This sally is counteracted by both Belinda and the Archdeacon's admiration for Eliot's spiritual poetry. In his Judgement Day sermon the Archdeavon reads from Eliot, but he fears that the poet is too obscure for his listeners. His friend the distinguished librarian Dr Nicholas Parnell replies, 'I think people prefer the more obvious aspects of the Christian teaching. . . . Simple sentiments in intelligible prose.' 'Yes, one appreciates that', the Archdeacon responds, 'and yet, why shouldn't Eliot express those sentiments?' (p. 118). In a fit of melancholy the young curate of *Crampton Hodnet* sees himself as a hollow man and quotes,

> This is the way the world ends,
> Not with a bang but a whimper.

Learning that her Member of Parliament feels that he *ought* to travel by train sometimes, Jane asks,

> 'You mean you want to know what your constituents have to endure? The tea too weak or too strong, the stale sandwich, the grimy upholstery, the window that won't open, the waiting on the draughty platform. . . .'
> Jane could have gone on indefinitely, feeling like one of our great modern poets.   (*Jane and Prudence*, p. 219)

The poetry of Sir John Betjeman, however, especially attracted Barbara Pym. Describing, in a talk for the BBC entitled 'Finding a Voice', the influence on her career as a writer, she listed

Betjeman's poems, particularly his 'Hymn' and 'Death in Leamington'. 'Betjeman's glorifying of ordinary things and buildings and his subtle appreciation of different kinds of churches and churchmanship made an immediate appeal to me', she said.³ A line from his poem 'How to Get on in Society' is quoted in *A Few Green Leaves*. When Graham Pettifer takes a cottage near hers, Emma remarks to her mother, a professor of English, that she must go round to see whether he has everything he wants. 'Are the requisites all in the toilet?' her mother quips (p. 130).

A phrase from Philip Larkin's poem 'Ambulance' is tucked into *Quartet in Autumn* as an ambulance bears the dying Marcia to a hospital. '"Unreachable inside a room" she may have been, yet there was no sense of that little room becoming an everywhere, in the fantasy of an earlier poet' (p. 172).

Only one allusion to an American poet other than Eliot occurs. Afloat on the river with Francis Cleveland and a bottle of wine, Barbara Bird in *Crampton Hodnet* quotes from Edgar Allen Poe's 'The City in the Sea': 'The viol, the violet, and the vine'.

Barbara Pym's characters are not passionate devotees of the novel as they are of poetry. Many novelists, Victorian, contemporary and Russian, are casually mentioned. Either the characters have read them, are reading them, or have always intended to read them. Only four novelists are consistently used in the novels, either to characterise or to further the plot. They are, in ascending order, Anthony Trollope, Charlotte M. Yonge, Charlotte Brontë and Jane Austen. None, it may be noted, appears in *Crampton Hodnet* or *Some Tame Gazelle*.

In the second novel, *Excellent Women*, the narrator, Mildred, uses Trollope to characterise a committee of excellent women quarrelling over the placement in St Mary's of the flowers for Whit Sunday. As she and Sister Blatt struggle to attach wire to old potted-meat jars in order to fill them with flowers, Mildred writes, 'There was a good deal of chatter, and I was reminded of Trollope's description of Lily Dale and Grace Crawley, who were both accustomed to churches and "almost as irreverent as though they were two curates"' (p. 118).

Jane of *Jane and Prudence* recalls both the characters of Trollope and Charlotte M. Yonge to mourn her failure as a clergyman's wife:

When she and Nicholas were engaged Jane had taken great

pleasure in imagining herself as a clergyman's wife, starting with Trollope and working through the Victorian novelists to the present. . . . But she had been quickly disillusioned. . . . Jane's outspokenness and her fantastic turn of mind were not appreciated; other qualities which she did not possess and which seemed impossible to acquire were apparently necessary. And then, as the years passed and she realised that Flora was to be her only child, she was again conscious of failure, for her picture of herself as a clergyman's wife had included a large Victorian family like those in the novels of Miss Charlotte M. Yonge. (p. 8)

Later, after she has blundered into a private meeting of the Parochial Church Council, Jane wails to her husband, 'I was going to be such a splendid clergyman's wife when I married you, but somehow it hasn't turned out like *The Daisy Chain* or *The Last Chronicles of Barset*' (p. 212).

Wilmet of *A Glass of Blessings*, named after the heroine of Charlotte Yonge's *Pillars of the House*, alludes to Trollope in characterising Father Thames as he begins his rambling retirement speech:

As some of you know, I am shortly leaving for a holiday in Italy. There seems something a little unsuitable, does there not, about a clergyman going for a holiday in Italy in these difficult days? When we hear about such a thing perhaps we remember our *Barchester Towers* – the older ones among us, that is. . . . We think of Canon Vesey Stanhope and his villa on the shores of Lake Como – or was it Maggiore? *Not* Garda, I think – I forget the details. As I was saying, we remember that, and it might be thought that there was a parallel there. (p. 211).

In *A Few Green Leaves*, Beatrix, the heroine's mother and a tutor in English literature, fills her bookshelves with Miss Yonge's novels and those of other lesser Victorians. As she reflects that since her husband was killed at Dunkirk no other man has been interested in her, she weighs the reasons. 'A young, academically inclined widow with a child, as she had been, was not immediately attractive or accessible, and then there had been her work, the Victorian fiction', she adds, doubtfully. 'Charlotte M. Yonge's novels contained more than one attractive young widow' (p. 100).

Charlotte Brontë also serves as an aid to characterisation in five of the novels. Interestingly, both Mildred of *Excellent Women* and Catherine of *Less than Angels* compare their appearance to Miss Brontë's most famous heroine's. Introducing herself as 'mousy and rather plain', Mildred writes, 'Let me hasten to add that I am not at all like Jane Eyre, who must have given hope to so many plain women who tell their stories in the first person, nor have I ever thought of myself as being like her' (p. 7). Catherine, on the other hand, 'was small and thin and thought of herself, with a certain amount of complacency, as looking like Jane Eyre' (p. 7).

Catherine also thinks 'that it isn't only we poor women who can find consolation in literature. Men can have the comfort of imagining themselves like Heathcliff or Mr Rochester' (p. 224). Jane does imagine Prudence's employer to be 'a big, tall, dark man, a sort of Mr Rochester' (p. 79), and is perplexed to find him little, short and grey. The name of the heroine of *The Sweet Dove Died*, Leonora Eyre, is used with satiric intent.

Emma of *A Few Green Leaves* uses Charlotte Brontë's later novel *Villette* to explain to her mother her relation to Graham Pettifer: 'we have the work experience in common', she says impatiently, aware that her mother sees Graham as a prospective husband for Emma. 'In the Victorian novel' her mother replies pedantically, 'a young woman had nothing like this. A hero could hardly share the work experience of a governess.' 'You don't think in *Villette*, perhaps?' Emma counters, obviously remembering Lucy Snowe and M'sieur Paul Emmanuel, colleagues in a girls' school in Brussels (pp. 163–4).

Four of Jane Austen's six novels (that is, all of them except *Northanger Abbey* and *Sense and Sensibility*) are used in five of Barbara Pym's novels: in *The Sweet Dove Died*, *Jane and Prudence* and *A Few Green Leaves* to characterise; and in *Less than Angels* and *No Fond Return of Love* to draw the plot to a close. The characterisation in *The Sweet Dove Died* is slight and general, almost a slip of the pen if the author were not Barbara Pym. At a cat show James attends with Leonora, Miss Pym adapts the opening sentence of *Pride and Prejudice* to portray his boredom: 'It is a truth now universally acknowledged that owners grow to look like their pets, and it was certainly impressed upon him as he and Leonora pushed their way through the crowds surrounding the cages' (p. 65).

Emma is used far more definitely to characterise Prudence and

Jane: 'Prudence disliked being called "Miss Bates"; if she resembled any character in fiction, it was certainly not poor silly Miss Bates' (p. 36). Jane, on the other hand, humbly acknowledges her resemblance to Emma Woodhouse in her misguided efforts at match-making for Prudence (p. 96).

In *A Few Green Leaves*, Emma, named after Emma Woodhouse, thinks of Jane Austen's novel as she hard-boils eggs for Graham: 'A too-soft-boiled egg would be awkward to manage, slithering all over the place in the way they did. Not to be coped with by a person in an emotional state, though Mr Woodhouse in that novel about her namesake had claimed that it was not unwholesome' (p. 82). The final reference to *Emma* in *A Few Green Leaves* slightly characterises the church organist: 'Geoffrey Poore was not a believer, but he appreciated the opportunity of playing on a fine instrument, like some Jane Austen heroine, Jane Fairfax, perhaps, and her gift of a pianoforte' (p. 238).

As Barbara Pym was writing *Jane and Prudence*, and thinking of *Less than Angels* as well, she wrote herself a note: 'Read some of Miss Austen's last chapters and find out how she manages all the loose ends.'[4] Yet in the first of the novels, *Less than Angels*, in which she uses an Austen novel for the resolution of the plot, she disposes of Tom Mallow's first love, Elaine, by the somewhat cavalier suggestion that she might have copied from *Persuasion* Anne Elliot's words:

> We certainly do not forget you so soon as you forget us. It is, perhaps, our fate rather than our merit. We cannot help ourselves. We live at home, quiet, confined, and our feelings prey upon us. You are forced on exertion. You have always business of some sort or other to take you back into the world immediately, and continual occupation and change soon weaken impressions. (p. 186)

Elaine is a minor character in *Less than Angels*, and so perhaps the way Barbara Pym disposes of her may be justified. But the denouement for the two major characters in *No Fond Return of Love* is puzzling: involved with other women across the novel, Aylwin Forbes abruptly turns to Dulcie Mainwaring on the penultimate page of the novel. Miss Pym explains his sudden conversion:

> As for his apparent change of heart, he had suddenly remembered the end of *Mansfield Park*, and how Edmund fell

out of love with Mary Crawford and came to care for Fanny. Dulcie must surely know the novel well, and would understand how such things can happen.   (p. 253)

A survey of Miss Pym's allusions to the English poets reveals not only her devotion to and remarkable familiarity with them, but also her especial kinship with Matthew Arnold and her preference for the Metaphysicals, particularly Donne. Among the older novelists, she read and reread Jane Austen and Trollope, the lives of whose characters resemble those of her own, and vividly remembered the more dramatic characters in the novels of Charlotte Brontë and Charlotte M. Yonge. Among the moderns, she said in her talk for the BBC, she was most influenced by Aldous Huxley in *Crome Yellow*, and, later, by Ivy Compton-Burnett.[5] As her own novels tell the reader, she liked a novel of the kind that her Prudence enjoyed, 'well written . . . with a good dash of culture and the inevitable unhappy or indefinite ending, which was so like life' (*Jane and Prudence*, p. 156).

14

The Narrative Sense of Barbara Pym*

Robert J. Graham

'Nothing, like something, happens anywhere.'[1]

I wanted to buy a copy of *Some Tame Gazelle*, the quintessential gift for a friend about to leave for the International Women's Conference in Kenya. Peopled by an irrepressible spinster, an ungallant bishop resting in England from the rigours of his African mission, and Oxford librarians who had, unbelievably, dunned tribal chiefs for contributions to the university libraries, Barbara Pym's first published novel offered the marvellous excesses of a Wodehouse or Henry Green and the bitter-sweet realities of a Coppard, Bates or Ashton-Warner. The novel was out of stock, but the assistant assured me that there were other Pym novels on the shelves. 'We try not to run out. Those books are really in demand. Oh, but I love to read Barbara Pym, and you're going to like this novel; it's her latest.'

Pressed to explain why Pym's fiction delighted her, the young woman had difficulty answering. She enjoyed the characters but didn't identify with them; she liked reading about England but recognised that Pym's England consisted mostly of London parishes and rarely visited villages. Exasperated, she declared, 'I'm not sure why I read them because, you know, nothing ever really happens in the stories. But when I'm reading *I feel as if I'm there.*'

To a remarkable degree, sophisticated reviewers – Eve Auchincloss among them – have echoed this naïve reader's comments, though few have gone on to acknowledge the

* The author wishes to acknowledge the National Endowment for the Humanities Travel to Collections Grant which provided research support for this essay.

uncommon ability Pym has to place readers *there*, to make them feel comfortable and at home, to set them among friends in a milieu that piques curiosity and sustains interest. She succeeds, as fine novelists do, not only in creating a microcosm – that 'self-contained world' Hazel Holt mentions in *A Very Private Eye* (p. xiii) – but also in making us care about the shades of difference in her world, especially about the gradations and modulations produced by her characters' inconsequential actions.

Historian Barbara Tuchman has observed how artist Edward Hopper catches people *between* the events in their lives, or at moments when they are *without* purpose. Barbara Pym depicts exactly the same landscape.

From Pym's perspective, I would suggest, the trivia of life count in proportion to the accretion of their effects. To her, the endless joys and tribulations of these accumulations reveal more about character than the dramatic moments of life. What results for the reader is a detailed picture of how those without career or distinction, often without mates or family of any kind, face the need to love and be loved, to connect with others in ways which bring some sense of usefulness and happiness. What results is a landscape of interstices: moments alone, moments spent looking out of windows.

In *A Very Private Eye* Hazel Holt notes, 'It is now possible to describe a place, a situation or a person as "very Barbara Pym"' (p. xiii). Although this self-contained world has begun to receive considerable critical attention, little has been written about what constitutes a 'Pym novel' – in which, one hears it claimed, nothing happens – or about how the novels unfold whatever the story they are or are not telling. My intention in this essay is to describe selected aspects of Barbara Pym's narrative manner and to examine the key elements responsible for the effects she achieves. A central premise throughout is that Pym's fiction is more consciously crafted and more purposely substantive than readers, reviewers or critics have generally recognised.

Among Pym's eleven novels, the structural frame for parish, village or city settings is, in most cases, similar; its design closely follows from writing-practices recorded in Pym's notebooks and diaries. Nearly half the novels have twenty-two or twenty-three chapters; only one, *A Few Green Leaves*, has as many as thirty-one;

over half have approximately the same number of pages. Even though her notebooks record her concern that the novels were too thin and needed fleshing out, her shortest novels, *Quartet in Autumn* and *The Sweet Dove Died*, are, to my mind, among her most artful.

Except for *Quartet in Autumn*, where she is brilliantly experimental, Pym structures chapters after the same pattern in all her novels. Narration begins with incisive observations later to be transformed from impression to idea. Certain ideas, subtly recurring throughout her books or clustering within individual works, form the dominant themes of her fiction: the need to connect; the search for love; the vagaries of male–female relationships; the power of the commonplace, custom and ritual. In each book a detached observer bolsters the narrative, which, in all but two of the novels, is fashioned through a third-person point of view. This central intelligence knows more than other characters about matters at hand. Usually female, the narrator skilfully links mundane actions, observations, musings and ideas – all within a tightly restricted time span.

The most technically accomplished narration in all of Pym's fiction can be found in Chapters 12 and 13 of *Quartet in Autumn*, almost exactly in the middle of the novel. Up to this point the narrative has moved inexorably toward the day when Marcia and Letty will retire. In scenes worthy of V. S. Naipaul's *Mr Stone and the Knight's Companion*, chapter 12 describes the retirement party provided by their employer. The scene opens with commentary on their pension situation, then shifts to the official ceremony, a progressively demeaning, sad story of redundancy and anonymity which all but erases the women's meager integrity. Extraordinary objectivity results from a detached tone and from ambiguities of time, place and purpose. With precisely measured intensity, spare details dramatise a relentless obliteration of individuality: the firm is never named; the nature of the women's work is never revealed; other offices in the building are seldom mentioned and never regarded as contributing to a sense of place. What *is* known is that, after the women's male co-workers retire, the office will be eliminated. Nor have Marcia and Letty, Norman and Edwin succeeded in penetrating the surface of their personal interrelationships – except as those great levellers, retirement and death, intervene. Thus, the retirement party's effect, tragically, is effacement, as though these lives, specks in a continuum, have had no fixed locus in human history.

Cogently written and stirring as this scene is, the artful brilliance of the following chapter extends its effect by chronicling Marcia and Letty's separate experiences on their first day of retirement. Organised into three major sections, chapter 13 depicts (1) Marcia coping with the initial realisation that she need not go to work that Monday morning or any other; (2) Letty facing the same actuality; (3) Norman and Edwin, at the office, speculating about what the 'girls' are doing on their first free day. Two economical paragraphs follow and act as coda: Letty, tired, postponing the 'serious reading' that had been her goal; Marcia, the day lost, no memory of it remaining, sitting in the dark listening to Radio 1. Binding the chapter sections is the ironic refrain, 'A woman can always find plenty to occupy her time' (pp. 114, 116, 112).

Symbolically, little occurs on the long-awaited day; furthermore, nothing happens in the ways Marcia or Letty had expected. The hours mirror the emptiness of their working days and foreshadow hardships to come. Now, there seems no one to dress for, no ritual journey to make, no schedule to consider. Since no one is filling her place or doing her work, whatever that work may have been, Letty feels 'that what cannot now be justified has perhaps never existed, and it [gives] her the feeling that she and Marcia had been swept away as if they had never been' (p. 114). Set in a microcosm of nameless offices and spinster living-quarters, the chapter's compelling symmetry, striking contrasts, terse narrative line and lean dialogue heighten the dramatic tension between illusion and reality, thereby achieving social realism at a high level: the actualities of retirement as experienced by myriad faceless pensioners.

Yet, for Letty Crowe, Mildred Lathbury and other excellent women, life goes on – not through plodding endurance after major trauma but through quiet acceptance steeped in genuine understanding of daily joys and modest possibilities. Although partial acceptance resolves conflicts in most people's lives, in Pym's narratives resolution is elusive and subtle because it is tied to the mundane. While depicting the daily round may risk tedium, Pym turns the risk to advantage by selectively layering comic details for splendid and telling effects. In *Excellent Women*, for example, Mildred Lathbury habitually tidies up her cupboards and drawers each Easter and Whit Monday. She begins by attacking the pigeon-holes of her desk. This ordinary chore leads to re-examining old letters and photos, a device enabling the author to provide the reader with information about Mildred's family, friends and her single, long-past experience of falling in love. Soon, however, ritual housekeeping becomes more than sorting and discarding objects: Mildred tidies too her attitudes and inclinations. A routine domestic activity evolves into a process of psychological ordering, which then becomes an annual inventory of experiences, emotions and commitments. To anchor the scene, Pym uses a church holy day, a device as natural to her narrative time schemes as are the hours or seasons. Still, although Easter triggers the action, Mildred's tidying-up 'seemed to be connected with fine weather rather than the great Festivals of the Church – a pagan rather than a Christian rite' (p. 121).

In this scene, as in numerous others, Pym masterfully builds the commonplace into the universal. Yet for readers an undeniable sense of loss remains. Although Mildred reminisces about her parents, joyful days at Oxford and a past love, a subdued tone, coupled with a distinct series of word choices, catalogues a pattern of embarrassment, fear, suffering and cruelty – all indicating the hardship she has weathered in coming to terms with rejection. This brief scene, by adding a further dimension to Mildred's conscious decision to remain more an observer than a participant in life's major events, explains to some degree her reluctance to become involved with Julian Malory or Everard Bone.

All Pym novels are concerned with variations on a single theme: life as a succession of large and small privations. After *Excellent Women*, novels that deal centrally with this theme include *Less than Angels, No Fond Return of Love, Quartet in Autumn,* and *The Sweet Dove Died.* In these, loss – not only what protagonists may have possessed and then forfeited, but also loss of what is unrealised – is an essential part of the primary or secondary plot structure. Catherine Oliphant releases a lover, Dulcie Mainwaring suffers a broken engagement, Edwin's beloved wife dies. These are overt deprivations, disappointments courageously confronted, but nevertheless ones which influence action and characterisation throughout the ensuing narrative.

More interesting, however, are those situations dealing with progressive diminishment: for instance, repeated occasions where loss is related to the inability to make contact. This is the case, as we have seen, in *Quartet in Autumn* when the four principals fail to make known their true feelings, when Norman stops short of genuine contact with Edwin or Marcia, when neither men nor women can communicate openly – not even with their own sex. Indeed, Norman and Edwin find every gesture which might involve them meaningfully with others to be 'altogether too difficult'. It is 'easier for them all to go their separate ways assuming a vague future together' (p. 107).

In Pym's writing, vagueness and subtlety overlay the substance, tone and voice of a novel and join with the theme of loss to function as part of a particular narrative technique. Again, this method depends upon the layering of small details. Rather than add information gradually to the point where a mass of knowledge about character and event has accumulated, Pym constructs tiers of *background* information, parcelling out with supreme control what she reveals about protagonists or the most crucial events in their past. Like the bystander in Philip Larkin's 'The Whitsun Weddings', Pym's major figures function 'as if out on the end of an event'; the momentous happenings in their lives normally occur on the periphery of the narrative frame.[2] Consequently, like a minimalist painter, Pym achieves marvellous effects with deliberately arranged white spaces. What readers don't know about Mildred Lathbury and Marcia Ivory makes what is known all the more important and increases the complexity of their situations. It is in *Quartet in Autumn* that Pym makes fullest use of the device of gradually uncovering information: for example, the protagonists' full names are not provided until well into the novel and then are offered parsimoniously, one by one.

In this novel and others where information is stringently withheld and the overriding theme is progressive deprivation, Pym attains maximum subtlety through this process of parcelling out the diverse losses her main characters experience. This gradual process of loss is at the core of her thematic development and enables the novelist to dramatise refinements difficult to present otherwise. For women such as Belinda, Mildred, Dulcie, and the Jessie Morrow of *Crampton Hodnet* (as opposed to the same character in *Jane and Prudence*) progressive deprivation dissolves into an irony peculiar to Pym's fiction: presented as positive figures (with rare exceptions, they are not defeated by circumstances), these characters are nevertheless linked to negative forces. In fact, the narratives which support them depend upon successive attempts at staving off deprivation. To avoid being unloved, unattached, unmarried, to refrain from the unsuitable and the improper – these are recurring objectives that turn into a way of thinking about life. Though at one juncture Mildred Lathbury affirms singleness as a positive state, at another she decides that what really counts is having a husband, no matter how dull.

To convey essential distinctions, Pym employs a variety of methods. Whether such modes rely upon her celebrated humour, cutting irony or the various tensions she wrings from thematic polarities, they are enhanced by her notable skill with cleverly crafted language devices. Often, selected ideas, words or phrases act as narrative agents. That men might *not* be superior beings worthy of special attention is one conception subversively angled into numerous novels. Cunning questions about why males receive favoured treatment, why they are thought to be erudite rather than merely obtuse, and why they are accepted as strong when their actions are weak pervade much of Pym's fiction.

Just as ideas repeated in diverse forms through book after book build cumulatively, so too do repeated key words and phrases. Veteran Pym readers generally expect to find in the novels 'excellent' and 'formidable' women and behaviour judged by whether it is 'suitable' or not – the tension between a given character and a certain behaviour propelling the plot forward. Furthermore, they understand each phrase to be redolent with meaning: that is, multiple connotations have accrued precisely because certain words or phrases have a prior history of general or specific use in Pym's fiction. Thus, *An Unsuitable Attachment* focuses on the matter of social propriety through Ianthe's romance with John Challow – an adventurous, even heroic act on her part. Conversely, in *Jane and Prudence*, Fabian Driver loses grace and stature when he decides that an evening walk through the village with Prudence would be unseemly; and in *Quartet in Autumn* Letty Crowe imagines her death will be 'something more "suitable" for a person like herself' (p. 58).

In like manner, Pym establishes a selective, personal imagery throughout her work by linking ideas to key words which, repeatedly used, elicit expected but ever-widening responses from the reader. 'Grey' – often applied to offices, government buildings, civil servants or other office workers – aids in maintaining a sombre tone and evoking dour circumstances. *Quartet in Autumn* presents the most pervasive and dismal evocations: the four protagonists work in a 'grey monolithic building' and Marcia Ivory believes herself 'greyer than ever, crushed and dried up by the weak British sun' (pp. 114, 9).

In order to sustain further the tentativeness crucial to plot and mood in her fiction, Pym employs a curious pattern of qualifying words, a way of composing that appears early in her diaries and notebooks. For example, she uses a qualifying phrase when recording the date on which she parted with her virginity: 'Today I must always remember I suppose' (*A Very Private Eye*, p. 17). She also speaks of being 'in love with Friedbert *in a way*' (p. 47, emphasis added). In time, qualification appears, especially in the journals, to reflect a way of looking at experience which underscores impermanence – in the comic, courageous manner that was and remains vintage Pym. More importantly, in the novels the use of qualifiers, particularly adverbs such as 'almost' and 'too', attain the level of a conscious, though judicious, stylistic technique designed to convey more precise, subtle shades of meaning than otherwise possible. *A Glass of Blessings* offers numerous examples. Wilmet reacts to Mary Beamish 'almost with dislike' and finds a letter to be 'almost beautiful' (pp. 84, 186). She later describes Mary's attire as 'too sensible' (p. 252). Things are usually sensible or not, beautiful or unbeautiful; but for Pym the sensible can be overdone, and for her protagonists – from *Some Tame Gazelle* to the posthumously published *Crampton Hodnet* – life is not that absolute or even definite. For Belinda Bede, Jessie Morrow and a bevy of heroines in between, attaining close relationships has proved a precarious undertaking, one to be generally evaded.

Another quality of Pym's narrative style attractive to readers is one influenced by her lifelong interest in poetry: a special poetic sensibility including delight in the commonplace and in the potential of colloquial speech. In a 1972 letter to Philip Larkin, Pym speculates on the most likely candidate for Poet Laureate following the death of Cecil Day-Lewis. After naming Larkin himself and 'Poor old Auden', she comments,

Betjeman might be the best choice? I liked your article on him in the *Cornhill*, but I think women (I at any rate) do enter into what he describes more fully than you perhaps realise, even the business girls in Camden Town and even perhaps 'And now dear Lord I cannot wait, because I have a luncheon date!' (*A Very Private Eye*, p. 269)

The Camden Town poem she cites is entitled 'Business Girls':

> From the geyser ventilators
>   Autumn winds are blowing down
> On a thousand business women
>   Having baths in Camden Town.
>
> Waste pipes chuckle into runnels,
>   Steam's escaping here and there,
> Morning trains through Camden cutting
>   Shake the Crescent and the Square.
>
> Early nip of changeful autumn,
>   Dahlias glimpsed through garden doors,
> At the back precarious bathrooms
>   Jutting out from upper floors;
>
> And behind their frail partitions
>   Business women lie and soak,
> Seeing through the draughty skylight
>   Flying clouds and railway smoke.
>
> Rest you there, poor unbelov'd ones,
>   Lap your loneliness in heat.
> All too soon the tiny breakfast,
>   Trolley-bus and windy street![3]

A student of poetry and a longstanding reader of Betjeman, Pym found much to admire in his work. A poet with a magnetic sense of place and prodigious knowledge of the Anglican Church, Betjeman naturally appealed to a reader with Pym's sensibility. That she entered 'fully' into poetry such as 'Business Girls', however, suggests an attraction beyond the expected to form, substance and other matters related to her sense of narration.

'Business Girls' establishes a musing tone, partly elegiac, and reads throughout like a meditation. An unidentified voice, presumably the poet's, selects as his vehicle the morning bathing-rituals of nameless working women within a specific London district. An ordinary moment distilled is then made poignant as an illuminating representation of loneliness. In much the same way such crystallised moments are indispensable to Pym's narratives, and are usually conveyed in meditative fashion by women more put upon than assertive, women who ordinarily leave their thoughts nominally unspoken or half-expressed. 'Business Girls' is a poetic cameo about the circumstances of exactly such figures. To sustain its mood and create an expression of loneliness, Betjeman relies on a particular but ordinary setting and common objects – ventilators, drainpipes, bathroom walls, a trolley-bus. The speaker mentions morning sounds, emphasises the diurnal round and concludes with a sympathetic recognition of women not merely alone but unappreciated. If Pym were assigning names to figures in the poem, she might include Letty Crowe or Marcia Ivory. And 'chuckle', as Betjeman uses it, is a verb Pym would admire.

In notebooks and diaries, Barbara Pym frequently recorded her current reading as well as named authors who had influenced her writing. While John Betjeman may not have had the effect credited Aldous Huxley, Ivy-Compton Burnett or the English Romantic poets, his name appears intermittently in her journals for almost forty years. Pym thinks of Weston as 'a Betjeman place', cites an early Betjeman scene – 'a nun coming out of a telephone box . . . Mount Zion in touch with the Infinite' – and admits to complete immersion in the subjects his poetry dramatises (*A Very Private Eye*, p. 195). She also quotes Betjeman and writes a poem for 'Jay', which she acknowledges to be in the Betjeman manner. It is telling that use of poetic quotation in description and dialogue, a device that every Pym reader associates with her work, far outpaces allusion to prose writing – an indication, I believe, of a poetic receptiveness crucial to the development of her narrative art.

The essence of such responsiveness resides, of course, in an intelligence attuned to the natural rhythms of language. It also signifies an openness to impressions as well as the capacity to be deeply affected emotionally or intellectually. These qualities Pym had in abundance; moreover, they were appropriately concentrated in her extraordinary powers of observation, a strength she recognised early and always valued. In fact, throughout the journals she alludes to the many ways in which she uses recorded observations in her novel-writing. As she writes in a letter to Richard Roberts, 'with a little polishing life could become literature, or at least fiction!' (*A Very Private Eye*, p. 231).

The process through which Pym's notebook jottings become fiction is discernible from her earliest entries onward. From the surrogate 'Sandra', the name she gave herself at university, and the pseudonym 'Lorenzo', which she assigned her first serious love there, to lively descriptions of academic and social scenes, the mark of a developing novelist is apparent. Evidence that these propensities are maturing appears in the journals with the emergence of incisive characterisation, as where she notes that Lorenzo is growing 'more affected – his smile of self-conscious fatuity is sweet – but one day it may seem silly'. It was not to be long before she began sustained work on her 'novel of real people', *Some Tame Gazelle*, where Lorenzo emerges as Archdeacon Henry Hoccleve (*A Very Private Eye*, pp. 30, 11).

Throughout her long career as a novelist, Pym continued to depend on her notebook and diary entries to supply the stuff of her fiction. Describing her working-method, she frequently cited the importance of recorded observations. A consummate storyteller, she developed a natural talent for depicting the simple and the concrete. While long descriptive sections are found rarely in the novels, brilliant passages do occur in her journals and are readily identifiable when transformed into fiction:

Walking in Mayfair just before eleven on a Sunday morning (21st May), the air soft and warm and lovely, trees in leaf and red hawthorns in flower. There is a delicious nostalgic smell of churches and new paint and later a Sunday dinner coming up from the basements. His [Jay's] house is newly painted in cream and royal blue and a window-box next door has petunias in it. How all things are in tune to a poor person in love. A fine, sunny afternoon in May, Beethoven and German lieder. I go to my irises, thinking to throw them away, but find that each dead flower has a fat new bud at the side of its stem. And so I take off the dead flowers and the new flowers begin to unfold. The photograph of him at the Union stands on the mantelpiece and in front of it a spray of red roses – but they are artificial ones from Woolworth's. (*A Very Private Eye*, p. 91)

This 1939 entry illustrates a number of Pym hallmarks – an acute sense of season and weather, painstaking attention to flowers and trees, emphasis on the sensory spectrum, a sentimental tone. The occasion, a walk past the home of a former lover, finds its way into *No Fond Return of Love*. Moreover, the unsentimental ending, a self-deprecatory contrast between newly budding iris and artificial red roses, foreshadows those chapter tailpieces which, so often, control sentiment and save Pym's heroines from self-pity.

Although typical notations such as the above reflect the novelist's eye at work in the service of her art, Pym also paid close attention to tone and voice, for she balanced sharp vision with an acute ear.

The evidence available in her diaries, notebooks and manuscripts clearly shows her to have been a dedicated artist, hard-working and skilled in her craft. Although Hilary Pym says she doesn't recall ever feeling that her sister isolated herself – going off to garret or library for long hours away from the world – Barbara did somehow complete an amazing amount of writing despite the demands of her position at the International African Institute. Obviously she did some work on her novels at the office, as Hazel Holt readily and bemusedly testifies. Her draft manuscripts were often typed there, on the reverse side of official correspondence carbons – letters to scholars, university and society officials – a delicious irony when one remembers the opening scene of *No Fond Return of Love*.

With the expected exception of *Quartet in Autumn*, Pym's novels impress readers by their casualness and calm: the narratives appear to unfold effortlessly. Her manuscripts, notebooks and diaries reveal the aesthetic transformation she undertook to achieve this effect. A complete writer's manual exists among these materials. About revising she comments, 'I love cutting out bits and crossing out whole pages' (*A Very Private Eye*, p. 88). Often she muses over how much sustenance her art afforded: 'I honestly don't believe I can be happy unless I am writing' (p. 86); and at one point she admits she could enjoy revising for ever (p. 234).

Barbara Pym's working drafts, notes, lists and jottings, all of which indicate ways of recasting scenes, adding characters or reordering narrative sequence, form a voluminous part of the Bodleian collection of her papers. An early draft of *Some Tame Gazelle*, for example, has Harriet in her middle forties and attracted to Henry Hoccleve's son; in this version Agatha has written 'a dull but scholarly book'.[4] A 1945 notation advises, 'Go over all the characters and make them worse – as Proust did. Especially the Archdeacon (and Mr Parnell).'[5] Further on, she reminds herself to add 'more plot, less quotation, more household detail'.[6] Additionally, there are topical outlines for all chapters of the novel, and a list entitled 'The Blackening of Characters' to aid her in emulating Proust's subtle irony.[7]

On 20 March 1972 the first in a chain of fascinating notebook entries announced the basic idea for *Quartet in Autumn*, stimulated by the International African Institute's enforced move to new offices. Drawing on her colleagues' reactions to the disruption, on her experience of being treated for breast cancer in 1971, and on her feelings as she approached retirement, *Quartet* was to be the novel she would write for herself. By April 1972 she was making regular substantive annotations, discovering more and more rich material within the High Holborn office setting. Soon she added larger, detailed entries on character and plot, gradually uncovering the connected images of *leaves* and *death* at the novel's centre.

5 November. Walking in Oxford on a Sunday afternoon – to look at the changed St Hilda's from the outside, though the gardens look the same. Then to Addison's Walk and deer and beech trees shedding their leaves. A good place to lie down waiting for death covered in leaves by the still streams.

8 December. The woman with the dogs very much in Baker St station these days. This morning the almost unbearable pathos of seeing the two of them curled up together asleep in a carrier bag.

A lonely person found dead with no food in the house (but what else would be there?). A cultured woman who has worked in an office, who realises that she is in danger but is too late to stop herself.

January 1973. There could be talk in the office about elderly people being found dead with no food in the house.
    'One might have a tin of soup but lack the strength to open it, or even to tear away the cellophane from a packet of biscuits.'

(*A Very Private Eye*, p. 272)

To achieve its masterful drama and commendable tautness, the manuscript of the novel passed through numerous partial revisions, ending with the addition of two chapters summarised as 'Edwin going to a memorial service and the three of them, with Father G, having lunch after Marcia's funeral at the crematorium' (*A Very Private Eye*, p. 295). On 7 February 1977 – nearly five years after its genesis – *Quartet in Autumn*, under the working-title *Four Point Turn*, arrived at Macmillan.

One concludes from the evidence to hand – the literary notebooks, the exacting revisions, the masterful writing – that this accomplished novelist knew intuitively what she was doing. While still in her teens, she commented on Huxley's *Crome Yellow*, 'Not actually about anything – of course not – the best novels never are – but full of witty and intelligent conversation.'[8] To say that nothing happens in Pym's novels is far from true: everything happens and much of it is consciously planned, brilliantly evocative and refreshingly authentic. The commonplace *is* the universal. With Philip Larkin's narrator in 'I Remember, I Remember', who passes through his birthplace and recounts all the things that did not happen to him there, Pym recognised that the spaces between are every bit as valuable as the events they separate. For 'Nothing, like something, happens anywhere' and deserves its day.

15
The Pym Papers[*]

Janice Rossen

In 1978 Barbara Pym wrote to Philip Larkin to request his advice about the disposal of her private papers. The immediate occasion for her inquiry was the fact that an American university wished to make an offer for them. In the role of both friend and librarian, Larkin suggested various alternatives. Pym responded by choosing the path of least resistance: 'I. (do nothing)' she wrote to him, announcing her decision. She continued her letter with a description of her 'literary remains', which were 'all in a large cardboard box in my bedroom – more like a novel by J. I. M. Stewart than *The Aspern Papers!' (A Very Private Eye*, pp. 316–17). The main requirement for the final disposal of the collection was that it stay in England. She wrote conclusively to this effect to Larkin: '[I] wouldn't like any of my MS handwritten material to go to USA to be pored over by earnest Americans (not even Jake Balokowsky)' (p. 315). In due course the papers were donated to the Bodleian Library, an altogether fitting repository, as Pym herself was a graduate of St Hilda's and had had a longstanding love for Oxford University.

In this essay I should like to provide an overview of the collection of Pym's papers in the Bodleian Library, the contents of which have been listed in Tim Rogers's typescript catalogue. I shall briefly summarise its contents and suggest what I believe to be the relative usefulness to scholars of its various parts. In conclusion I shall address practical considerations with regard to reading in the collection. Categories of the collection will be

* I am indebted throughout this essay to conversations I had with the following people regarding the Bodleian collection: Hazel Holt, Hilary Pym, Tim Rogers, Robert Smith and Philip Larkin. In addition I should like to thank especially Colin Harris, Serena Surman and others of the Bodleian staff in Room 132 for their help in practical matters.

addressed in the following order: fiction, diaries and notebooks, correspondence and miscellaneous writings.

The fiction in the manuscript collection may be categorised as follows: early unpublished novels dating from before 1950, which exist mostly in draft form: early drafts of published fiction; the untitled 'academic novel', written in the 1960s and not submitted for publication; and short stories.

The earliest of Pym's unpublished novels is *Young Men in Fancy Dress*, which she composed at the age of sixteen, inspired by reading Aldous Huxley's *Crome Yellow*. Her novel follows the adventures of Dennis, a young man who longs to become an artist. He feels constricted and embarrassed by his humble origins; he is the heir of a wealthy bourgeois 'Sausage King'. None the less, he finds his way to the Bohemian setting of Chelsea and befriends several artists as well as embarking on two passionate romances. Full of youthful exuberance, the novel seems occasionally strained in its satire, but reveals early evidence of Pym's sense of comedy. The manuscript is particularly notable for its dedication: 'To H. D. M. G. [a friend] who kindly informed me that I had the makings of a style of my own'[1] – a pronouncement which seems most suitable and auspicious with regard to her later writing. The novel is also notable for the author's own fondness for it. She referred to it with affection in autobiographical talks about her fiction late in her life, and described it in a letter to Philip Larkin as perhaps the 'prize' of her manuscript collection (*A Very Private Eye*, p. 315).

Next in chronological order of composition is an early typescript of *Some Tame Gazelle*, her first published novel, begun in July 1934 after she went down from Oxford. This first manuscript is especially interesting in comparison with the final published version of 1950. The initial draft is substantially longer than the later one, and it is characterised by a more defensive treatment of Belinda Bede's relationship with Henry Hoccleve. The character of Henry appears more fatuous and that of Belinda more vague than in the published version of the novel, which draws much of its comedy from Belinda's insight into and perceptiveness about Henry's character.

The fair copy of a novel entitled *Civil to Strangers* dates from 1936. This appears to be the only manuscript from this early period which Pym sent to publishers – other than *Some Tame Gazelle*, which was eventually accepted by Jonathan Cape in 1949. Set in a small English village, *Civil to Strangers* revolves around Cassandra, a young married woman of twenty-eight who is at once level-headed and slightly dissatisfied with her role as 'excellent housekeeper' when the novel opens. The book is light-hearted and clever, and is graced by several delightful vignettes of minor characters. It stresses English virtues as opposed to dubious foreign ones, and takes as its central theme the comfort and stability offered by marriage and the corresponding tendency of husbands to take their wives for granted.

Next in chronological order of composition is the draft of a novel provisionally entitled *Beatrice Wyatt* or *The Lumber Room*. The first title is the heroine's name; the second title refers to the author's conception of the human memory as a lumber room or attic where treasures are stored.[2] This novel is especially interesting because it offers the first introduction to the figure of Jane Cleveland, who later appears in *Jane and Prudence*. In this earlier novel she is more neatly categorised by the characters around her. One of them describes her as 'brilliantly clever' and 'really wasted as a clergyman's wife'.[3] The heroine, Beatrice Wyatt, is an Oxford don who divides her time between the University and the small village where her mother and unmarried sister live. The novel contains some moving and poignant passages about unrequited love, as well as some comic scenes set in the village, to which Beatrice returns during vocation.

An untitled novel set in Finland and composed about 1938 offers fascinating reading. Like *Beatrice Wyatt* it is primarily a novel about unrequited love, taking as its subject the struggles of the heroine with an indecisive hero: Flora follows Gervase to Finland, where he has gone to teach English at a university. After showing the draft of this novel to her friend Robert Liddell, Pym seems to have abandoned the manuscript: 'On Monday Jock depressed me about my Finland novel', she wrote in her diary, and concluded further that 'my own life seemed pointless and just a waste of time, if I wasn't even going to be able to write'.[4] Though the Finnish novel represents only an initial draft and not a polished reworking, it is valuable in showing the creative use which Pym made of her rejection by Henry Harvey (the original of the Gervase figure) as well as the way her imagination formed a picture of his life abroad. The vigorous speeches by the heroine,

Flora, offer insight into Pym's conception of the rejected heroine.

In 1939 Pym began to write a war novel which describes a wealthy older woman whose life is brightened by the arrival of children who have been evacuated to the country. This plot apparently incorporates some of Pym's own experience doing relief work in the early part of the war; a few of her short stories deal with similar subjects related to the war, such as air-raid warden duty. Pym abandoned the manuscript part-way through and left the novel unfinished.

Most lively among Pym's early novels is *Crampton Hodnet*, which has been edited by Hazel Holt and was published posthumously in 1985.

'Something to Remember', begun in June 1940, is a novelette of seventy handwritten leaves. It seems to have been an early experiment for *Excellent Women*, because it is narrated by a spinster who reminds us of Mildred in the later novel.

In 1941 Pym began a spy novel. It contains moments of comic genius offset by ironic understatement. At one point the heroine is chloroformed by German agents; later she describes the experience as 'a nasty turn'.

Since they are not heavily revised, Pym may have regarded many of these early, unpublished novels as vigorous warm-up exercises for the carefully crafted – though no less exuberant – work which was to follow in the 1950s. Several of the works are handwritten first drafts with virtually no revisions. Some remain unfinished. Thus they represent a special part of the collection of her 'literary remains', having been used for a particular purpose: to begin to formulate themes which would reappear in later fiction and to create characters who would step ready-made into her published novels.

The next part of the manuscript collection listed in the typescript catalogue consists of early drafts of the published novels (all except *Jane and Prudence*, the first draft of which has been lost). These drafts are generally interesting in terms of the creative process which they demonstrate. Pym often began composing a new novel from a list of characters, as a gratuitous comment in a draft of *A Glass of Blessings* indicates: '"Oh, I like a crowded canvas", says BP.'[5] Whereas the 'little notebooks' served to catch ideas in their formative stages, early drafts of novels represent an effort to set them down systematically in sustained narrative. Pym did prune and revise and excise for her final versions; yet the first drafts often seem surprisingly close to the finished form in substance.

An intriguing addition to Pym's later fiction is a novel which she began in 1965 and to which she referred in letters to friends as an 'academic novel'. Set at a redbrick university, the book describes various rivalries among faculty members in a department of sociology and anthropology, and the domestic traumas of one lecturer and his wife in particular. The novel sheds some valuable light on the aims which the author set for herself at this period in her writing, as witness the following note scribbled in the margin of a draft: 'But keep it sharp, acid and uncosy!'[6] In accordance with this, the novel deals with such subjects as divorce, abortion and student riots. The relationship between Caro, the heroine, and Coco, a homosexual man whom she befriends, shows a distinct connection with Pym's treatment of the relation between Leonora and James in *The Sweet Dove Died* and might well repay further study in this regard. Although Pym revised the manuscript in several subsequent drafts, she never submitted it for publication.

Pym's unpublished fiction is augmented by twenty-seven short stories, most of which were submitted for publication but rejected. They survive largely as fair copies in neatly typed drafts. Though less complex and well-rounded than her novels, the stories contain several clever passages. They incorporate many of the themes she uses later: regret, nostalgia, middle age, timidity, spinsterhood and life's occasional absurdity. Of particular note is 'A Few Days before the Winter', which has appeared in the magazine *Woman's Own*. In their delicacy and wry wit the stories offer a delightful counterpoint to the author's novels.

Mention should also be made here of a notebook containing some stories written while the author was still in her teens. It contains amusing vignettes and offers ample evidence of early talent as a writer. Characteristically, one of the best of these stories describes a hero who wants to be an artist; another work, a long satiric poem, describes the entrance of a 'curate on a motorbike'.

These early manuscripts contain much of the raw material which was subsequently reworked into the rich complexity of Pym's later novels. Hazel Holt is preparing an anthology of sections from these works as well as an official biography of the author.

I turn now to Pym's private diaries and notebooks, which fall into three main classes: personal diaries, daily calendars and 'little notebooks'.

With the publication of *A Very Private Eye*, much of the contents of the personal diaries have been made available to the reading public. The most intimate and revealing diaries are those kept at Oxford, which describe Pym's three years at the University and her relationship with Henry Harvey; and those written in 1943, which describe Pym's response to the end of her affair with Gordon Glover. These are informally titled by Pym: the Oxford notebooks comprise the 'Adventures of Sandra', the fictitious name which Pym chose to describe one aspect of herself. The wartime diaries are designated 'After Christmas', and refer to the specific episode Pym entitles 'Tears on the Bridge'. This refers to a conversation she had during which Glover requested that they separate for a year.

These two sets of diaries reveal much about the author's private life, stressing as they do two periods of intense suffering. They show the author's vulnerability, and they alternate between rationalising, posing and occasional despairing. The Oxford diaries represent an effort to capture the fleeting golden days of youth. To emphasise this function Pym inscribes one notebook with a quote from Boswell: 'There is a waste of good if it be not preserved.' When she embarked on her troubled relationship with Henry Harvey, the diaries in turn modulate from confidence to uncertainty. Pym was in turn exasperated and exalted by his attentions. On the stage provided by the diaries she confided her hopes and fears, and alternately railed against Henry's indifference and accused him. At one point she mocks her own efforts by deploring the monotony of the diaries, which must, she says, 'be dull reading with nothing but the falseness of Henry' in them. Yet this element provides a fascinating subject indeed.[7] Thus she used the Oxford diaries both to vent her frustrations and to formulate a theory of unrequited love.

The 'After Christmas' diaries represent a more sustained narrative and single-minded purpose. Confiding in them her feelings over a long period of misery caused by her disappointment in love, Pym writes to justify herself, either to an audience of unknown readers or to Gordon himself: 'Well, I ramble on and you Reader will wonder at it. But Gordon would understand.'[8]

The main subject of these notebooks is the author's grieving for lost happiness.

These two sets of personal diaries are the most compelling documents in the manuscript collection. The more mundane diaries offer their own perspective, though, which is equally interesting. The diaries from Pym's period of service in the Wrens contain fewer emotional outbursts and more descriptions of daily life in their cataloguing of dinner parties and routine office work. Much of the substance of these can be found in *A Very Private Eye*. In addition there are several years' worth of diaries in the purely practical sense of daily records – small pocket calendars with appointments listed: trips to the hairdresser and the dentist, luncheon engagements with friends, and who among the Finstock villagers was to read the lessons in church on Sunday.

One of the central, most significant parts of the collection of Pym's papers is the small, spiral-bound 'little notebooks', which act as part diary and part working-notebooks for novel-writing. She habitually carried one of these in her handbag as a useful repository for thoughts, possible plot summaries, grocery lists, details of expenses, and humorous descriptions of people.[9]

The notebooks contain a variety of miscellaneous jottings. As Pym describes them, 'my diaries are mostly bits and ideas for my novels rather than events'.[10] And in them one can see the novels taking shape, from the cry of 'WHAT IS MY NEXT NOVEL TO BE?' to subsequent ideas for characters and plots (*A Very Private Eye*, p. 194). The notebooks are perhaps most helpful in illustrating the close connection between autobiography and fiction. Many of the events recorded in the diaries eventually find their way into the novels. The ringing telephone which Pym hears during a service in 'Freddie Hood's church' appears on the opening page of her novel *A Glass of Blessings*, and the walk she takes past a furniture depository finds its way into the novel as well.

As with her fictional prose style, irony is the author's forte in these private jottings. Pym describes herself in one notebook entry as sitting alone self-consciously in a restaurant with a book of poetry, and this passage later becomes the character Prudence's perspective on herself in *Jane and Prudence*. Little self-mockeries of this kind are sprinkled throughout the notebooks, and add to their charm.

As editor Hazel Holt points out in *A Very Private Eye*, Pym delighted in the 'rich comic material' provided by her job at the

International African Institute. Many observations and speculations sparked off by the daily routine are included in the notebooks, as when she quips, for instance, 'Archaeology – a dig is not "amusing".'[11] These entries can strike a haunting note as well, as when she describes the 'desolate feeling' she experienced on one occasion when she saw two women friends giggling together in a restaurant. Also notable in these entries is Pym's abiding love of trivial detail which conjures up a picture of the absurd, as when she imagines a 'revolting thing in the oven' made with beans and potatoes. The notebooks also include the occasional revealing epigram, such as 'With the years men get more bumbling and vague, but women get sharper.'[12]

The author considered these little notebooks as comprising perhaps the most valuable part of her private papers, and they do offer a marvellous portrait of the artist at work. As such, they provide not only insight into the creative process but delightful reading as well.

I shall begin my description of Pym's correspondence with a chronological survey of her correspondence with friends, focusing on its highlights, and then turn to a consideration of her correspondence with publishers. Brief mention should also be made of some miscellaneous letters regarding her fiction – including correspondence from thesis-writer Tullia Blundo, scholar Lord David Cecil, and officials of the Romantic Novelists Association.

The Bodleian collection includes several letters from Rupert Gleadow, written during Pym's first year at Oxford and his third. These reveal much about the climate of her time there, especially when read in conjunction with her own contemporary diaries. Gleadow's letters are lively, affectionate and charming. Pym pronounced him to be 'brilliant – in all sorts of ways' (*A Very Private Eye*, p. 15). Dating from 1945–6 there are a few letters written by Captain Alan R. Davis, a friend of Pym's from her Wren days in Italy. These touch on the difficulties of resettling into civilian life after the war. Letters to Barbara Pym from novelist Elizabeth Taylor are few and generally short, as are letters to Pym from her friend Richard Roberts.

The longest and most complete correspondence is that between Pym and Robert Smith, both sides of which have survived

virtually complete. These letters span the period between their
first meeting in 1952 and the time of her death in 1980. Smith
lectured in history for several years at various universities in
Africa, and this separation in distance accounts for the length and
regularity of their correspondence. Smith's letters show him a
faithful admirer of Pym's work, ready to encourage her and often
inquiring when her readers would have the pleasure of a new
novel. In 1965 he wrote to her, 'And do, do keep on writing. One
day the BP cult will broaden out. If only I taught Eng. Lit. I would
introduce you as a Special Subject.'[13] Their letters discuss the
progress of Pym's work, her later difficulties in finding a publisher,
Smith's varied experiences in African culture, and news of mutual
friends.

Letters to Pym from Philip Larkin date from 1962, when he first
wrote to her and offered to write a review of her next novel. This
letter initiated a correspondence between the two which lasted
until her death. For those who are familiar with Larkin's published
poetry and prose, the letters offer further delights in their wry wit
and deft turns of phrase.

The correspondence relating Barbara Pym's dealings with
publishers offers rich ground for exploration. Responses to her
work ranged from printed rejection slips to personal testimonies
of unbounded enthusiasm. Especially noteworthy are the
numerous letters relating to manuscripts which she submitted
between 1961 and 1977. The correspondence relating to
unsuccessful attempts to place *An Unsuitable Attachment*, *The Sweet
Dove Died* and *Quartet in Autumn* is remarkable for its sheer
volume. The Bodleian reader may well feel increasingly appalled
in turning over the stack letter by letter. One can only imagine the
effect of such a steady stream of rejection notices on the author,
who received them one at a time over a period of several years.
The correspondence with publishers reveals, above all, Pym's
own determination to keep sending out her work. It shows
indifference on the part of many presses, as one might expect, yet
the exchange also shows respect and even affection from some
editors.[14]

Since Pym's publishing-history has drawn so much attention,
the first-hand record offered by these letters is most interesting
and will allow the reader to form his own opinion of the situation.
It is also pertinent to an understanding of Pym's conception of
herself as a writer. Her determination to write and to publish her

work is evidenced by her passing remark in the notebooks that she had sent one novel alone to twenty-two publishers. Commenting on the 'rediscovery' of her fiction in 1977, she often referred to her 'good luck' in having had such excellent friends to speak for her at the right time. It can only be said in conclusion that Pym's personal good fortune became that of her readers as well.

The miscellaneous part of the manuscript collection includes a variety of material. Although hardly any of Pym's *juvenilia* are extant, there is an 'operetta' entitled 'The Magic Diamond' which she wrote at the age of nine. In addition to the libretto of twelve leaves, photographs of the actors, who included Barbara and Hilary Pym and some male cousins, survive. The snapshots show the children attired in capes and crowns; as leading lady, Barbara is seen in a dashing pose with her arm thrown about the hero's neck. Other stray bits of memorabilia include a map of Naples (where she was stationed briefly during her term in the Wrens), programmes for various opera performances, and the menu and seating-arrangements for a college dinner at St John's which she attended with a friend. This experience provided the setting for her story 'Across a Crowded Room' which appeared in the *New Yorker* in 1979, as references to the evening's menu indicate. Also included in the collection is the typescript of a doctoral thesis in Italian by Tullia Blundo of the University of Pisa.

Of immense value in understanding Pym's view of her craft are typescripts of various autobiographical talks which she delivered to literary societies and on radio programmes. In these she describes her early interest in writing and the difficulties she experienced at various points in finding a publisher for her work. She urges fellow writers not to be discouraged by similar experiences. The script of the radio programme *Finding a Voice* is especially helpful, as is that of a talk ('The Novelist's Use of Everyday Life') given during the 1950s. In it she summarises aspects of the novel such as character and plot and provides long extracts from her own favourite novels as examples. The radio scripts also include revised-for-broadcast versions of Pym's novels *Excellent Women* and *No Fond Return of Love*, plus a very few pieces written by Pym specifically for radio, including *Something to*

Remember, which was broadcast, and *Parrots' Eggs*, a spoof of anthropologists, which was not.

The index of Barbara Pym's library made by her sister at the time of Pym's death in 1980 provides invaluable information about the novelist's tastes and interests. The list represents an erudite collection indeed. Pym owned a full library of classics in English literature from her education at St Hilda's in the 1930s. Subsequent additions were made, and these reveal a continuing interest in literature and a tendency to collect books on particular figures. The index shows seventeen books by or about Thomas Hardy, for instance; in addition, there are five Keats books, nine Byron books, sixteen Betjeman books, nine Charlotte M. Yonge novels and a complete set of Austen novels. Pym also owned seventeen Ivy Compton-Burnett novels and several poetry anthologies. Among books written by her personal friends, she possessed eight by Larkin, nineteen by Robert Liddell and fifteen by Elizabeth Taylor. A discussion of Pym's private library might be best concluded with a mention of the book which she chose as sufficiently complex to be a fitting companion in hypothetical exile: Henry James's *The Golden Bowl* – chosen when she was interviewed on the radio programme *Desert Island Discs*.

Access to the manuscripts in the Bodleian collection can be obtained only through written permission from Barbara Pym's literary executor, Mrs Hazel Holt, whose address is Tivington Knowle, Minehead, Somerset TA24 8SX. In addition it is extremely helpful both to the reader and to the Bodleian staff if readers write ahead to announce their arrival. A copy of the typescript catalogue can be ordered from the library in advance. The library will also send information on what documents a prospective reader needs to gain admission, the hours when the library is open and (most important) days on which the library is closed. Pym manuscripts are consulted through the Department of Western Manuscripts in Room 132 of the New Bodleian Library, and the staff is exceptionally helpful and efficient.

Permission to quote from material in the collection must be obtained by writing both to the Bodleian Library and to Mrs Holt, and, in the case of letters *to* Pym, to the individual authors or their executors. A few sections of the collection are closed to readers until further notice, including PYM 93, 146 and 153–7.

Material included in *A Very Private Eye* which is not in the Bodleian collection includes letters from Pym to Larkin, Harvey and Roberts.

Part III
In Retrospect

Part III
In Retrospect

16

The Rejection of Barbara Pym

Philip Larkin

'I sent my novel to Cape last week', Barbara Pym wrote to me in February 1963. 'It is called (at present) *An Unsuitable Attachment.*' It was her seventh, 'which seems a significant number'. The significance was to prove greater than she could have ever imagined.

Barbara Pym was then in her fiftieth year. Her previous books had been well received by reviewers, and she had gained a following among library borrowers; it was time for a breakthrough that would establish her among the dozen or so novelists recognised as original voices and whose books automatically head the review lists. With this in mind, I had written to her in 1961 saying how much I liked her novels and suggesting I should do an article about them to coincide with the publication of her next, hinting that she should let me know when it was ready. She replied amiably, but was clearly in no hurry, and our correspondence lapsed; the letter I have quoted was the first for over a year.

She did not write again until May, and then, after a courteous page of generalities, it was to say that *An Unsuitable Attachment* had been rejected. Although she strove to maintain the innocent irony that characterised all her letters, for once it broke down:

I write this calmly enough, but really I was and am very upset about it and think they have treated me very badly.

Of course it may be that this novel is much *worse* than my others, though they didn't say so, giving their reason for rejecting it as their fear that with the present cost of book production etc. etc. they doubted whether they could sell enough copies to make a profit.

To have one's seventh book turned down by a publisher who has seemed perfectly happy with the previous six is a peculiarly wounding experience, and she felt it as such. It is also damaging: another publisher can be approached only from a position of weakness, weaker than if the novel were one's first. A second publisher sent it back saying, 'Novels like *An Unsuitable Attachment*, despite their qualities, are getting increasingly difficult to sell', while a third simply regretted it was not suitable for their list.

What was to be done? I wanted to try it on my own publisher, but Barbara demurred: she wanted to put it aside, to rewrite it, to write something else, and several years went by in which she did all these things, but to no avail. The new book, *The Sweet Dove Died*, was rejected as firmly as its predecessor, and the revised *Attachment* was unsuccessfully sent to a second round of publishers, including my own. I wish I had gone ahead and written my article; the honour of publishing the first independent appreciation of her work went instead to Robert Smith, whose 'How Pleasant to Know Miss Pym' appeared in *Ariel* in October 1971.

It was a strange and depressing time – strange, because (as Mr Smith's article indicates) her books retained their popularity. *No Fond Return of Love* was serialised by the BBC in 1965, while Portway Reprints, that infallible index of what people want to read instead of what they ought to want to read, reissued five others. Depressing, because the wall of indifference she had run up against seemed as immovable as it was inexplicable. For over ten years she had been a novelist: now, suddenly, she was not. The situation was galling. 'It ought to be enough for anybody to be the Assistant Editor of *Africa* [which is what she was], especially when the Editor is away lecturing for 6 months at Harvard,' she wrote, 'but I find it isn't quite.'

In 1971 she had a serious operation, and in 1973 retired to live with her sister near Oxford. There her disappointed silence might have ended, but for an extraordinary accident. 'In about ten years' time, perhaps somebody will be kind enought to discover *me*', she had written at the end of 1967, and this was precisely what happened. In 1977 *The Times Literary Supplement* published a symposium on the most over- and underrated writers of the century, and two contributors named her as the second – the only living writer to be so distinguished. The rest is, as they say, history. Her next novel, *Quartet in Autumn*, was published before the year was out, followed by *The Sweet Dove Died*. Cape began to reissue her earlier books, Penguin and Granada planned a series of paperbacks. She was widely interviewed, and appeared on *Desert Island Discs* and in a TV film called *Tea with Miss Pym*. All this she sustained with unassuming pleasure, but the irony of the situation was not lost on her.

An Unsuitable Attachment, now that it is finally before us, clearly belongs to Barbara Pym's first and principal group of novels by reason of its undiminished high spirits. For, although the technique and properties of her last books were much the same, there was a sombreness about them indicative of the changes that had come to her and her world in fifteen years' enforced silence. Here the old confidence is restored: 'Rock salmon – that had a noble sound about it', reflects the vicar, Mark, at the fish and chip shop, buying supper for his wife Sophia and their cat Faustina, and the reader is back among self-service lunches and parish bazaars and the innumerable tiny absurdities to be found there (p. 15). It is perhaps the most solidly 'churchy' of her books: Mark and Sophia in their North London vicarage are at its centre, and the Christian year – Harvest Thanksgiving, Advent, Christmas, Lent and Easter – provide both its frame and background. 'One never knew who might turn up in church on Sunday', Sophia thinks, and it is this kind of adventitious encounter that once again sets her narrative moving (p. 21).

The book's chief failing is that the 'unsuitable attachment' between Ianthe Broome, the well-bred librarian with ladylike stockings and brown court shoes, and the younger John Challow, whose own shoes 'seemed to be a little too pointed – not quite what men one knew would wear' (p. 49), is not sufficiently central to the story and not fully 'done', as Henry James would say. Potentially the situation is full of interest: John's soppy, rather common advances, coupled with his borrowing money from her, seems faintly threatening ('John had been intended to be much worse', Barbara wrote apologetically), and their relation at one time looks poised for disaster. When this does not happen, its 'unsuitability' becomes rather academic, something felt more by the other characters than Ianthe herself, who lets 'love sweep over her like a kind of illness' rather than agonise over differences of age and class (p. 147).

Then again, it is a somewhat self-indulgent book, full of echoes. Sophia and her sister Penelope recall *Jane and Prudence*, or even

Dulcie and Viola from *No Fond Return of Love;* Sister Dew resembles Sister Blatt from *Excellent Women;* but other parallels are more explicit. Barbara Pym was always given to reintroducing characters she had used before, and sometimes this is fully justified (the conversation between Wilmet and Rowena in *A Glass of Blessings* about Rocky Napier is only fully meaningful if we have met him in *Excellent Women*), but the concluding chapters of *An Unsuitable Attachment* are a real *omnium gatherum*: Esther Clovis and Digby Fox from *Less than Angels,* Everard Bone from *Excellent Women,* Wilf Bason from *A Glass of Blessings,* and perhaps most extravagantly of all an older but otherwise unchanged Harriet Bede (complete with curate) from *Some Tame Gazelle.* It is all rather like the finale of a musical comedy.

Do these blemishes (if blemishes they are) mean that Cape's rejection of the book in 1963 was justified? Recently I wrote to their Chairman, who at that time had been their literary adviser and in his late twenties, asking whether Barbara Pym had been 'dropped', as she believed, simply because her books did not suit the spirit of the decade and would not make money. He replied readily:

When *An Unsuitable Attachment* came in it received unfavourable reports. Indeed they must have been very unfavourable for us to decide to reject a new manuscript by an author for whom we had published several books. At that time we had two readers, both of whom had been here for many years: William Plomer and Daniel George. Neither then nor at any time since has this company rejected a manuscript for commercial reasons 'notwithstanding the literary merit of a book'. Though of course the two must be relative to some extent.

The reports by Plomer and George were subsequently found and they confirmed that one was 'extremely negative' and the other 'fairly negative'.

The reader must make what he can of these two accounts. If her publishers are correct, it is surprising there was not someone at Cape prepared to invite Barbara Pym to lunch and say that, while they had enjoyed publishing her books in the past and hoped to continue to do so in the future, this particular one needed revision if it was to realise its potential value. It was the blank rejection, the implication that all she had previously written stood for nothing, that hurt.

But there is still much in *An Unsuitable Attachment* to cherish. The increasingly hilarious appearances of Faustina, for instance, and the role she plays in Sophia's marriage ('she's all I've got' – p. 138), are original and penetrating; at times, indeed, one wonders if the book's title would not be more applicable to this relation than to Ianthe and John. Nor does it lack the occasional plangent sentence of the kind that give her books their special quality:

Oh, this coming back to an empty house, Rupert thought, when he had seen her safely up to her door. People – though perhaps it was only women – seemed to make so much of it. As if life itself were not as empty as the house one was coming back to. (p. 43)

Barbara Pym made no further move to publish this unlucky seventh novel during her lifetime, preferring to concentrate on new books, but now that there will be no more of these it is right that it should be issued. If its confidence, or over-confidence, was its own undoing, it is still richly redolent of her unique talent as it was before that confidence was so badly shaken. Her followers will need no further recommendation.

17
A Success Story

Robert Liddell

The first thing to be said about the life and work of Barbara Pym is that it is a success story. After a slow beginning she was able to publish her work, and had appreciation for her first six novels – to which I shall refer as the 'canon'. Thereafter came rejection, and years in the wilderness, the first threat of cancer and a major operation; but, in the long remission that followed, her name came back into a revived literary reputation more considerable than she had ever enjoyed, and she was to bring out her strongest novel, *Quartet in Autumn*. Her last years were passed in happy retirement in a country village with a much loved sister, and in contentment at being rediscovered.

Nevertheless some readers of her 'autobiography' have spoken of her as 'frustrated', and have made the further mistake of supposing that she wasted her affections on unworthy people; one reviewer calls them 'cads'.

It will here be maintained that we must go to her novels to correct any false impressions derived from her 'autobiography'.

This would seem the wrong way round. The material out of which *A Very Private Eye* is composed is nearly all from the hand of Barbara herself, who was always sincere – and it has been arranged by those who best knew and loved her.

Are the critics, then, to blame? Just a little, perhaps, but not much.

The old-fashioned idea that an unmarried woman is 'frustrated', or at least a 'failure', is not only a masculine prejudice – though no such language is ever used about an unmarried man. One of Barbara's heroines, going to an old girls' reunion at her former school, was aware of eyes looking to see who was wearing a wedding-ring. Another heroine did not like visiting her mother, whose friends seemed always to hope for news of an engagement. And it was a distinguished woman novelist (the authoress of

Elizabeth and her German Garden) who wrote that every woman hopes to be a widow – the finished article.

Barbara's hobby (generally enjoyable) of 'unrequited love' is misunderstood. Some people think she was badly treated by her 'chaps', as she called them – it will not do to call them 'lovers', or simply 'friends', and certainly not 'suitors'. Unrequited love is at least love, and warming; it is interesting, and the lover always has something to think about – for him it is no penance to sit alone in a waiting-room. The beloved, on the other hand, can find unwanted love chilling and boring; it can embarrass him, and put him in a disadvantageous position. 'All the world loves a lover', and he gets all the sympathy; and yet Estella in *Great Expectations* deserves pity as much as Pip, for she badly needs friendship and not that tormenting passion – and it was dreadful (and finally lethal) to Catherine Linton to have Heathcliff's cruel love.

Barbara, of course, did not torment her 'chaps'. With her 'private eye' she investigated them, found out all she could from books of reference, and haunted streets where they lived or worked. This harmless manhunt was more a sport than anything else, and she was in most cases the pursuer rather than the pursued. Were the 'chaps', once caught, to be blamed for making some use of her to darn their socks or type their theses in return for their company? She liked it.

Her editors, I think, made use of the wrong word (an easy thing to do) when they said that Barbara was 'hurt' by the marriage of her beloved 'Lorenzo'. That seems to imply that she had counter-claims. She was grieved no doubt, for marriage like death can put an end to a day-dream – she would probably have liked 'Lorenzo' to be forever single – but she had no reason to feel aggrieved, and was too sensible to be so.

Barbara's point of view is better revealed in the novels. It will not always be necessary to distinguish authorial remarks from the thoughts or utterances of her characters, even if these are characteristic or dramatic. The same view of life always emerges.

The heroine of *Excellent Women*, herself a most excellent woman, defines the function of her kind: 'They are for being unmarried . . . and by that I mean a positive rather than a negative state' (p. 190). The same heroine, Mildred, remarked, 'Women like me really expected very little – nothing, almost' (p. 37). But she had observed 'that men did not usually do things unless they liked doing them' (p. 9). In *No Fond Return of Love* some men stood

apart: 'those are the people from whom one asks no return of
love. . . . Just to be allowed to love them is enough' (p. 75). Or
(this is Mildred again) 'I realised that one might love him secretly
with no hope of encouragement, which can be very enjoyable for
the young or inexperienced' (*Excellent Women*, p. 92).

A minor character in *Jane and Prudence* who is getting on in
years says gravely that men are very passionate and 'only want
one thing' (p. 70). She knows nothing about it. In Barbara's novels,
'the right true end of love' to most of the men is 'one thing to
their purpose nothing'. They want a great many other things,
such as washing, sewing and darning – some of them have taught
women 'early in life what it is to bear love's burdens, listening
patiently to their men's troubles and ever ready at their
typewriters, should a manuscript or even a short article get to the
stage of being written down' (*Less than Angels*, p. 49).

Men, who are here the 'fair' and certainly not the 'strong' sex,
want flattery as well as service. In *Jane and Prudence*,

> Oh, but it was splendid the things women were doing for men
> all the time. . . . Making them feel, perhaps sometimes by no
> more than a casual glance, that they were loved and admired
> and desired when they were worthy of none of these things –
> enabling them to preen themselves and puff out their plumage
> like birds and bask in the sunshine of love, real or imagined, it
> didn't matter which.   (p. 75)

This, then, is a major theme of the novels in the 'canon' – and
when, in *Excellent Women*, Mildred and her charwoman 'laughed
together, a couple of women against the whole race of men'
(pp. 23–4), men can join in their kindly laughter, unless they have
an overweening sense of their own dignity. If they have, it is
probably a woman's fault for spoiling them. This theme, and the
controlled tone in which it is conveyed, is what chiefly
distinguishes Barbara's work.

We turn back in surprise to those who have thought her
'frustrated'! A main cause for misunderstanding is this: Barbara,
who was always sincere, often delighted in not being serious. We
meet her too early in life as a *Backfisch*, 'Still young enough to
suffer disappointments in love as commonly as colds or headaches'
(*A Very Private Eye*, p. 71). Her early journals are not really
'writing' – and show no signs of her being a 'born writer' (though

she was). They are like recorded talk – and those who can still
hear her voice in them, or see the expression in her eyes will not
be taken in. Had they been written for printing – she appears to
have authorised their printing, but that is another thing – we
could complain of their faulty tone. As it is, we may think it a pity
that what stemmed from the speaking voice should have been
given the permanence of print. We turn again in gratitude to the
novels, where the tone is always right.

If the unrequited love sometimes ended in tears, it was soon
succeeded by all passion (almost) spent. Already in her first
novel, Belinda (a portrait of herself thirty years on) 'was sure that
our greater English poets had written much about unhappy lovers
not dying of grief, although it was of course more romantic when
they did' (*Some Tame Gazelle*, p. 130). She had not done so; she
found

> there was a certain pleasure in not doing something; it was
> impossible that one's high expectations should be disappointed
> by the reality. To Belinda's imaginative but contented mind this
> seemed a happy state, with no emptiness or bitterness about
> it. She was fortunate in needing very little to make her
> happy.   (p. 89)

As Mildred said later, 'life was like that for most of us – the small
unpleasantnesses rather than the great tragedies; the little useless
longings rather than the great renunciations and dramatic love
affairs of history or fiction' (*Excellent Women*, p. 101).

Nevertheless, the excellent woman is apt to be put upon and
not only by men. Practically anything may be the business of an
unattached woman with no troubles of her own, who takes a
kindly interest in those of her old friends. If she marries, she
assumes other burdens: besides, 'typing a man's thesis' and
'correcting proofs', there is 'putting sheets sides-to-middle,
bringing up children, balancing the house-keeping budget', and,
if she is a vicar's wife, as she is apt to be (for not all Anglican
clergy are celibate) she will have to attend three services every
Sunday, sitting in her dowdy clothes too near the front of the
church (*Jane and Prudence*, p. 127).

Like most people of her class and generation, Barbara must
sometimes have looked back with nostalgia to the days when one
had living-in servants; and on no one have the social and

economic changes of the last forty years fallen more heavily than upon the excellent women. Some minor characters remark hypocritically that it is 'better so'. The comment is never authorial, for the hearts of the excellent women know their own bitterness, but a bitterness as gentle and uncomplaining as the rest of them. Some of the fortunate men characters are hardly at all affected, so excellent are their women.

Comparing frustration in love with frustration in letters, 'Miss Pym who like Tiresias though really not at all like him had known both' once told me that the latter was by far the worse. Certainly her sufferings in this sort went deeper and lasted longer. But happily, as I shall try to show, they were the making of her as a writer, and did her far more service after 'love' was no more important. *God moves in a mysterious way* – that was her favourite hymn.

It seemed that she was going to make an early start. Jonathan Cape showed an interest in *Some Tame Gazelle* in 1936; but, 'falser than false Cressid', he decided against it. Yet it must have remained in his mind, for he spoke of it to me after the war and asked me to urge Barbara to revise it and send it in again. It was not published until 1950, and then was substantially the original book, though already some of the humours learned in her work at the African Institute enter into her picture of a colonial bishop.

Thereafter, throughout the 1950s, followed the other novels of the 'canon' – delightful comedy set in closely defined environments, which allow for delicate and minute observation. Like *Some Tame Gazelle*, one of its successors is set in an English village, but 'so many parts of London have a peculiarly village or parochial atmosphere', and this enters into the other books. The clergy often occupy a central position, but the International African Institute contributes anthropologists – who are a fit subject for study as their life is spent in studying even more primitive tribes. There are always excellent (often Anglo-Catholic) women, and a few less excellent – Prudence, whose recreation was having love affairs, was a favourite (she has told us) of the author's.

The last published novel of the 'canon', *No Fond Return of Love*, owes the most to exercise of the 'private eye': 'Investigation – some might have said prying – into the lives of other people, the kind of work that involved poring over reference books, and street and telephone directories' (p. 44). And indeed it is remarkable how much you find out that way, even things that people might like to conceal. 'It seemed . . . so much safer and more comfortable to live in the lives of other people – to observe their joys and sorrows with detachment as if one were watching a film or a play' (p. 108) – though, as we are told in *Less than Angels*, 'Curiosity has its pains as well as pleasures, and the bitterest of its pains must surely be the inability to follow everything to its conclusion' (pp. 8–9).

There are other pains: 'one goes on with one's research, avidly and without shame. Then suddenly a curious feeling of delicacy comes over one. One sees one's subjects – or perhaps victims is a better word – as being somehow degraded by one's probings' (*No Fond Return of Love*, p. 171). Dulcie's research in *No Fond Return of Love* takes her to evensong in one suburban church, to a jumble sale in aid of the organ fund for another church, to a hotel in Cornwall, a cemetery and a castle.

This was to be the end of the 'canon' – a series of novels admirably picturing a section of middle-class society at that period, and started off by the great comic character Archdeacon Hoccleve. Would the inspiration have continued? It has seemed to me after study of *No Fond Return of Love*, where there is no longer the same unity of place and action as in earlier novels, that it might have been failing.

In 1963 Barbara, who thought of herself as a safely established writer, had a real shock when *An Unsuitable Attachment* was rejected by her publishers. Philip Larkin rightly says that someone in the firm ought to have softened the blow, by taking Barbara out to luncheon and telling her that something had to be done about the book. She ought not (after all she had done) to have been obliged to face the brutality of a downright rejection, and had Jonathan Cape been alive I think he would have spared her this and asked her to revise the book. I do not, however, think she could have brought it into an acceptable form. If we may compare smaller with greater things, I believe that, like another rejected novel, *Northanger Abbey*, it had a fatal flaw in its structure. They both survive as posthumous books, and we are thankful to have them. We could not bear to be without Catherine and the washing-bills, or without Barbara's Sophia and her cat Faustina – 'she's all I've got' (p. 138). Nevertheless, we cannot see how Jane Austen could have rendered General Tilney plausible, nor what Barbara could have done to give an interest to the 'unsuitable attachment' between the canon's daughter and the young man whose shoes 'seemed to be a little too pointed – not quite what men one knew would wear' (p. 49). He had good looks, but good looks, so important in life or on stage or screen, do not even come into existence in the novel.

There followed the years of neglect, but (as one reviewer said) worse might have happened. *An Unsuitable Attachment* might have come out, with hostile reviews, followed by one or two other novels with dwindling confidence, and then final silence. As it was, the 'canon' remained, cherished and reread by a number of admirers, owing its continued life to its own sharp flavour and to the fact that it is not merely a group of novels but an oeuvre. The whole is greater than the sum of its parts. Some readers have expressed irritation at the reappearance of characters from book to book, but many of us were glad to have news of old friends.

Barbara took rejection as a challenge; she seems never to have been resigned to silence or to have given up attempts at writing. But gradually there was a development. She was now fifty, and sadder, and had faced a new emotional experience, an attachment to a man much younger than herself. 'Nothing', of course, 'could come of it.' But something did. It was the inspiration of her most deeply felt novel, *The Sweet Dove Died*. Though every book of hers must have made someone laugh aloud, I do not think she has ever drawn a tear from a reader. Nevertheless this book, which ends in tears, has an atmosphere of tender melancholy.

Leonora, the heroine, is an elegant rather than an excellent woman. The two types had always existed side by side in the 'canon', and each expressed part of the author's nature. In this book, though we hear the bell ringing, no one goes to church. Leonora is too attentive to a young man, who feels the need for escape. Like Wilmet, in *A Glass of Blessings*, she has become interested in a man who is basically homosexual. This need not have been an impediment to a happy friendship between them, had she been content with less and had not scared him away by her attempts at domination. The affair between the two young men is most delicately done, neither for nor against – and the author takes refuge in silence only after twice bringing it to a pitch following which nothing but the vulgarity of asterisks or of consummation would have been possible. The portrait of Leonora contains almost poignant self-criticism, expressed in the title of the book:

> I had a dove, and the sweet dove died;
> And I have thought it died of grieving;
> O, what could it grieve for? its feet were tied
> With a single thread of my own hand's weaving.

But Keats did not only give her an analysis of the situation. At his house she saw a middle-aged woman with 'the brightly coloured packet of a frozen "dinner for one" ' in her shopping-bag. After a moment's contempt 'she saw the woman going home to a cosy solitude' (p. 155). Perhaps she will learn this solution. This was the last book published in Barbara's lifetime, but it was written before *Quartet in Autumn*, her most original and strongest novel.

The 'quartet', two men and two women, work in the same office; they are near to retirement, which indeed overtakes the women. Their lives interweave and separate, and show all the minute, unsparing but charitable observation that we know from the 'canon'. This time Barbara has again created a really memorable character. Marcia, as a tragic character, is as great a creation as the comic Archdeacon, and rather more plausible. She is an independent, eccentric solitary who has triumphantly slipped 'through the net' of the Welfare State (p. 187), and fights off the attentions of social workers and those who are eager to 'fall over backwards' to do her unwanted good. Her one (platonic) passion is for the surgeon who performed her 'major surgery'. She dies, almost of starvation, although she has a large store of tinned food to which she has regularly added in case of 'emergency' (pp. 152, 64).

A Few Green Leaves, published posthumously, is a charming account of some months in the life of an Oxfordshire village, not unlike that to which Barbara and her sister had retired. It is pleasantly readable as a notebook or chronicle of country life, but sharpened by the author's skill as a novelist, and the observation of her principal character, Emma, who is an anthropologist.

Thus all the external parts of Barbara's life seem to have come together in her work – and of all the distinguished *alumnae* of St Hilda's College none has had more right to take to herself the college motto *Non frustra vixi*.

It is often said that every novelist is consciously or unconsciously a propagandist; this is no more than a half-truth. Every novelist is to some extent expressing his ideas about life; he prefers 'some ends, some means', and Barbara was quite conscious that she did.

But a propagandist is trying to impose these preferences on others, and this Barbara has never done. In general she has exhibited the lifestyle of more or less excellent women of the middle-class, most of them with some degree of culture and none of them an advocate of any cause – their moral values are mainly right. All she is saying is that it is pleasant to spend some time with such people – so it is, for there is an absence of stress, and a tonic fresh air.

For Barbara was a good woman – brave and patient and firmly religious. A good parishioner at a rather dull church, she would not despise a handsome High Mass and Procession, or a Solemn Evensong and Benediction, or clouds of 'the most expensive incense', or 'glamorous acolytes' – but like one of the characters in her last book she was not given to 'self-indulgent churchgoing' (*A Few Green Leaves*, p. 121). Nevertheless she could sympathise with another of the characters in the same book who had left the Anglo-Catholics – who might have said, in the words of a once-popular song,

> We play the Lambeth way,
> Not like you, but a bit more gay.

Now poor Adam, used to something more seemly, was condemned to the ugliness of the 'dreadful vernacular Mass', imposed by a philistine hierarchy on us, members of the 'Roman persuasion'.

It is significant that the elegant and rather worldly Wilmet in *A Glass of Blessings* is the character who comes nearest to showing spirituality:

> One or two people were kneeling in the church, and I knelt down too and began to say one of those indefinite prayers which come to us if we are at all used to praying, and which can impose themselves above our other thoughts, so often totally unconnected with spiritual matters. (p. 25)

Few other novelists of our time, or their characters, are 'used to praying', or know what it means.

18

The Importance of Connecting

Frances H. Bachelder

Eleven published novels – all similar, but, like stitches in a hand-knitted sweater, each is slightly different and therein lies the beauty of the human touch. Every novel is a vital part of the whole picture and therefore dependent upon the others for a better understanding of the lifestyle Barbara Pym portrays.

Her books lend contentment and comfort to us. They are down-to-earth, folksy, with day-to-day details, reminding us of the people we have known – good folk, helpful, impish, sometimes critical and gossipy, not perfect, but always good friends.

For instance, in *Some Tame Gazelle* Belinda, a particularly lovable lady, is unhappy with any kind of *'atmosphere'*. Even when she has a wicked little thought she feels guilty, but somehow pleased with herself. She and her sister Harriet, as well as the other characters in the novel, enjoy provincial living – and what is wrong with that? Their troubles, thoughts, actions, joys and worries are the same as others'; and yet they are like sheep happily involved in their own little world surrounded by a protective fence. Life goes on while they gently and skilfully handle the problems and irritations that arise each day. Except for an occasional dark cloud, the sun shines on and on. This is only one of the joys of reading Pym.

There are many examples to which we can relate, as in the following scene from *No Fond Return of Love*:

'I don't think I closed my eyes till dawn and then I slept until you came in with the tea' [Viola remarks].

'I hope I didn't wake you', said Dulcie anxiously. 'I thought you might like to have a cup.' That was the worst of trying to be helpful, she reflected; so often one did the wrong thing. (pp. 29–30)

Another example: 'Again [Dulcie's] thoughts wandered to her home and all that needed to be done there, and she began to wonder why she had come to the conference when she had so many better ways of occupying her time' (p. 30). At times we wonder why we follow certain paths. Then when our efforts are rewarded, we look back and understand the reasons for this. Or, as Dulcie thinks, 'It might be that the absurd conference had served some useful purpose after all' (p. 44).

From such passages we might smugly decide that Barbara Pym's novels are going to be light reading with little substance. But wait. It's not long before we realise she has a surprise in store for us – she makes us think! The thoughts that come to mind depend a lot upon our backgrounds, and for this reason her books might not appeal to some of us. Nevertheless, it is evident we have much in common with her characters and in many instances are the ones she is writing about.

Beneath the trivia and amusing comments there is an undercurrent of seriousness. Her simplest sentences are so enriching that the deeper meanings show through and cannot be ignored. We are reminded perhaps of Beethoven's *Für Elise*, which is not difficult if played for the notes only, yet has greater depth when studied further. For some of us, skimming a stone over the water to see the steps it makes is enough; for the rest of us, discovering what happens beneath the ripples is more satisfying.

While minor details are prominent throughout the novels, we have to agree that life is composed of trivia and from this stockpile come results that might never occur but for the accumulation and solidifying of minutiae. As the housekeeper remarks in *No Fond Return of Love*, 'Oh, I know it's a trivial detail . . . but those are the things that make up life, aren't they' (p. 248). Or, as Alexander Pope wrote, 'What mighty contests rise from trivial things'.

There are of course trivia that waste our time – as when Dora in *Excellent Women* fights over a little matter such as 'wearing hats in chapel'. It was not the hats that bothered her so much – there was another reason for her feeling this way, hidden meanings misunderstood by some. In this case it was partly her objection to 'organised religion of any kind' (p. 101).

Although Pym's satire is reminiscent of Pope's, her remarks are not cutting or personal and her descriptions of life and absurd or comical situations show little if any bitterness. Many examples of her humour are worth noting. In *A Glass of Blessings* Wilmet sits in church and remarks, 'I could not at first decide whether the rustling sound came from their natural age and brittleness or whether they were whispering together about something' (p. 99). Mark in *Less than Angels* feels that 'Tom had gone too far' when he died (p. 235). In the same novel Mabel Swan thinks,

> It was nice when the warm weather came and they could have salads for supper, . . . though why it was nice she didn't really know. Washing a lettuce and cutting up the things to go with it was really almost as much trouble as cooking a hot meal. (pp. 34–5)

In *Some Tame Gazelle*, ' "Well, hardly that", ventured Belinda, growing a little more confidential, for the Ovaltine had loosened her tongue' (p. 155). And, later in the same novel,

> 'But didn't he say *anything*? Surely you weren't just reading poetry *all* the time?'
> 'No, not all the time.' Belinda smiled as she remembered their conversation. 'We talked about the dust on the mantelpiece.' (p. 156)

Because every paragraph in Barbara Pym's books is a story in itself, what might seem like humdrum events become real and exciting. We wonder how she can hold our interest in day-to-day situations which are true to life, not only in detail but also in form. Aylwin Forbes in *No Fond Return of Love* 'took a sip of tea. It tasted strong and bitter. Like Life?' (p. 25).

Her characters speak often of living a full life, which raises the question of what is meant by this. In *Jane and Prudence*, Prudence feels that, although Jane is married, her own life 'seemed rich and full of promise. She had her work, her independence, her life in London and her love for Arthur Grampian. But tomorrow, if she wanted to, she could give it all up and fall in love with somebody else' (p. 83).

At a class reunion Prudence is reminded that she is one of three in her year who never married. In spite of this, at the conclusion of the book she realises that two men are interested in her and is 'suddenly overwhelmed by the richness of her life' (p. 222).

Then we read in *Less than Angels* that Rhoda (who is single) is 'not in the least envious of her sister's fuller life' – a 'fuller life' here meaning that her sister Mabel is married with two children. Since the two sisters are now 'in their fifties', Rhoda feels there is 'very little difference between them' (p. 36).

Unquestionably many styles of living are important, otherwise life as we know it would be incomplete. If a person believes he is living up to his potential and is satisfied with the results, then there is no reason to change that pattern, regardless of the opinions of others. In Pym's novels the characters who are not married or never have been are the ones who seem to be more concerned about living a full life. But it also applies to those who are married when they discover limitations such as daily family responsibilities and less freedom in other ways.

Therefore it is possible that the meaning of a full life often lies in the mind of the individual. We all know the part the mind plays in our lives. Much satisfaction is derived from contemplating our mind-made experiences whereby we can project ourselves as we want to be, and then find enjoyment in that likeness. As Mary says in *A Glass of Blessings*, 'Oh, Wilmet, life is perfect now! I've everything that I could possibly want. I keep thinking that it's like a glass of blessings – life, I mean' (p. 253). After thinking about Mary's 'description of life', Wilmet decides that perhaps her own 'always had been [a glass of blessings] without [her] realising it' (p. 256).

As mentioned previously, this theme runs throughout most of Barbara Pym's books. It makes us wonder how often she might have thought about this with regard to herself; but after reading her eleven published novels it is apparent that she felt she *was* living a full life. Then, again, perhaps she was so filled with courage, humour, hope and positive thoughts that she completely fools us. Now that is quite an accomplishment – giving us much pleasure yet at the same time not revealing any unhappiness or uncertainties she might have had. Pym shares her wonderful gift to the fullest.

In her 'autobiography', *A Very Private Eye*, we read, 'she realised that she would only just live long enough to complete *A Few*

Green Leaves' (p. xv). Could this novel, as well as *Quartet in Autumn* (which is quite bleak) be an outpouring of Barbara Pym's feelings with which she does not want to burden others – a sort of placebo? Bringing thoughts into the open is often a relief. In both novels there is much preoccupation with death, graveyards (churchyards), aging and doctors – although not in a morbid way – and this is understandable. We wonder if Pym ever wished she could take some of her characters with her. If so, such thoughts may have been comforting to her, as she probably had moments of feeling very much alone.

Although the lives of ordinary people are the highlights of her novels, occasionally there are hints that something strange or unusual is imminent. This applies especially to *A Few Green Leaves*, in which there is an odd build-up of activities. Miss Grundy has a 'kind of turn – more like an *experience* – she says she's *seen* something, some person from the past' (pp. 113–14). Perhaps she only wanted attention – she was often put down by Miss Lee. She describes the young man she saw as one 'with long hair, wearing a brightly coloured coat – rather in an Oriental style'. Miss Lee is 'irritated by the fuss' over Miss Grundy and dismisses the matter (p. 114). And Daphne, who is riding in a bus, hears 'songs with an Oriental strain' coming from the driver's radio (p. 118).

Later in the same novel there is a sense of foreboding when Miss Vereker 'took the train from Paddington to the station nearest to the village, not telling her nephew and his wife what she was doing.' Then 'She set out to walk to the village . . . she could easily manage that' (pp. 204, 206). The suspense builds: 'she seemed to have strayed some way off the direct path' (p. 216), and later Dr Gellibrand says, 'I thought you ought to know . . . that Miss Vereker has been found wandering in the woods' (p. 223).

Another example – also from *A Few Green Leaves* – gives us a shock:

In the next-door cottage Miss Lickerish had not bothered to put on the light at the normal time. She boiled a kettle on the fire and then sat in her chair with a cup of tea at her side and a cat on her knees. But some time during those dark hours the cat left her and sought the warmth of his basket, Miss Lickerish's lap having become strangely chilled. (p. 227)

These sections of suspense and foreboding lead us to believe that Pym would have been a good mystery-writer. The death of Miss Lickerish is euphemistically portrayed, but in such a clever way we can almost see the mercury falling in the thermometer.

In *The Sweet Dove Died* Pym for the most part seems to stray from her usual pattern. Perhaps she intended to, but it comes as a surprise to us. This fascinating but unsettling story is in keeping with the times, however, and here again we are made aware of Pym's sensitivity toward and understanding of life. James is a sweet young man who really cares for Leonora. But he is tied to her by conscience and by the care and comfort he receives rather than by true love. He is unsure how to escape his situation without hurting her or himself: she's afraid of losing him if she holds on too tightly. Obviously Leonora makes the right decision, although difficult for herself as well as James. The ending for the two of them is Shakespearean: both are figuratively stabbed in the heart, and death comes to something beautiful, to a relationship which it is impossible should continue. She deserves the flowers with which she presents herself after a perfect performance.

An important factor that ties Pym's novels together is the appearance of characters from earlier ones. This could be a problem for someone reading the books for the first time but not following the order in which they were written. In her tenth and final novel, *A Few Green Leaves*, published posthumously in 1980, we find that Esther Clovis has died. If we follow with her seventh novel, *An Unsuitable Attachment*, published posthumously in 1982, we note that Rupert plans to invite Esther to his party. Aside from that, though, it is fun to meet former characters who are by now old friends. Also, at times there are so many names with which we must acquaint ourselves that it is a relief to recognise familiar ones.

We can imagine Pym smiling to herself when four of our friends from *A Glass of Blessings* appear again in *No Fond Return of Love* and she writes, ' "No wonder she's tired in those ridiculously high heels", said Viola sourly, as they waited for the bus back. "What odd people they were! Like characters in a novel" ' (p. 193).

As we continue our search for deeper meanings, there is one aspect we almost overlook: what are the sources from which she has drawn her characters' names? An extensive study could be made on this subject, but it will suffice here to explore a few examples, provided by the names of Dr Grampian (*Jane and Prudence*), Belinda (*Some Tame Gazelle*) and Faustina (*An Unsuitable Attachment*). Prudence is 'a sort of personal assistant to Dr Grampian' (*Jane and Prudence*, p. 10), an 'insignificant-looking little man' (p. 75) whom she loves and looks up to as one would to the Grampian mountains which rise in the Highlands of Scotland. The name Belinda might have been taken from Pope's poem *The Rape of the Lock*, in which Belinda is one of the principal characters. Although there are many shining stars in *An Unsuitable Attachment*, Faustina the cat has her own little footlights. If anyone lives a full life, and is unconcerned one way or the other, it is she. Treated royally and allowed to do as she pleases, she is truly an empress and could have been named after Faustina, the widow of Constantius II, emperor, son of Constantine the Great.

Another sidelight is shed by the use of the word 'suitable' and its derivatives. In *An Unsuitable Attachment*, *Quartet in Autumn* and *A Few Green Leaves* these words occur, in all, more than a hundred times – sixty-six in *An Unsuitable Attachment* alone. It becomes a game to see how many more such uses we can find in the other novels – without letting this interfere with our reading and enjoyment of the novels, of course. Is it feasible that the author is teasing or testing us? Is 'suitable' a favourite word or, when she uses it, *the* word that expresses exactly what she wants to say? For us to overlook a sentence, phrase, word or punctuation mark is to take a chance on missing some important effect or idea.

Of special interest is the way each of the novels begins, immediately catching us up in the fairytale pattern of 'once upon a time'. The opening sentence of *Crampton Hodnet* is a typical example: 'It was a wet Sunday afternoon in North Oxford at the beginning of October' (p. 1). She captures our attention and holds it as she describes the laurel bushes, flowers drooping in the rain, the house with its stained-glass window, and, inside, the peace and quiet for Miss Morrow as long as Miss Doggett rests upstairs in her bedroom.

Crampton Hodnet (published in 1985) was written in 1939–40 when Barbara Pym was in her late twenties. Since this novel is the latest to be published – but one of the earliest to be completed – it is easy for us *now* to compare it with those novels she wrote as a more mature author. We feel that this book is as exciting and well done as her later ones, though perhaps lacking depth and subtlety. It is written with youthful enthusiasm and with an amazing understanding of the ways of people much older than the author at the time of writing.

From her excellent description of Mr Cleveland's marital uneasiness and the rationalising ways of meddling gossips, we realise she was born to be a writer. Furthermore, there is no limit to the number of times Pym's novels may be read and enjoyed. Many interesting points are certain to have escaped us in the first reading. She is a writer for all times.

Whether or not it is the author's intention, we find a smooth transition from one book to the next, as though turning a page will reveal tomorrow. As Pope writes in the *Essay on Criticism*:

> what affects our hearts
> Is not th'exactness of peculiar parts;
> 'Tis not a lip or eye we beauty call,
> But the joint force and full result of all.

Let us picture the eleven novels as the cars of a train, eleven in all, with communicating doors enabling us to step with ease from one to the next. We pass many friends, some of whom are recognised as those encountered earlier. Having reached the last car and final seat, we step out onto the observation deck. The train pulls into the station; it is hard to leave. We are sorry to see our journey end, especially because we shall be taking leave of Barbara Pym and her friends for a while. Suddenly it is our turn to be overwhelmed by that elusive feeling of fulfilment, as, for a short time, we have been allowed to share in the lives of some very special folk.

The whistle blows, the train pulls away and disappears; but there remains the memory of this gleaming array of cars, each reaching for the next, which is tugging at the one behind, all closely related and blending into one.

Barbara Pym did her work well, thereby leaving her spirit behind, and as a result enriching the traditions of mankind.

No lesson is so effective as the lesson of a person's life.

19

Years of Neglect

Gail Godwin

If I weren't going to be in Europe in September, I would love to join in a celebration of Barbara Pym. I just finished *A Very Private Eye*, and I found it very engrossing and poignant – especially the spirit in which she met her 'years of neglect'.

If I were to contribute any words to her day of celebration, I would like those words to take the tone of vindicated indignation: If there are any publishers out there who still tremble at the tenor of the times, let them not shake so much that they lose their hold on the kind of writing that endures the madness and turbulence of the ever-fickle *Zeitgeist*. Barbara Pym recorded and preserved a corner of English life that was important to her while the sixties raced by on the highroad. Now the sixties are gone, but her valiantly civilised and unpretentious landscapes remain vividly before us. That should tell us something.

Notes

Numbers prefixed PYM are items in the collection of Barbara Pym's papers lodged at the Bodleian Library, Oxford.

PREFACE

1. 'Reputations Revisited', *The Times Literary Supplement*, 21 Jan 1977, pp. 66–7.
2. Jill Powles to Dale Salwak, 24 Aug 1984.
3. Bob Redston to Dale Salwak, 25 Aug 1984.
4. Vladimir Nabokov, 'Good Readers and Good Writers', in *Lectures on Literature*, ed. Fredson Bowers (New York and London: Harcourt Brace Jovanovich, 1980) pp. 5–6.
5. Lisa Schwarzbaum, 'A Cup of Pym', *The Real Paper*, 14 June 1980, p. 16.
6. John Halperin to Dale Salwak, 12 Jan 1984.
7. Delmore Schwartz, quoted by Lance Morrow, 'We Need More Writers We'd Miss', *Time*, 26 July 1982, p. 64.
8. 'Symposium: Books that Gave Me Pleasure', *New York Times Book Review*, 5 Dec 1982, p. 61.

CHAPTER 2. THE QUEST FOR A CAREER
Constance Malloy

1. Pym to Robert Smith, 8 Feb 1977. The previous day she had noted in her journal, 'Duncan Druce (the violinist of Ramsden [village next to Finstock]) is apparently getting up a petition to protest against Concorde which we saw flying over last week. She soars beautiful above us but our road is full of potholes as it might be in the 16th century' (PYM 76, fols 16–17). Many anecdotes and observations that appear in Barbara Pym's personal letters and her novels were originally recorded in her journal.
2. Barbara Pym, 'A Year in Oxfordshire', in *My Britain, 1979*, ed. Helen and David Titchmarsh (London: Jarrold, n.d.) p. 108. The entry on Finstock further notes, 'Described by John Wesley, who visited it three times (1774–7–8), as "this delightful solitude", its inhabitants being "a plain and artless people" (no doubt a compliment coming from J. W.). Finstock today is a fragmented village, with a fine gabled manor house

and a plain Victorian church.' The church contains a plaque commemorating T. S. Eliot, who was baptised there in 1927, and a plaque in memory of Barbara Pym herself.

3. In 1922, at the age of eight, Barbara composed and staged 'The Magic Diamond', an 'operetta' (by virtue of many tra-la-las). It starred Princess Rosebud (Barbara), who offers to save her beloved Prince George (her cousin, Neville Selway) from the evil wizard's curse. Even as a romantic child Barbara had reversed the fairytale in which the man comes to the woman's rescue.

4. In the original draft of *Some Tame Gazelle*, all the characters bear the names of the actual people on whom they are modelled. In addition to the Pym sisters and 'Archdeacon' Henry Harvey, the cast includes the librarian Robert ('Jockie') Liddell, now known for his critical work on Jane Austen, George Eliot and Ivy Compton-Burnett. Though Liddell went to live in Greece, he and Barbara continued to exchange letters and visits.

5. Long before Henry Harvey married Elsie, Barbara had written,

> This evening it occurred to me that perhaps I don't really love Gabriel [her name for Henry] anymore. How satisfactory if I could really think that – but how empty my life would be without a consuming passion. They are delightful when they aren't too intense – my love for Gabriel has been by no means all honey – in fact no honey at all, except the amusement of seeing him and speculating as to what he was like before I knew him. (22 Dec 1933, PYM 102, fol. 27)

In 1931, when she was twenty-one, she copied into her commonplace book this excerpt from Virginia Woolf's *To the Lighthouse*: 'it had flashed upon her that she . . . need never marry anybody, and she had felt an enormous exultation' (PYM 83, fol. 32).

6. Pym to Henry Harvey, 5 Apr 1938.
7. Pym to Elsie Harvey, 20 July 1938.
8. On 10 October 1938, she wrote in her diary, '[The six children evacuated from Birkenhead] were running about like Bears in the kitchen. Too tired to write my great novel' (PYM 105, fol. 154). On 14 September 1941, she noted, 'Started to write my spy story which I must and will finish' (PYM 107, fol. 81).
9. Diary entry (PYM 109, fols 74–5).
10. Models for Rocky probably included Michael Cashman, Alan Davis, Iain Watson ('Starky') and especially Edward Astleigh-Jones. See *A Very Private Eye* (pp. 167–80) for Barbara's diary entries regarding these men and her Naples adventures.
11. Diary entry (PYM 111, fol. 49).
12. Address to the Senior Wives Fellowship, Headington, Oxfordshire, 15 May 1978. The group, which may seem an unusual one for a spinster to address, calls itself

> a society of educated women over the age of 45 whose object is to uphold Christian principles in marriage, motherhood, and

citizenship. Apart from this it holds no corporate opinions, and is interdenominational and non-political. There are branches all over the country whose members hold meetings for talks and discussions on a wide variety of topics, their objects being intellectual and spiritual refreshment. (PYM 172, fol. 6)

13. In *Jane and Prudence*, Jane takes up the piano-tuner's hat and pirouettes around the hall singing 'O Donna Clara' (p. 144). When Barbara was a girl, Irena Pym had done this very thing, besides performing other Jane-like capers.
14. Coincidentally, Barbara had written a novel (unpublished) entitled *Beatrice Wyatt* in 1938, long before she had heard of the Beatrice Wyatt who was Secretary of the IAI.
15. Pym to Henry Harvey, 9 Feb 1946.
16. Address to the Senior Wives Fellowship, 15 May 1978.
17. Pym to Henry Harvey, 1 May 1950.
18. Henry Harvey wrote to Barbara on 25 September 1950 saying that he had lent out *Some Tame Gazelle* before reading it, then had given it to his second wife, Susi, who he says was jealous of his former intimacy with Barbara (PYM 167, fol. 41).
19. On 24 May 1950 Ivy Compton-Burnett wrote to Barbara Pym, 'I have been greatly entertained by *Some Tame Gazelle*' (PYM 167, fol. 27). Elizabeth Taylor wrote in similar vein in November (PYM 167, fol. 64). On 24 November 1953 Lord David Cecil wrote, 'Forgive a total stranger writing to tell you how much he enjoys your books. . . . You have so much sense of reality and sense of comedy, and the people in your books are living and credible and likeable. I find this rare in modern fiction. Please do not answer this' (PYM 147, fol. 148). In 1961 Philip Larkin wrote to praise Barbara's work and to suggest that he write a review when her next novel was published (see *A Very Private Eye*, p. 210). Unfortunately, sixteen years of rejection were to intervene before another Pym novel was published.
20. Address to the Senior Wives Fellowship, 15 May 1978.
21. G. Wren Howard to Pym, 19 Mar 1963 (PYM 164, fols 130–1).
22. Pym to Robert Smith, 19 Mar 1963 (PYM 161, fol. 28b).
23. Ibid. Charles Monteith of Faber, to whom Barbara sent *An Unsuitable Attachment* in 1965, corroborates many of these theories. He mentions that 'novels have become increasingly difficult to sell, partly because of 'the paperback revolution' and partly because of the collapse of lending-libraries such as Boots. In addition, paperback firms 'tend, I fear, to go for something rather more violent and sensational' (PYM 164, fols 152–3).
24. *Finding a Voice*, BBC radio talk, transmitted 18 Apr 1978, tape no. TLN06/103L4356/103L435.
25. Crampton was the middle name of Barbara's father, as it was of both Hilary and Barbara. Hilary speculates in *A Very Private Eye* (pp. 1–2) that it may have been the name of her paternal grandfather, who did not marry her paternal grandmother, Phoebe Pym. Barbara explained the use of a pseudonym to Jean Mossop of Cape in a letter of 5 July

1976: 'My heart sinks at the idea of having to approach more publishers, either telling them that I have published novels before or pretending to be a new writer. I have tried both approaches in the past and have found that the second is more likely to succeed' (PYM 165, fol. 73).

26. Pym to Rowena Lawson, 6 Apr 1978 (PYM 171, fol. 143).
27. Address to the Romantic Novelists Association, 8 Mar 1978.
28. Valerie Sullivan to Pym, 11 May 1978, speaking of a letter from Cape in 1970 (PYM 172, fols 54–5).
29. Pym to Jean Mossop, 6 Dec 1971 (PYM 166, fol. 28).
30. Address to the Senior Wives Fellowship, 15 May 1978.
31. Pym to Miss Abbott, 22 Mar 1977 (PYM 169, fol. 2). A typical diary entry from this period is that of 22 May 1975:

> Three days of fine weather, cuckoos, buttercups, cow parsley, etc. and sun. Writing novel in morning then went to Northleigh, lingered in the churchyard, then went to buy some plants. Tuesday went to Oxford. Wednesday afternoon a beautiful walk over the field at the side of the Plough, then to Wilcote. . . . In the evening CPRE [Council for the Protection of Rural England] meeting at Kiddington Hall with wine and cheese and a lecture by Frank Emery, author of the Oxfordshire Landscape' (PYM 74, fols 1–2).

32. Pym to Robert Smith, 20 Oct 1966 (PYM 161/1, fol. 69).
33. Pym to Jean Mossop, 25 May 1976 (PYM 165, fol. 68).
34. Pym to Henry Harvey, 6 Apr 1976.
35. Diary entry, 6 May 1976 (PYM 75, fol. 10).
36. Pym to Robert Smith, 26 May 1971 (PYM 162/2, fol. 12).
37. Diary entry, 7 Apr 1974 (PYM 72, fols 13–15). On 31 August 1975, while attending a cocktail party at the home of novelist Gilbert Phelps in Finstock, Barbara suffered an asphasia attack (apparently related to the earlier stroke) that left her tongue-tied (see *A Very Private Eye*, p. 283). Mortified, she wrote in her journal the following day, in an allusion to T. S. Eliot's 'Prufrock', 'Summer still? I shall wear the bottoms of my trouser rolled and avoid social gatherings' (PYM 74, fol. 14).
38. Hilary Walton to Robert Smith, 4 Apr 1974 (PYM 162/2, fol. 32).
39. Pym to Robert Smith, 24 May 1963 (PYM 161, fol. 29).
40. Perhaps seeing herself as Leonora and Richard Roberts as James, she noted on 10 September 1964, 'She [Leonora] thinks perhaps this is the kind of love I've always wanted because absolutely *nothing* can be done about it!' (PYM 59, fol. 8).
41. Pym to Robert Smith, 22 Sep 1964 (PYM 161/1, fols 39–40).
42. Pym to Robert Smith, 16 Feb 1967 (PYM 162/1, fol. 72).
43. Pym to Robert Smith, 9 Aug 1967 (PYM 161/1, fols 74–5).
44. Robert Smith to Constance Malloy, 21 Oct 1983.
45. Philip Larkin, 'The World of Barbara Pym', *The Times Literary Supplement*, 11 Mar 1977, p. 260.
46. Diary entry, 20 Nov 1975 (PYM 74, fol. 19). In 1979 the *New Yorker*

did publish one of Barbara Pym's short stories, 'Across a Crowded Room', based on the Rawlinson dinner that she attended in April 1978.
47. Address to the Senior Wives Fellowship, 15 May 1978.
48. 'Reputations Revisited', *The Times Literary Supplement*, 21 Jan 1977, pp. 66–7.
49. Pym to Robert Smith, 8 Feb 1977 (PYM 162/2, fols 53–5).
50. Ibid.
51. Pym to Henry Harvey, 27 Jan 1977.
52. Address to the Romantic Novelists Association, 8 Mar 1978.
53. Address to the Senior Wives Fellowship, 15 May 1978.
54. Pym to Robert Smith, 1 Apr 1977 (PYM 162/2, fol. 58). It was Tom Maschler whom Barbara seemed to resent most in the rejection of her novels. In her 1963 journal she described him as a strong modern invention out to ruin the delicate remnants of a bygone era: 'The name "Mas[c]hler" could easily be that of a firm of demolition contractors, perhaps destroyed [*sic*] a church or a delicate Georgian house' (27 Mar 1963, PYM 57, fol. 7).
55. Address to the Senior Wives Fellowship, 15 May 1978.
56. Pym to Robert Smith, 1 Apr 1977 (PYM 162/2, fol. 58).
57. Pym to Robert Smith, 8 June 1977 (PYM 162/2, fol. 59). In a Dutton publicity release in 1978, Bayley is quoted as saying, 'I first encountered the novels of Barbara Pym in 1954 and was at once enchanted with what then seemed to me – and still seems now – a wholly new and original talent.' In the same release Iris Murdoch says, 'Barbara Pym is one of the quietest but most accomplished English novelists writing today' (PYM 166, fol. 172).
58. Pym to Robert Smith, 8 June 1977 (PYM 162/2, fol. 59).
59. Address to the Senior Wives Fellowship, 15 May 1978.
60. Macmillan author's publicity form, 8 Mar 1977 (PYM 165, fols 99–100).
61. Pym to David Powell of Northampton Literature Group, 15 Mar 1978 (PYM 172, fol. 1).
62. Pym to Paul De Angelis, 13 Jan 1979 (PYM 166, fol. 186).
63. Diary entry (PYM 77, fol. 17).
64. Pym to Robert Smith, 14 Aug 1977 (PYM 162/2, fol. 62).
65. Address to the Senior Wives Fellowship, 15 May 1978.
66. Caroline Moorehead, 'How Barbara Pym was Rediscovered after 16 years out in the Cold', *The Times*, 14 Sep 1977, p. 11.
67. Address to the Senior Wives Fellowship, 15 May 1978.
68. Pym to Paul De Angelis, 1 June 1978 (PYM 166, fol. 169).
69. Address to the Senior Wives Fellowship, 15 May 1978.
70. Pym to Tullia Blundo, 7 Oct 1977 (PYM 147, fol. 23).
71. Pym to Robert Smith, 24 June 1977 (PYM 77, fol. 17).
72. Pym to James Wright, 17 Oct 1979 (PYM 165, fol. 63).
73. James Wright to Pym, 11 Dec 1979 (PYM 165, fol. 160).
74. Paul De Angelis to Pym, 9 Jan 1980 (PYM 165, fol. 164).

CHAPTER 3. THE NOVELIST IN THE FIELD: 1946–74
Hazel Holt

1. Pym to Philip Larkin, 12 May 1963.
2. Pym to Robert Smith, 16 Feb 1967.
3. Pym to Philip Larkin, 21 Aug 1965.
4. Notebook entry, 17 May 1967.
5. Pym to Robert Smith, 20 Jan 1972.
6. Pym to Robert Smith, 9 Feb 1968.
7. Pym to Henry Harvey, 5 June 1946.
8. Pym to Robert Smith, 3 Dec 1969.
9. Pym to Robert Smith, 9 Aug 1967.
10. Pym to Robert Smith, 25 May 1970.
11. Pym to Hazel Holt, 8 Feb 1975.
12. Jan Vansina, *The Kingdoms of the Middle Congo, 1880–1892* (London: Oxford University Press for the International African Institute, 1973).
13. Pym to Robert Smith, 4 May 1979.
14. Pym to Philip Larkin, 24 Oct 1972.
15. Pym to Robert Smith, 19 Nov 1974.
16. Notebook entry, 16 June 1965.
17. Pym to Richard Roberts, 27 Nov 1964.
18. Notebook entry, 21 Feb 1973.
19. Notebook entry, 20 Mar 1972.
20. Pym to Philip Larkin, 1 Dec 1974.

CHAPTER 5. BARBARA PYM'S NOVELISTIC GENIUS
Joyce Carol Oates

1. *A Very Private Eye*, p. 267.
2. Ibid., p. 262.
3. Ibid., p. 306.

CHAPTER 6. THE WORLD OF BARBARA PYM
Penelope Lively

1. Philip Larkin, 'The World of Barbara Pym', *The Times Literary Supplement*, 11 Mar 1977, p. 260.
2. 'Women of Character', *The Times Literary Supplement*, 7 July 1950, p. 417.

CHAPTER 8. HOW PLEASANT TO KNOW MISS PYM
Robert Smith

1. 'Family Failings', *The Times Literary Supplement*, 2 Oct 1953, p. 625.

CHAPTER 10. LOVE AND MARRIAGE IN THE NOVELS
Mary Strauss-Noll

1. PYM 167, fol. 105.
2. *The Complete Poems of Emily Dickinson*, ed. Thomas H. Johnson (Boston, Mass.: Little, Brown, 1960) p. 283.
3. Robert Liddell, 'Two Friends: Barbara Pym and Ivy Compton-Burnett', *London Magazine*, xxiv (Aug–Sep 1984) 59.
4. Charlotte Brontë, *The Professor* (Edinburgh: J. Grant, 1911) pp. 360–1.
5. PYM 7, fol. 130.
6. PYM 151, fols 22–3.
7. *The Complete Poems of Emily Dickinson*, p. 94.
8. Rosemary Dinnage, 'Comic, Sad, Indefinite', *New York Review*, 16 Aug 1984, p. 15.
9. PYM 98, fol. 32.
10. PYM 58, fol. 12.
11. PYM 6, fol. 44.
12. PYM 92, fol. 18.
13. 'Barbara Pym (Mary Crampton)', in *World Authors 1970–1975*, ed. John Wakeman (New York: H. W. Wilson, 1980) p. 664.
14. *The World of Barbara Pym*, BBC Radio 4, 16 Sep 1984.

CHAPTER 11. BARBARA PYM AND THE WAR OF THE SEXES
John Halperin

1. Hazel Holt to John Halperin, 14 Jan 1985.
2. Ibid.
3. Barbara Brothers, 'Women Victimized by Fiction', in *Twentieth-Century Women Novelists*, ed. Thomas F. Staley (London: Macmillan, 1982) pp. 69, 71.

CHAPTER 12. THE NOVELIST AS ANTHROPOLOGIST
Muriel Schulz

1. Diane Lewis, 'Anthropology and Colonialism', *Current Anthropology*, xiv (1973) 581–602.
2. Derek Freeman, *Margaret Mead and Samoa: The Making of an*

Anthropological Myth (Cambridge, Mass.: Harvard University Press, 1983).
3. Lewis, in *Current Anthropology*, XIV, 590.
4. Claude Lévi-Strauss, 'Anthropology: Its Achievement and Future', *Current Anthropology*, VII (1966) 124–7.

CHAPTER 13. LITERARY ALLUSIONS IN THE NOVELS
Lotus Snow

1. Jeremy Treglown, 'Puff Puff Puff', *New Statesman*, 94 (23 Sep 1977) 418.
2. PYM 11, fol. 46.
3. PYM 96.
4. PYM 43.
5. PYM 96.

CHAPTER 14. THE NARRATIVE SENSE OF BARBARA PYM
Robert J. Graham

1. Philip Larkin, 'I Remember, I Remember', *The Less Deceived* (New York: St Martin's Press, 1965) p. 39.
2. Philip Larkin, *The Whitsun Weddings* (New York: Random House, 1964) p. 22.
3. John Betjeman, *John Betjeman's Collected Poems* (London: John Murray, 1980) pp. 226–7. Reprinted with the permission of John Murray (Publishers) Ltd.
4. PYM 2, fol. 1.
5. PYM 3.
6. Ibid.
7. Ibid.
8. PYM 1, fol. 3.

CHAPTER 15. THE PYM PAPERS
Janice Rossen

1. PYM 1, fol. i.
2. Hazel Holt has commented on the initial difficulty experienced in dating this manuscript, as Beatrice Wyatt happened also to be the name of the Secretary at the International African Institute, where Pym found a job after the war. Indeed, it was through Beatrice Wyatt, aunt of a friend of hers, that she obtained the job.
3. PYM 6, fol. 10.

4. PYM 103, fol. 69.
5. PYM 17, fol. 34.
6. PYM 23, fol. 15.
7. PYM 103, fol. 63.
8. PYM 108, fol. 27.
9. One gathers that such notebooks formed an indispensable part of the Pym sisters' life, for Hilary Pym is still in the habit of carrying such a spiral-bound notebook in her handbag.
10. PYM 100, fol. 88.
11. PYM 40, fol. 3.
12. PYM 45, fol. 23.
13. PYM 160, fol. 97. Robert Smith did, in fact, write the first published article about her fiction. It appeared in the October 1971 issue of *Ariel* and is reprinted as Chapter 8 above.
14. For further information about why the firm of Jonathan Cape rejected *An Unsuitable Attachment*, see Philip Larkin's Foreword to the British edition of the novel, which was published posthumously by Macmillan in 1982. Larkin's essay is reprinted as Chapter 16 below.

Select Bibliography

PRIMARY SOURCES

Some Tame Gazelle (London: Cape, 1950, 1978; New York: Dutton, 1983).

Excellent Women (London: Cape, 1952, 1978; New York: Dutton, 1978).

Jane and Prudence (London: Cape, 1953, 1978; New York: Dutton, 1981).

Less than Angels (London: Cape, 1955, 1978; New York: Dutton, 1980).

A Glass of Blessings (London: Cape, 1958, 1977; New York: Dutton, 1980).

No Fond Return of Love (London: Cape, 1961, 1979; New York: Dutton, 1982).

Quartet in Autumn (London: Macmillan, 1977; New York: Dutton, 1978).

The Sweet Dove Died (London: Macmillan, 1978; New York: Dutton, 1979).

A Few Green Leaves (London: Macmillan; New York: Dutton, 1980).

An Unsuitable Attachment (London: Macmillan; New York: Dutton, 1982).

A Very Private Eye: An Autobiography in Diaries and Letters, ed. Hazel Holt and Hilary Pym (London: Macmillan; New York: Dutton, 1984).

Crampton Hodnet (London: Macmillan; New York: Dutton, 1985).

An Academic Question (London: Macmillan; New York: Dutton, 1986).

SECONDARY SOURCES

Benet, Diana, 'The Language of Christianity in Pym's Novels', *Thought*, \LIX (1984) 504–13.

Benet, Diana, *Something to Love: Barbara Pym's Novels* (Columbia: University of Missouri, 1986).

Binding, Paul, 'Barbara Pym', in *British Novelists Since 1960: Dictionary of Literary Biography*, ed. Jay L. Halio, xiv (Detroit: Gale Research, 1983) 604–7.

Brothers, Barbara, 'Women Victimized by Fiction', in Thomas F. Staley (ed.), *Twentieth-Century Women Novelists* (London: Macmillan, 1982) pp. 61–80.

Broyard, Anatole, 'Overflowing her Situation', *New York Times Book Review*, 15 Aug 1982, p. 27.

Burkhart, Charles, 'Barbara Pym and the Africans', *Twentieth Century Literature*, xxix (1983) 45–53.

Calisher, Hortense, 'Enclosures: Barbara Pym', *New Criterion*, i (1982) 53–6.

Finlayson, Iain, 'An Interview with Barbara Pym', *Literary Review*, 23 Feb 1980, pp. 2–5.

Graham, Robert J., 'Cumbered with Much Serving: Barbara Pym's "Excellent Women"', *Mosaic*, xvii (1984) 141–60.

Howe, Pamela, 'The "Cruelly Perceptive Eye" of a Born Novelist', *Listener*, 5 July 1984, pp. 14–15.

Kapp, Isa, 'Out of the Swim with Barbara Pym', *American Scholar*, lii (1983) 237–42.

Keener, Frederick M., 'Barbara Pym Herself and Jane Austen', *Twentieth Century Literature*, xxxi (1985) 89–110.

Kirk-Greene, Tony, 'Barbara Pym 1913–1980', *Africa*, l (1970) 94–5.

Larkin, Philip, 'The World of Barbara Pym', *The Times Literary Supplement*, 11 Mar 1977, p. 260.

Liddell, Robert, 'Two Friends: Barbara Pym and Ivy Compton-Burnett', *London Magazine*, xxiv (1984) 59–69.

Long, Robert Emmett, *Barbara Pym* (New York: Ungar, 1986).

Miller, Karl, 'Ladies in Distress', *New York Review of Books*, 9 Nov 1978, pp. 24–5.

Moorehead, Caroline, 'How Barbara Pym was Rediscovered after 16 Years out in the Cold', *The Times*, 14 Sep 1977, p. 11.

Nardin, Jane, *Barbara Pym*, ed. Kinley E. Roby (Boston, Mass.: Twayne, 1985).

'Pym, Barbara (Mary Crampton)', in *World Authors 1970–75*, ed. John Wakeman (New York: H. W. Wilson, 1980) pp. 663–6.

Rossen, Janice, 'Love in the Great Libraries: Oxford in the Work of Barbara Pym', *Journal of Modern Literature*, xii (1985) 277–96.

Rowse, A. L., 'Austen Mini?', *Punch*, 19 Oct 1977, pp. 732–4.

Sadler, Lynn Veach, 'Spinsters, Non-Spinsters, and Men in the

World of Barbara Pym', *Critique: Studies in Modern Fiction*, XXVI (1985) 141–54.

Salwak, Dale, 'Barbara Pym', in *Survey of Long Fiction*, ed. Frank A. Magill, IV (Englewood Cliffs, NJ: Salem Press, 1983) 2178–85.

Schofield, Mary Anne, 'Well-Fed or Well-Loved? – Patterns of Cooking and Eating in the Novels of Barbara Pym', *University of Windsor Review*, XVIII (1985) 1–8.

Shapiro, Anna, 'The Resurrection of Barbara Pym', *Saturday Review*, IX (1983) 29–31.

Snow, Lotus, 'The Trivial Round, the Common Task: Barbara Pym's Novels', *Research Studies*, XLVIII (1980) 83–93.

Stetz, Margaret Diane, '*Quartet in Autumn*: New Light on Barbara Pym as a Modernist', *Arizona Quarterly*, XLI (1985) 24–37.

Tyler, Anne, Foreword to '*Excellent Women*', '*Jane and Prudence*', '*An Unsuitable Attachment*' (New York: Quality Paperback Book Club, 1984) pp. v–xviii.

Updike, John, 'Books: Lem and Pym', *New Yorker*, 26 Feb 1979, pp. 115–21.

Wymard, Eleanor B., 'Secular Faith in Barbara Pym', *Commonweal*, 13 Jan 1984, pp. 19–21.

Index